How to Access the Federal Government on the INTERNET

Fourth Edition

BRUCE MAXWELL
bmaxwell@mindspring.com

Congressional Quarterly
Washington, D.C.

ISBN 1-56802-387-1
ISSN 1088-7466

To my parents, Bill and Sue Maxwell,

and to the memory of my grandparents,

Leon and Eunice Maxwell.

SUMMARY CONTENTS

Preface xxiii

Introduction 1

The Internet Resources 7

 Access to Information 9

 Agriculture 31

 Arts and Museums 39

 Business, Trade, and Economics 45

 Children and Families 67

 Computers 73

 Defense 77

 Demographic Data 91

 Education 95

 Emergency Response and Fire Safety 115

 Energy 119

 Environment 127

 Foreign Affairs 143

 Government 161

 Health and Medicine 183

 History 223

 Jobs and Employment 229

 Law and Justice 237

 Science and Technology 253

 Space 269

 Transportation 283

Glossary 288

Index 291

CONTENTS

Preface xxiii

Introduction   1

The Internet Resources   7

Access to Information   9

Gateways   10

    The Center for Information Law and Policy   10
    The Federal Information Center   10
    FedLaw   11
    FedStats   11
    FedWorld   11
    Frequently Used Sites Related to U.S. Federal Government
      Information   12
    GOVBOT   13
    Government Information Exchange   13
    INFOMINE   13
    Meta-Index for U.S. Legal Research   14
    NonProfit Gateway   14
    U.S. Consumer Gateway   14
    U.S. Federal Government Agencies Directory   15
    United States Government Information   15
    U.S. State and Local Gateway   15
    University of Michigan Documents Center   16
    Yahoo!—U.S. Government   16

Government Publications   17

    Colorado Alliance of Research Libraries (CARL) Databases   17
    Consumer Information Center   17
    Core Documents of U.S. Democracy   18
    Department of Housing and Urban Development   18
    Federal Bulletin Board   18
    Federal Register Mailing Lists   19
    Federal Trade Commission Home Page   19
    Freedom of Information Act   20
    Government Information Sharing Project   20
    GOVINFO   21
    GOVNEWS   21
    How to Effectively Locate Federal Government Information on
      the Web   22
    National Academy Press   22

Uncle Sam 23
U.S. Government Documents Ready Reference Collection 23
U.S. Government Printing Office 24
U.S. House of Representatives Internet Law Library 26

Libraries 27

Library of Congress Home Page 27
Library of Congress Information System (LOCIS) 28
LM_NET 28
National Institutes of Health Library Catalog 29
NLM Locator 29
Online Library System (OLS) 29

Agriculture 31

Agricultural Research Service 32
Alternative Farming Systems Information Center 32
Animal Welfare Information Center 32
Current Research Information System (CRIS) 33
Economic Research Service 33
National Agricultural Library 34
North Carolina Cooperative Extension Service 34
Rural Development 35
Rural Information Center 35
USDA Economics and Statistics System 36
USDA Home Page 36
USDA Reports Electronic Mailing List 36
Water Quality Information Center 37

Arts and Museums 39

The First 150 Years: The Traveling Exhibition 40
The John F. Kennedy Center for the Performing Arts 40
National Air and Space Museum 40
National Endowment for the Arts 40
National Gallery of Art 41
National Museum of American Art 41
National Museum of Natural History 42
National Portrait Gallery 42
Smithsonian Institution 42
Smithsonian Institution Research Information System (SIRIS) 43

Business, Trade, and Economics 45

Business 46

The Bureau of Export Administration 46
Federal Electronic Commerce Program Office 46
IBM Patent Server 46
Office of Economic Conversion Information 47
Office of the United States Trade Representative's Homepage 47

Online Women's Business Center   47
SBA PRO-Net   48
Tourism   48
U.S. Business Advisor   49
U.S. Department of Commerce   49
U.S. Department of the Treasury   50
United States Government Electronic Commerce Policy   50
U.S. International Trade Commission   50
U.S. Patent and Trademark Office   51
USPTO Patent Databases   52
United States Postal Service   52
U.S. Securities and Exchange Commission   52
U.S. Small Business Administration   53
WhoWhere? Edgar   53

Economic Data   54

Board of Governors of the Federal Reserve System   54
Bureau of the Public Debt on the Net   54
Federal Reserve Banks   54

Government Contracts, Grants, and Sales   56

Acquisition Reform Network (ARNet)   56
CBD Net   56
daily-sales, gov.us.fed.doc.cbd.forsale   56
Federal Acquisition Regulation   57
Ginnie Mae: Government National Mortgage Association   57
govsales, gov.topic.forsale.misc   57
List of Defaulted Borrowers   58
Loren Data Corp.   58
Marshall Space Flight Center Procurement Site   59
NAIS Email Notification Service   59
NASA Acquisition Internet Service (NAIS) Home Page   59
National Endowment for the Humanities   60
National Science Foundation   60
U.S. General Services Administration   60
The U.S. Mint   61

Specific Businesses and Industries   62

Federal Communications Commission   62
Federal Deposit Insurance Corporation   62
Federal Financial Institutions Examination Council   63
HomePath   63
National Credit Union Administration   63
National Gambling Impact Study Commission   64

Taxes and Social Security   65

The Digital Daily   65
Digital Dispatch   65
IRIS (Internal Revenue Information Services)   65

Social Security Online   66
Taxing Times   66

Children and Families   67

The Administration for Children and Families   68
ChildStats.gov   68
Coming Up Taller: Arts and Humanities Programs for Children and Youth at
   Risk   68
National Child Care Information Center (NCCIC)   69
National Clearinghouse on Child Abuse and Neglect Information   69
National Parent Information Network (NPIN)   69
Office of the Assistant Secretary for Planning and Evaluation   70
PARENTING-L   70
Safe Places to Play   71
Web Pages for Kids around the Federal Government   71
YouthInfo   71

Computers   73

CIAC-Bulletin   74
Computer Incident Advisory Capability   74
Computer Security Resource Clearinghouse   74
FedCIRC   75
Federal Y2K Commercial Off-the-Shelf (COTS) Product Database   75
IT Policy On-Ramp   75
President's Council on Year 2000 Conversion   76

Defense   77

Chemical and Biological Weapons   78

The Nuclear, Biological, and Chemical Medical Defense Information Server   78
U.S. Army Chemical and Biological Defense Command   78
The United States Army Medical Research Institute of Chemical Defense   79
United States Army Medical Research Institute of Infectious Diseases   79

General   80

ACQWeb   80
Air Force Link   80
Air Force News Service   81
BosniaLINK   81
Critical Infrastructure Assurance Office   81
Defense Intelligence Agency   81
Defense Technical Information Center (DTIC) Home Page   82
DefenseLINK   82
DefenseLINK News by Email   83
Department of Defense Inspector General   83
Department of Veterans Affairs   83
Intelligence Reform Program   84
MarineLINK   84

National Security Agency   84
National Security Council   85
The Pentagon Book Store Online   85
President's Commission on Critical Infrastructure Protection   85
Selective Service System   86
U.S. Arms Control and Disarmament Agency   86
U.S. Army Homepage   86
United States Army Recruiting Web Site   87
U.S. Coast Guard   87
U.S. Navy   87

Nuclear Weapons   88

Defense Nuclear Facilities Safety Board Server   88
Department of Energy Nevada Operations Office   88
Environment, Safety, and Health Technical Information Services   88
Explorer   89

Demographic Data   91

Bureau of Labor Statistics   92
censusandyou, i-net-bulletin, press-release, and *product-announce*   92
Current Population Survey   93
FERRET   93
Geospatial and Statistical Data Center   93
U.S. Census Bureau   94
United States Historical Census Data Browser   94

Education   95

ARTSEDGE   96
AskERIC   96
Civnet   96
Computers for Learning   97
ECENET-L   97
ECPOLICY-L   97
EDInfo   98
EDSITEment   98
Educational Resources Information Center (ERIC)   98
ERIC Clearinghouse for Community Colleges   99
ERIC Clearinghouse for Social Studies/Social Science Education   99
ERIC Clearinghouse on Adult, Career, and Vocational Education   100
ERIC Clearinghouse on Assessment and Evaluation   100
ERIC Clearinghouse on Disabilities and Gifted Education   100
ERIC Clearinghouse on Educational Management   101
ERIC Clearinghouse on Elementary and Early Childhood Education   101
ERIC Clearinghouse on Higher Education   102
ERIC Clearinghouse on Information and Technology   102
ERIC Clearinghouse on Languages and Linguistics   102
ERIC Clearinghouse on Reading, English, and Communication   103
ERIC Clearinghouse on Rural Education and Small Schools   104

ERIC Clearinghouse on Teaching and Teacher Education 104
ERICNews   104
FAFSA on the Web   105
FCCsend, FCCshare, and edtech   105
Federal Resources for Educational Excellence (FREE)   106
LingNet   106
MIDDLE-L   107
National Center for Education Statistics   107
National Clearinghouse for ESL Literacy Education (NCLE)   108
National Education Goals   108
National Institute for Literacy Home Page   108
National Literacy Advocacy   109
Project EASI (Easy Access for Students and Institutions)   109
Quest   109
READPRO   110
ReadyWeb   110
Smithsonian Education   110
This is MEGA Mathematics!   111
U.S. Department of Education   111
U.S. Department of Education Search Page   112
Urban Education Web   112

Emergency Response and Fire Safety   115

Federal Emergency Management Agency   116
National Interagency Fire Center   116
U.S. Fire Administration   116

Energy   119

Alternative Fuels Data Center   120
Bioenergy Information Network   120
Biofuels Information Center   120
Clean Cities   121
DOE Information Bridge   121
DR-NRR, GC-NRR, and PR-OPA   121
EIA Email Lists   122
Energy Efficiency and Renewable Energy Network (EREN)   123
Energy Information Administration   123
International Nuclear Safety Center   124
International Nuclear Safety Program   124
National Renewable Energy Laboratory   124
Office of Scientific and Technical Information   125
Tennessee Valley Authority   125
U.S. Department of Energy Home Page   125
United States Nuclear Regulatory Commission   126

Environment   127

General   128

Agency for Toxic Substances and Disease Registry   128
Biological Resources Division   128
The Chemical Scorecard   129
Congressional Research Service Reports   129
Envirofacts Warehouse   129
environb-l, epa-press, internetnb-l and oppt-newsbreak   130
EPA Federal Register Mailing Lists   131
EPA Sector Notebooks   131
fws-news   132
National Marine Fisheries Service   132
National Wetlands Inventory   132
NOAA Web Sites   133
North American Reporting Center for Amphibian Malformations   133
RTK NET   134
Sector Facility Indexing Project   134
State of the Coast   135
United States Environmental Protection Agency   135
United States Fish and Wildlife Service   136

Nuclear Waste   137

Office of Civilian Radioactive Waste Management   137
U.S. Nuclear Waste Technical Review Board   137
Yucca Mountain Site Characterization Project   137

Parks and Public Lands   139

Alaska Public Lands Information Centers   139
America's National Parks Electronic Bookstore   139
Bureau of Land Management National Homepage   139
Grand Canyon National Park   140
National Wildlife Refuge System   140
NatureNet   140
ParkNet   141
Park Search   141
Recreation.GOV   142
USDA Forest Service Home Page   142
U.S. Fish and Wildlife Service Region 7—Alaska   142

Foreign Affairs   143

Bosnia Report   144
Bureau of Consular Affairs Home Page   144
Bureau of Diplomatic Security   144
Caucasus Report   145
Center for the Study of Intelligence   145
The Central Intelligence Agency   145
CIA Electronic Document Release Center   146

Foreign Affairs Network Listservs   147
International Broadcasting Bureau Servers   147
Overseas Security Advisory Council   148
Peace Corps   148
Radio Free Asia   148
Radio Free Europe/Radio Liberty   149
RFE/RL Newsline   149
Secretary of State   149
Travel-Advisories Mailing List   150
U.S. Agency for International Development   150
U.S. Department of State Electronic Reading Room   150
U.S. Embassies and Consulates   151
United States Information Agency   158
United States Institute of Peace   158
U.S. State Department   159

Government   161

Congress   162

Committee Hearings   162
Congress Today   162
Congressional Budget Office   162
Congressional Quarterly VoteWatch   163
Congressional Quarterly's American Voter   163
FEDNET   164
GAO Daybook   164
HillSource   164
Independent Counsel's Report to the United States House of Representatives   165
The Office of the Clerk On-line Information Center   165
Office of the Majority Whip   165
Office of Technology Assessment Archive   166
The OTA Legacy   166
Penny Hill Press   166
Subcommittee on Rules and Organization of the House   167
THOMAS   167
United States General Accounting Office   168
U.S. House of Representatives   168
U.S. Legislative Branch   169
The United States Senate   169
Vote Smart Web   170
The Whip Notice and *The Whipping Post*   170

Elections   171

Campaign Finance Data on the Internet   171
Center for Responsive Politics   171
FECInfo   172
Federal Election Commission   172
Federal Voting Assistance Program (FVAP)   173

Policies, Regulations, and Operations   174

   FinanceNet   *174*
   National Partnership for Reinventing Government   *174*
   Office of Governmentwide Policy   *174*
   Plain Language Action Network   *175*
   Project on Government Secrecy   *175*
   REGINFO.GOV   *176*
   U.S. Consumer Product Safety Commission   *176*
   United States Immigration and Naturalization Service   *177*
   U.S. Office of Government Ethics Home Page   *177*
   U.S. Office of Special Counsel   *177*

White House   178

   E-mail to the White House   *178*
   The Independent Counsel and Impeachment   *178*
   Office of Management and Budget   *179*
   Office of National Drug Control Policy   *179*
   Welcome to the White House   *179*
   White House Publications   *180*

Health and Medicine   183

AIDS   184

   AIDS Clinical Trials Information Service   *184*
   AIDS in the Workplace   *184*
   AIDSNews   *184*
   CDC National Prevention Information Network   *185*
   HIV/AIDS Treatment Information Service   *185*

Alcohol and Drug Abuse   186

   National Institute on Alcohol Abuse and Alcoholism   *186*
   National Institute on Drug Abuse   *186*
   PREVline (Prevention Online)   *187*

Bibliographic Information   188

   Combined Health Information Database   *188*
   Dr. Felix's Free MEDLINE Page   *188*
   Internet Grateful Med   *189*
   National Library of Medicine   *190*
   PubMed   *191*

Cancer   192

   CancerNet   *192*
   Cancer Trials   *192*
   National Action Plan on Breast Cancer   *192*
   National Cancer Institute   *193*

Directories and Search Engines   194

   Department of Health and Human Services   *194*
   healthfinder   *194*

National Health Information Center   194
National Institutes of Health   195
NIH Web Search   195

Disabilities   196

ABLEDATA   196
The Access Board   196
Disabilities and Managed Care   196
National Council on Disability   197
National Rehabilitation Information Center   197
Trace Research and Development Center   198

Environmental Health   199

National Institute of Environmental Health Sciences   199
National Pesticide Telecommunications Network   199
National Toxicology Program   200

Food and Nutrition   201

Center for Food Safety and Applied Nutrition   201
Food and Nutrition Information Center   201
The National Food Safety Database   202
Nutribase   202
Office of Dietary Supplements   202

General   204

Administration on Aging   204
Agency for Health Care Policy and Research   204
Centers for Disease Control and Prevention   205
CDC Diabetes and Public Health Resource   205
CDC Travel Information   205
CDC's Tobacco Information and Prevention Source (TIPS)   206
CDC WONDER   206
Committee on Commerce Tobacco Documents   207
Consumer Health Information   207
Diabetes in America   207
Health Care Financing Administration   208
The Initiative to Eliminate Racial and Ethnic Disparities in Health   208
Internet FDA   209
LTCARE-L   209
Medicare   209
National Bioethics Advisory Commission   210
National Eye Institute   210
National Heart, Lung, and Blood Institute   210
National Human Genome Research Institute   211
National Institute of Allergy and Infectious Disease (NIAID)   211
National Institute of Arthritis and Musculoskeletal and Skin Diseases   211
National Institute of Dental Research   212
National Institute of Diabetes and Digestive and Kidney Diseases   212
National Institute of Neurological Disorders and Stroke   212

National Sudden Infant Death Syndrome Resource Center   213
National Women's Health Information Center (NWHIC)   213
Office of Alternative Medicine   214
Office of Animal Care and Use   214
Office of Disease Prevention   214
Office of Disease Prevention and Health Promotion   215
Office of Minority Health Resource Center   215
Office of Rare Diseases   215
Organ Donation   216
Osteoporosis and Related Bone Diseases National Resource Center   216

Gulf War Illness   217

GulfLINK   217
The Missing GulfLINK Files   217
Presidential Advisory Committee on Gulf War Veterans' Illnesses   218

Human Radiation Experiments   219

Human Radiation Experiments Information Management System (HREX)   219
Office of Human Radiation Experiments   219

Mental Health   220

ALZHEIMER   220
ALZHEIMER Page   220
Alzheimer's Disease Education and Referral Center   220
National Institute of Mental Health   221
National Mental Health Services Knowledge Exchange Network   221
Substance Abuse and Mental Health Services Administration   222

History   223

Advisory Council on Historic Preservation   224
American Memory   224
The Architect of the Capitol Home Page   225
Franklin D. Roosevelt Library and Museum   225
George Bush Presidential Library and Museum   226
Images from the History of Medicine   226
Jimmy Carter Library   226
John F. Kennedy Library Home Page   227
The Lyndon B. Johnson Library and Museum   227
National Archives and Records Administration   227
U.S. Colored Troops   228

Jobs and Employment   229

Jobs   230

America's Career InfoNet   230
America's Job Bank   230
The Corporation for National Service   231
Office of Personnel Management Home Page   231
Planning Your Future: A Federal Employee's Survival Guide   231
USA Jobs   232

Labor Laws and Regulations   233

Job Accommodation Network (JAN)   233
National Labor Relations Board   233
Occupational Safety and Health Administration Home Page   233
Pension Benefit Guaranty Corporation   234
President's Committee on Employment of People with Disabilities   234
Technical Links   235
United States Department of Labor   235
U.S. Equal Employment Opportunity Commission   236
WorkNet@IRL   236

Law and Justice   237

Courts   238

The Federal Judicial Center Home Page   238
The Federal Judiciary Homepage   238
FindLaw   238
Georgetown University Legal Explorer   239
Law Journal Extra!   239
Legal Information Institute   239
liibulletin   240
The Oyez Project   240
U.S. Bankruptcy and District Courts   241
United States Circuit Court of Appeals Decisions   241
U.S. Court of Appeals for the Federal Circuit   241
U.S. Court of Appeals for the Second Circuit   245
U.S. Court of Appeals for the Fifth Circuit   245
U.S. Court of Appeals for the Seventh Circuit   245
U.S. Court of Appeals for the Eighth Circuit   246
United States Courts for the Ninth Circuit   246
U.S. Court of Appeals for the Tenth Circuit   246
U.S. Federal Courts Finder   247

Justice   248

Bureau of Alcohol, Tobacco, and Firearms   248
Federal Bureau of Investigation Home Page   248
Federal Bureau of Prisons   249
Justice Information Center   249
Justice Information Distribution List (JUSTINFO) and Juvenile Justice Electronic
   Mailing List (JUVJUST)   250
National Archive of Criminal Justice Data   250
Office of Justice Programs   250
U.S. Customs Service Web Site   251
U.S. Department of Justice   251
United States Commission on Civil Rights Home Page   252
United States Sentencing Commission   252

Science and Technology   253

Earth Sciences   254

    Cascades Volcano Observatory   254
    Department of the Interior Home Page   254
    Earthquake Information   255
    Global Change Data and Information System   255
    National Ocean Service   255
    U.S. Geological Survey   256
    USGS Branch of Earthquake and Geomagnetic Information On-line
      Information System   256
    WINDandSEA   256

Technology   257

    Ernest Orlando Lawrence Berkeley National Laboratory   257
    Hybrid Electric Vehicle Program   257
    Intelligent Mechanisms Group   257
    JPL Robotics   258
    NASA Space Telerobotics Program   258
    National Institute of Standards and Technology   258
    Oak Ridge National Laboratory (ORNL)   259
    Partnership for a New Generation of Vehicles (PNGV)   259
    Rocky 7   259
    SCAN   260
    Time Service Department   260

Weather   261

    Interactive Weather Information Network (IWIN)   261
    National Hurricane Center/Tropical Prediction Center   261
    National Severe Storms Laboratory   261
    National Weather Service   262
    National Weather Service Alaska Region   262
    National Weather Service Offices   262
    River Forecast Centers   268

Space   269

Asteroids and Comets   270

    Asteroid and Comet Impact Hazards   270
    Comet Observation Home Page   270
    Near-Earth Asteroid Tracking Home Page   270
    Near-Live Comet Watching System   271
    Stardust   271
    Stardust Mailing List   271

General   272

    Earth from Space   272
    EXPRESS   272
    International Space Station   272

issnews   273

Jet Propulsion Laboratory   273

Kennedy Space Center   274

ksc-press-release and *shuttle-status*   274

Lunar Prospector   274

NASA Headquarters   275

NASA Homepage   275

NASA Image eXchange (NIX)   276

NASA Johnson Space Center Digital Image Collection   276

NasaNews   276

NASA Search   277

The NASA Shuttle Web   277

NASA Shuttle-Mir Web   277

NASA Spacelink   277

National Space Science Data Center   278

press-release   278

Space Calendar   279

Trading Post 3   279

Views of the Solar System   279

Planets   280

Center for Mars Exploration (CMEX)   280

Kepler Mission: A Search for Habitable Planets   280

Mars Missions   280

Mars Today   281

MGS-Status   281

PDS Mars Explorer for the Armchair Astronaut   281

Planetary Photojournal   282

Planetary Rings Node   282

Welcome to the Planets   282

Transportation   283

Amtrak   284

Bureau of Transportation Statistics   284

FAA Y2K Program Office   284

Federal Aviation Administration   285

Federal Transit Administration   285

National Highway Traffic Safety Administration   285

The National Transportation Safety Board   286

Office of System Safety Home Page   286

U.S. Department of Transportation Homepage   287

White House Commission on Aviation Safety and Security   287

Glossary   288

Index   291

PREFACE

No matter what your occupation, interests, or hobbies, you're bound to find valuable information at federal government Internet sites. With information from the sites, you can do everything from learning the ins and outs of buying a new home to investigating which businesses in your community are releasing toxic chemicals into the environment.

This fourth edition of *How to Access the Federal Government on the Internet* provides detailed descriptions of more than 900 federal government Internet sites, mailing lists, and other resources that you can access for free. It explains how to reach each site, describes what each one offers, provides searching tips for selected sites, and offers advice on where to start a search for federal government information on the Internet. The descriptions, tips, and advice are based on the hundreds of hours I've spent online examining the sites.

This book is aimed at all levels of Internet users, ranging from "newbies" to experienced pros. I'm a journalist by training—not a computer expert—so I've written the book in plain, straightforward language. To some extent, though, the Internet has its own vocabulary. If you see a strange word, you can turn to the glossary for a quick explanation.

This book does not list every Internet site that offers federal government information. Instead, it lists some of the most useful sites, some of the most interesting sites, and some sites that are just intriguing examples of what it's possible for the federal government to do with the Internet. Although most of the sites are operated by federal agencies and departments, some are operated by colleges, universities, or individuals. In fact, some of the best "federal government" Internet sites are run by universities, not by the federal government.

I plan to update this book regularly. If you have suggestions for sites that should be included in new editions, please send me an e-mail message at

bmaxwell@mindspring.com

If you'd like to be informed about new editions of this book, please visit my Web site at

http://bmaxwell.home.mindspring.com

I am indebted to many people who helped make this book possible. First among them is Dave Tarr, my editor at Congressional Quarterly, for his ongoing, enthusiastic support of this project. I'd also like to thank Ann Davies for her editing, Christopher Karlsten for shepherding the book through the production process, Debra Naylor for the design work, and Joan Stout for creating the index.

As always, I reserve my greatest thanks for my wife, Barbara. No writer could have a more supportive partner.

Bruce Maxwell

INTRODUCTION

The myth that federal government Internet sites offer only boring statistics and stuffy reports was forever laid to rest on September 11, 1998.

That's the day the report of Independent Counsel Kenneth Starr, who investigated President Bill Clinton's affair with Monica Lewinsky, was placed on the Internet by the House of Representatives. Millions of people read part of all of the X-rated document within days of its release, making it one of the most-read government publications in the nation's history.

The release of Starr's report focused attention on disseminating government information over the Internet. But the Internet's power was not news to the agencies throughout the federal government that have been using it for years to make a huge array of information available for free.

Through federal sites, Internet users can watch videos of NASA vehicles exploring Mars, read bills that are being debated by Congress, learn how to help their children do better in school, find a job, download tax forms, research health problems, apply for student financial aid for college, view treasures in the collections of the Library of Congress and the Smithsonian Institution, explore previously secret FBI files about everyone from Lucille Ball to Adolf Hitler, trace their ancestors, search the Library of Congress catalog, find solutions to common consumer problems, and much, much more.

Many federal Internet sites are enormously popular. In May 1998, according to the tracking firm Relevant Knowledge, 1.8 million people over age twelve visited NASA's main site. In that same month the main sites operated by the Library of Congress and the National Institutes of Health had 1.2 million visitors each.

Making federal information available to the public over the Internet has not been without problems and controversies. In some cases, agencies have been dragged kicking and screaming to the Internet. The most notable example is the Securities and Exchange Commission, which balked at placing its treasure trove of corporate data on the Internet. The SEC relented only after activist and Internet pioneer Carl Malamud shamed the agency by creating a nonprofit site offering all of its data. When Malamud's funding ran out, he challenged the agency to continue his work, and it reluctantly did. Malamud has also shamed other agencies into placing vast amounts of data online.

In other cases, federal agencies have claimed that documents placed online reveal secrets or threaten national security. In September 1998 the Department of Defense ordered a review of all DOD Web sites for sensitive information that might be useful to terrorists and other foes. The DOD's action plan said that some of its Web sites "provide our adversaries with a potent instrument to obtain, correlate and evaluate an unprecedented volume of aggregated information regarding DOD capabilities, infrastructure, personnel and operational procedures." The U.S. Army took the drastic action of temporarily shutting down all its Web sites until they could be checked and sensitive information removed.

The most controversial issue involves the huge amount of federal information that has not yet been placed online. Perhaps the most egregious offender in this regard is Congress. That's ironic, since in November 1994 Newt Gingrich, then soon to be Speaker of the House of Representatives, promised a new openness in government. He said House rules would be changed so that congressional information "will be available to any citizen in the country at the same moment that it is available to the highest paid Washington lobbyist."

Despite some moves in the right direction, Gingrich's promise remains largely unfulfilled. The full text of all bills introduced in Congress is now available on the Internet, but draft versions of bills circulating around Capitol Hill—and with lobbyists—are not. Nor can Americans turn online to watch how bills change during committee markups and other steps in the legislative process. Lobbyists have easy access to this information.

One of the most basic pieces of congressional information—how individual members vote on specific bills—is not available in a useful format on any congressional Web site. Nor is testimony at most congressional hearings, research reports by the Congressional Research Service, financial disclosure reports filed by members of Congress, or lobbyist disclosure forms filed with Congress—even though they're filed electronically.

WHAT'S NEW IN THIS EDITION

This fourth edition of *How to Access the Federal Government on the Internet* contains descriptions of more than 900 federal government Internet sites, hundreds of which are new in this book. Here are some highlights from the new sites:

- FedStats has links to federal statistical data at sites across the Internet that you can search or browse by topic.

- The GOVBOT database lets you search more than 800,000 Web pages at federal government and military sites.

- The U.S. Consumer Gateway has links to hundreds of consumer publications at dozens of federal Web sites.

- The U.S. Government Documents Ready Reference Collection from Columbia University provides links to dozens of the most popular federal government documents.

- The Online Women's Business Center, which is operated by the Small Business Administration, offers a great collection of information for women (and anyone else) starting a small business.

- Safe Places to Play offers an excellent collection of annotated links to Web pages for kids operated by a variety of federal agencies.

- The U.S. Army Chemical and Biological Defense Command site has fact sheets about chemical weapons stored at facilities across the United States.

- FAFSA on the Web provides an online form that students can use to apply for federal financial aid for college.

- Federal Resources for Educational Excellence (FREE) offers links to hundreds of teaching and learning resources developed by more than thirty federal agencies.

- The Chemical Scorecard lets you find out which manufacturing plants are releasing toxic chemicals into your community.

- The Bosnia Report distributes a weekly e-mail newsletter about events in Bosnia.

- Congress Today offers a searchable database of congressional votes from 1996 to the present.

- Cancer Trials has information about clinical trials of cancer therapies.

- The Food and Nutrition Information Center has a database that contains nutrient data for thousands of foods.

- The CDC Travel Information site offers health advice for travelers to any country in the world.

- The U.S. Colored Troops site has personal information about more than 230,000 soldiers who served in the U.S. Colored Troops during the Civil War.
- The NASA Image eXchange (NIX) links together hundreds of thousands of the best images from NASA.

HOW TO START A SEARCH

Searching for information on the Internet can be frustrating. It's not like looking for information at your local library, which has a catalog listing everything it owns and librarians who can help if you get lost. On the Internet, you're dumped into cyberspace and left to your own devices. There are millions of files out there—somewhere. How do you find them?

If you're looking for federal government information, you've made a good start by reading this book. The index should be particularly helpful in your search. But this book cannot list every federal Internet site or every document. If what you're looking for is not listed here, your best bet is to try one of the sites listed under "Gateways" in the "Access to Information" section of this book. Most of these gateway sites have huge collections of federal government documents, in addition to links to hundreds of other federal government Internet sites. Any one of them is an excellent starting point in a search for federal government information on the Internet.

You also can locate federal information by using search engines such as AltaVista, InfoSeek, or Lycos. But a word of caution: The search engines are most effective if you're searching for a narrow subject. A search on a broad topic can bury you in results. For example, a recent search of AltaVista on "Bill Clinton" returned 146,014 documents. Similarly, searches on "Social Security" returned 218,985 documents, "federal budget" turned up 47,075, and "Newt Gingrich" returned 40,760.

HOW TO USE THIS BOOK

The sites in this book are arranged alphabetically by subject as logically as possible. However, sites frequently have files about many subjects, so you should check the index for topics of interest.

Most sites have hundreds or thousands of files, making it impossible to describe fully what's available at each one. You should use this book as a general guide to a site, not as a catalog of every file and resource.

Some of the sites listed here are still being developed. This means they may not always be available, they may have bugs, or their offerings may be slimmer than you think upon first inspection. When you use the Internet, patience is a virtue. If you can't access a site because it has crashed, try it again another time. If the site has bugs, send an e-mail message to the system administrator reporting the problem. And if you find empty sub-directories at a Web site, try back in a few weeks after the site's manager has had more time to develop the resources.

The basic access information for each site is listed below its description. This access information varies from site to site, but you will find the following whenever it's applicable:

- Access method(s) The tool(s) you can use to access the site, such as the World Wide Web, FTP, Telnet, and E-mail.

- To access   The site's address(es) on the Internet.

- Login   The login you must type to access the site.

- Password   The password you must type to access the site.

- E-mail   The e-mail address where you can send questions about the site.

- Dial-in access   The telephone number you can dial with your communications software to access the site directly without going through the Internet.

- Available   The hours that the site is available. Sites are available twenty-four hours a day unless noted.

- Note   Special instructions for accessing or using the site.

Two other pieces of access information are provided for mailing lists:

- Subject line   The word(s) you must type on an e-mail message's subject line to subscribe to a mailing list. The words you must type are in **bold type.** If this line is blank in the instructions, leave it blank in your message as well.

- Message   The word(s) you must type in an e-mail message's message area to subscribe to a mailing list. The words you must type are in **bold type.** Any words that are in *italics* you must replace with the correct information. For example, if the message in the instructions reads **subscribe** *listname firstname lastname,* you must type **subscribe** followed by the list's name, your first name, and your last name.

A FINAL WORD

There's a widespread belief that "everything" is available somewhere on the Internet if you only know where to look. This isn't true for "everything," nor is it true for all federal government documents. Although vast quantities of federal information are available on the Internet—and more information is being placed online each day—much is still unavailable. The Internet is simply one tool in any search for federal information, just as books, paper documents, CD-ROMs, bulletin board systems (BBSs), and commercial databases are tools. Although the Internet is a wondrous tool, it is not a panacea. Nor is it a replacement for a good librarian. If you're serious about searching for federal government information, a good librarian remains your most valuable resource.

THE INTERNET RESOURCES

ACCESS TO INFORMATION

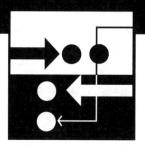

GATEWAYS

The Center for Information Law and Policy

The Center for Information Law and Policy provides the Federal Web Locator and the Federal Court Locator, which are great starting points in any search for federal information in general or federal court information in particular. The center is a joint project of the Villanova University School of Law and the Illinois Institute of Technology's Chicago-Kent College of Law.

The Federal Web Locator provides links to hundreds of Web sites operated by federal agencies and departments. You can browse through the listings by category or search them by using keywords. Use the address http://www.cilp.org/Fed-Agency/fedwebloc.html to reach the Federal Web Locator directly.

The Federal Court Locator provides opinions from the Third Circuit Court of Appeals and the Ninth Circuit Court of Appeals, in addition to links to sites that offer opinions from all the other circuit courts, many U.S. district courts, and the U.S. Supreme Court. Use the address http://www.cilp.org/Fed-Ct/fedcourt.html to reach the Federal Court Locator directly.

The Federal Court Locator also offers a fantastic database of U.S. Supreme Court opinions from 1937 to 1975. The database contains more than 7,400 opinions.

Another useful resource is the Tax Law Locator, which has dozens of links to federal and state tax laws, tax forms, and related information. Use the address http://www.cilp.org/tax/taxmaster/taxhome.htm to reach the Tax Law Locator directly.

Two interesting nonfederal resources offered by the center are the State Web Locator (http://www.cilp.org/State-Agency) and the State Court Locator (http://www.cilp.org/State-Ct).

Vital Stats:

Access method:	WWW
To access:	http://www.cilp.org
E-mail:	hallman@mail.law.vill.edu

The Federal Information Center

The Federal Information Center site offers contact information for federal agencies that can answer some of the public's most common questions. It's operated by the General Services Administration.

The contact information, which includes links to agency Web sites, is arranged into the following subjects: Congress, consumer issues, consumer product recalls, Freedom of Information and Privacy Acts, federal employment, federal loans or grants, federal taxes, savings bonds, government publications, protection of intellectual property, Selective Service, Social Security and Medicare/Medicaid, travel by Americans out of the country, and workplace issues.

Vital Stats:

Access method:	WWW
To access:	http://fic.info.gov
E-mail:	gix@gsa.gov

FedLaw

FedLaw is an amazing resource for federal legal and regulatory research. It provides no original information but has more than 1,600 links to legal-related information on the Internet. The site is operated by the General Services Administration.

The links provide federal laws and regulations, including presidential executive orders and Office of Management and Budget circulars and bulletins; decisions from the Supreme Court and federal circuit, district, and bankruptcy courts; the text of congressional bills and General Accounting Office reports; state and territorial laws; and much, much more.

The site's most useful feature is a topical and title index, which separates the links by hundreds of subjects. Another useful section arranges federal statutes and regulations by subject.

Vital Stats:

Access method:	WWW
To access:	http://fedlaw.gsa.gov
E-mail:	janice.mendenhall@gsa.gov

FedStats

FedStats is a one-stop source for statistical information produced by dozens of federal agencies. It offers no original information but has links to federal statistical data at sites across the Internet that you can browse by topic or search. FedStats is operated by the Federal Interagency Council on Statistical Policy.

Other pages provide links to regional statistics, links to Web sites operated by major federal statistical agencies, links to other statistical Web sites, and links to some of the most popular federal statistical publications, such as the *Statistical Abstract of the United States* and the *State and Metropolitan Area Data Book.*

Vital Stats:

Access method:	WWW
To access:	http://www.fedstats.gov

FedWorld

One of FedWorld's most popular features is its gateway to more than 100 federal bulletin board systems. However, FedWorld also has databases and thousands of files that offer everything from tax forms to information about federal job openings.

Here are some highlights of what's available:

- Hundreds of documents issued by the White House, including press releases, transcripts of news conferences and background briefings for reporters, and speeches by the president and vice president.

- A database of federal job openings that you can search by state and keywords. The database is updated daily Tuesday through Saturday at about 9:30 a.m. EST. The same job information is available through USA Jobs (p. 232).

- More than 500 tax forms and supporting publications from the Internal Revenue Services for individuals, corporations, and nonprofit organizations.

- A database containing U.S. Supreme Court decisions issued between 1937 and 1975. You can search the database, which contains more than 7,400 decisions, by case name or keyword.

- Nearly 1,000 files from the Federal Aviation Administration, including regulations, advisory circulars, and other types of documents.

Vital Stats:

Access methods:	WWW, Telnet, FTP, dial-in
To access:	http://www.fedworld.gov or telnet://fedworld.gov or ftp://ftp.fedworld.gov
Login (Telnet and dial-in access only):	**new** (you then must go through a registration procedure)
Login (FTP only):	**anonymous**
Password (FTP only):	your e-mail address
E-mail:	webmaster@fedworld.gov
Dial-in access:	703-321-3339

Frequently Used Sites Related to U.S. Federal Government Information

This excellent site offers links to dozens of federal Web sites that are among those used most frequently by government documents librarians. It's operated by the Federal Documents Task Force of the Government Documents Round Table, which is associated with the American Library Association.

The annotated links are arranged by subject: major government indexes, business and economics, census, Congress, consumer information, copyright and patents and trademarks, crime and justice, education, foreign countries, health and welfare, laws and regulations, natural resources, president and executive branch, scientific and technical reports, statistics, Supreme Court, tax forms, travel, and voting and elections.

Vital Stats:

Access method:	WWW
To access:	http://www.library.vanderbilt.edu/central/staff/fdtf.html
E-mail:	romans@library.vanderbilt.edu

GOVBOT

The GOVBOT database lets you search more than 800,000 Web pages at federal government and military sites around the country. GOVBOT's only drawback is that it does not say which sites it searches, so there's no way to know if your search was comprehensive.

GOVBOT was developed by the Center for Intelligent Information Retrieval at the University of Massachusetts.

Vital Stats:

Access method:	WWW
To access:	http://ciir2.cs.umass.edu/Govbot
E-mail:	info@ciir.cs.umass.edu

Government Information Exchange

The Government Information Exchange offers no original information, but it has hundreds of links to other Internet sites operated by local, state, federal, and foreign governments and international organizations. The site is operated by the General Services Administration.

The Yellow Pages section, where links are arranged by subject, is especially useful. Some of the subjects covered are applications/forms, benefits/assistance, business/commerce, consumer information, employment/workplace, laws and legislation, military, public safety, and year 2000.

The Federal Employees section also is strong. It provides information about federal jobs and employment, benefits, buyouts and downsizing issues, government travel, and accommodation of people with disabilities, among other topics. It also features a good set of links to government telephone directories.

Another especially nice section is the Kids Corner, which has links to federal Web pages for kids offered by dozens of federal agencies.

Vital Stats:

Access method:	WWW
To access:	http://www.info.gov
E-mail:	gix@gsa.gov

INFOMINE

INFOMINE is an attempt by librarians to tame the Internet and catalog its resources into subject directories. Although any such effort is by definition incomplete, INFOMINE is a great place to start a search for government information on the Internet. INFOMINE is provided by librarians at the University of California.

You can browse INFOMINE's government links by subject, title, or keywords. You also can search all the listings. Each listing provides a good description of what's available at the linked site. INFOMINE's "What's New" section is a particularly good way to keep up with new government Internet sites.

Vital Stats:

Access method:	WWW
To access:	http://lib-www.ucr.edu/govinfo.html
E-mail:	reasoner@ucrac1.ucr.edu

Meta-Index for U.S. Legal Research

The Meta-Index for U.S. Legal Research provides a simple interface to searchable databases of federal legal information maintained by various sites on the Internet. From the home page, you can search U.S. Supreme Court opinions from 1937 to the present, decisions from every federal court of appeals, the U.S. Code, bills introduced in Congress, the *Congressional Record,* and the Code of Federal Regulations. The site is operated by the Georgia State University College of Law.

Vital Stats:

Access method:	WWW
To access:	http://gsulaw.gsu.edu/metaindex
E-mail:	webmaster@gsulaw.gsu.edu

NonProfit Gateway

This site provides links to information for nonprofit organizations offered by dozens of federal departments and agencies. It is designed to be a starting point for nonprofit organizations to access federal information and services. The links provide information about grants, regulations, taxes, services, and many other topics.

Vital Stats:

Access method:	WWW
To access:	http://www.nonprofit.gov
E-mail:	gateway@comcat.org

U.S. Consumer Gateway

This site, which is a cooperative project of two dozen federal agencies, is a gateway to consumer information. It offers no original information but has links to hundreds of consumer publications at other federal Web sites.

The links are arranged by subject into directories and sub-directories. The top-level directories are food, product safety, health, home and community, money, transportation, children, careers and education, and technology.

The site also has special pages of links to consumer alerts from the Federal Trade Commission, information about privacy, and publications about online fraud and scams.

Vital Stats:

Access method: WWW
To access: http://www.consumer.gov
E-mail: gateway@ftc.gov

U.S. Federal Government Agencies Directory

The U.S. Federal Government Agencies Directory offers links to hundreds of federal government Internet sites. They're arranged by executive branch, judicial branch, legislative branch, independent agencies, quasi-official agencies, and boards, commissions, and committees. The links are not annotated, so you need to know what you're looking for. The site is operated by the Louisiana State University Libraries.

Vital Stats:

Access method: WWW
To access: http://www.lib.lsu.edu/gov/fedgov.html
E-mail: sbolner@lsu.edu

United States Government Information

The United States Government Information site is one of the best places to start a search for federal information on the Internet. It offers hundreds of annotated links to federal Internet sites, arranged by dozens of subjects.

Some of the available subjects include affirmative action and civil rights, climate and weather, consumer information, crime statistics and reports, demographics and statistics, economic and business information, education, environment, foreign affairs and international aid, health and medical information, historic documents and exhibits, legislation, patents and trademarks, and welfare and welfare reform, among others.

The site is operated by the Government Publications Library at the University of Colorado, which deserves three cheers for putting together this great resource.

Vital Stats:

Access method: WWW
To access: http://www-libraries.colorado.edu/ps/gov/us/federal.htm
E-mail: govpubs@colorado.edu

U.S. State and Local Gateway

This site provides links to federal documents arranged by subject. It's aimed at making it easy for state and local government employees to find federal information. The site is a federal interagency project in collaboration with the National Performance Review.

Some of the subjects covered are welfare reform, Year 2000, administrative management, communities and commerce, disasters and emergencies, education, environment and energy, health, housing, public safety, and workforce development.

The site also has links to federal press releases. You can browse them by subject or agency.

Vital Stats:

Access method:	WWW
To access:	http://www.statelocal.gov
E-mail:	don.elder@npr.gov

University of Michigan Documents Center

The University of Michigan Documents Center has a fantastic collection of links to federal government sites on the Internet. Each link is annotated, making this a great place to start a search for federal information on the Internet.

The links are arranged in more than a dozen categories: agency directories and Web sites, bibliographies, budget, civil service, copyright, executive branch, executive orders, General Accounting Office, grants and contracts, historic documents, judicial branch, laws and constitution, legislative branch, Office of Management and Budget, patents, president, regulations, taxes, and White House.

The site also has a special set of links to government documents related to recent news events. To reach these links directly, use the address http://www.lib.umich.edu/libhome/Documents.center/docnews.html.

In addition, the site has the best congressional directories available on the Internet—even better than those maintained by Congress. The directories list e-mail addresses and Web site addresses for all members of Congress who have them. Best of all, the directories are constantly updated. To reach the directories directly, use the address http://www.lib.umich.edu/libhome/Documents.center/congdir.html.

Vital Stats

Access method:	WWW
To access:	http://www.lib.umich.edu/libhome/Documents.center/federal.html
E-mail:	graceyor@umich.edu

Yahoo!—U.S. Government

Yahoo! offers links to thousands of sites operated by or about the federal government. The links are arranged into dozens of subject directories and sub-directories.

The top-level subject directories include the following: agencies, auctions, budget, civic participation, documents, embassies and consulates, employment, executive branch, federal employees, impeachment, intelligence, judicial branch, legislative branch, military, national security, national symbols and songs, politics, reengineering, research labs, statistics, and Web directories.

Vital Stats:

Access method:	WWW
To access:	http://www.yahoo.com/government/u_s__government

GOVERNMENT PUBLICATIONS

Colorado Alliance of Research Libraries (CARL) Databases

The Colorado Alliance of Research Libraries (CARL) Databases offer a catalog of federal government publications and information about domestic assistance programs.

The government publications catalog contains information about documents published by the Government Printing Office since 1976. You can search it by name, word, title, call number, or series.

The Catalog of Federal Domestic Assistance contains detailed information about federal loan, grant, and technical assistance programs aimed at various levels of government, Indian tribes, private institutions, and individuals. The catalog describes more than 1,300 programs operated by fifty-one agencies. You can search it by keyword or name.

Vital Stats:

Access method:	Telnet
To access:	telnet://database.carl.org
E-mail:	database@carl.org
Path:	*CARL System Library Catalogs/CARL Systems Libraries—Western U.S./CARL/Library Catalogs/Government Publications.* When you reach the *Government Publications* menu, choose either *U.S. Government Publications* or *Federal Domestic Assistance Catalog.*

Consumer Information Center

The Consumer Information Center offers hundreds of publications about cars, children, employment, the environment, federal programs, food and nutrition, health, housing, money, small businesses, travel, and hobbies. The server lists prices up to a couple of dollars for some of the publications. Ignore the prices—everything is free.

Some sample titles are *Books for Children, Choosing and Using Credit Cards, Civil War at a Glance, Consumer's Resource Handbook, Eating for Life, Federal Benefits for Veterans and Dependents, Guide to Choosing a Nursing Home, Helping Your Child Learn to Read, IRS Guide to Free Tax Services, Lesser Known Areas of the National Park System, Military Service Records in the National Archives, New Car Buying Guide, Questions to Ask Your Doctor Before You Have Surgery, Small Business Handbook,* and *Where to Write for Vital Records.*

The site also has lists of government properties for sale by the General Services Administration and includes a list of seized property for sale by the U.S. Marshal's Service.

Vital Stats:

Access methods:	WWW, Gopher
To access:	http://www.pueblo.gsa.gov *or* gopher://gopher.gsa.gov
E-mail:	catalog.pueblo@gsa.gov

Core Documents of U.S. Democracy

This site provides some of the most important current and historical government publications. It's part of the U.S. Government Printing Office site (p. 24).

Through its own files and links to other Internet sites, the site offers the *Federalist Papers*, Declaration of Independence, Bill of Rights, U.S. Constitution, congressional bills, the federal budget, public laws, selected Supreme Court decisions, U.S. Code, Code of Federal Regulations, *Congressional Record, Federal Register, Weekly Compilation of Presidential Documents, Statistical Abstract of the United States, Catalog of Federal Domestic Assistance, Commerce Business Daily, Economic Report of the President, United States Government Manual,* and other publications.

Vital Stats:

Access method: WWW
To access: http://www.access.gpo.gov/su_docs/dpos/coredocs.html
E-mail: gpoaccess@gpo.gov

Department of Housing and Urban Development

Just about anything you might want to know about home ownership is available from the Department of Housing and Urban Development site or through its links. It has extensive information about buying a home, obtaining a mortgage, buying a home from HUD or other federal agencies, fair housing laws, and consumer protection rules under the Real Estate Settlement Procedures Act.

The site also offers information about community projects around the country, community organizing, job training programs, federal programs for the homeless, HUD's programs, and contracting opportunities. Finally, it includes HUD handbooks and forms, decisions from HUD's Office of the General Counsel, and selected federal documents about housing policy.

Vital Stats:

Access method: WWW
To access: http://www.hud.gov
E-mail: Candis_B._Harrison@hud.gov

Federal Bulletin Board

The Federal Bulletin Board offers a strange hodgepodge of information. Much of it is outdated junk, but there are a few jewels if you have enough patience to slog through everything. The board is operated by the Government Printing Office.

The board offers Supreme Court opinions and orders back to the 1992–1993 term, numerous documents about federal depository libraries, selected Justice Department documents about the Americans with Disabilities Act, statements submitted at hearings by the Subcommittee on Regulations and Government Information of the Senate Committee on Governmental Affairs, decisions of the Federal Labor Relations Authority, selected regulations from the Food and Drug Administration, and test guidelines from the Environmental Protection Agency, among other documents.

Vital Stats:

Access methods:	WWW, Telnet, dial-in
To access:	http://fedbbs.access.gpo.gov *or* telnet://fedbbs.access.gpo.gov
E-mail:	gpoaccess@gpo.gov
Dial-in access:	202-512-1387

Federal Register Mailing Lists

Subscribers to the Federal Register Mailing Lists automatically receive items from specific sections of the *Federal Register* in their e-mail mailboxes. The eight lists, which are also available through Usenet newsgroups, are operated by Financenet.

The eight mailing lists (with the names of their newsgroup counterparts in parentheses) are:

- federal-register-announce (gov.us.fed.nara.fed-register.announce)
- fed-register-contents (gov.us.fed.nara.fed-register.contents)
- fed-register-corrections (gov.us.fed.nara.fed-register.corrections)
- fed-register-meetings (gov.us.fed.nara.fed-register.meetings)
- fed-register-notices (gov.us.fed.nara.fed-register.notices)
- fed-register-presidential (gov.us.fed.nara.fed-register.presidential)
- fed-register-proposed-rules (gov.us.fed.nara.fed-register.proposed-rules)
- fed-register-rules (gov.us.fed.nara.fed-register.rules)

Vital Stats:

Access methods:	E-mail, Usenet newsgroups
To access (e-mail):	Send an e-mail message to listproc@financenet.gov
Subject line:	
Message:	**subscribe** *listname firstname lastname*
To access (Usenet):	Read the appropriate Usenet newsgroup
E-mail (questions):	carl@chage.com

Federal Trade Commission Home Page

The Federal Trade Commission Home Page offers more than 100 consumer publications about consumer disputes, vehicle leasing, credit cards, credit repair scams, women and credit histories, diet programs, home financing and refinancing, mortgage discrimination, infomercials, toy ads on TV, career and vocational schools, funerals, income tax preparation services, telemarketing fraud, job ads, work-at-home schemes, and lots of other topics.

The site also has nearly a dozen publications for businesses about the mail and telephone order merchandise rule, the telemarketing sales rule, credit reports, office supply scams, and other topics.

In addition, it offers information about how to report complaints about fraud, news releases, the FTC's weekly calendar, speeches by FTC officials, FTC consent agreements and orders, information about FTC conferences and workshops, FTC staff reports about online privacy and other subjects, extensive information about antitrust and competition issues, addresses and telephone numbers for regional FTC offices, consumer protection rules, links to other Internet sites that offer consumer information, and much more.

Vital Stats:

Access method:	WWW
To access:	http://www.ftc.gov
E-mail:	consumerline@ftc.gov

Freedom of Information Act

This Justice Department page offers extensive information about how to make a request for federal documents under the Freedom of Information Act (FOIA).

Some of the available publications are *DOJ FOIA Guide, Your Right to Federal Records*, and *A Citizen's Guide to the FOIA*. The site also provides the full text of the FOIA, the full text of the Privacy Act, a quarterly newsletter about the FOIA, and Justice Department FOIA and Privacy Act regulations.

Two particularly interesting sections provide contact information for FOIA officers at agencies throughout the federal government and links to FOIA pages maintained by dozens of government agencies.

Vital Stats:

Access method:	WWW
To access:	http://www.usdoj.gov/04foia/index.html
E-mail:	web@usdoj.gov

Government Information Sharing Project

The Government Information Sharing Project provides a magnificent collection of online databases containing federal data on demographics, economics, education, and related subjects. The data are extracted from CD-ROMs published by the Bureau of the Census, Bureau of Economic Analysis, National Center for Education Statistics, and other organizations. The site is operated by the Oregon State University Libraries.

Most of the databases are very easy to use. With some, you just click on a map to obtain the data. The following databases are available:

- USA Counties 1996

- 1990 Census of Population and Housing

- Population Estimates by Age, Sex and Race: 1990–94

- Equal Employment Opportunity File: 1990

- Regional Economic Information System: 1969–1995

- 1992 Economic Census

- Census of Agriculture: 1982, 1987, 1992

- U.S. Imports/Exports History: 1992–1996

- Consolidated Federal Funds Report: 1987–96

- Earnings by Occupation and Education: 1990

- School District Data Book Profiles: 1989–1990

The site also has links to other sites that offer federal information, arranged by subject. A mailing list called GOVINFO (next entry) provides e-mail notices about updates to the system.

Vital Stats:

Access method:	WWW
To access:	http://govinfo.kerr.orst.edu
E-mail:	weblist@govinfo.kerr.orst.edu

GOVINFO

Subscribers to the GOVINFO mailing list receive news about updates to the Government Information Sharing Project site operated by the Oregon State University Library (see previous entry). The site provides numerous databases containing federal demographic, economic, and education information.

Vital Stats:

Access method:	E-mail
To access:	Send an e-mail message to listserv@mail.orst.edu
Subject line:	
Message:	**subscribe govinfo** *firstname lastname*
E-mail:	GOVINFO-request@mail.orst.edu

GOVNEWS

The GOVNEWS site provides information about the more than 200 Usenet newsgroups created by the International Govnews Project to disseminate government information and discuss government policies.

The project, which is a collaborative effort between public and private sector volunteers and is supported by the National Science Foundation's FinanceNet network, created a special government category on the Internet's Usenet news system. The category has more than 200 newsgroups, some devoted to particular topics and others to particular government agencies. Some of the newsgroups simply deliver government information, such as official notices, reports, and publications, while others allow people to discuss government issues.

Most of the groups are devoted to the U.S. federal government. The newsgroups provide information about government privatization, sales of government property, aviation, the Central Intelligence Agency, foreign trade, federal job openings, grant opportunities, natural resources, and numerous other topics. Other newsgroups distribute the full text of bills introduced in Congress, reports from the General Accounting Office, various sections of the *Congressional Record* and the *Federal Register,* announcements from specific government agencies, and other types of documents. Use the address http://www.govnews.org/govnews/site-setup/gov.allgroups to get a list of all the available groups.

Besides the list of groups, the site offers information about the project, how to access the newsgroups, and how to create new newsgroups.

Vital Stats:

Access method:	WWW
To access:	http://www.govnews.org
E-mail:	webmaster@govnews.org

How to Effectively Locate Federal Government Information on the Web

This page offers a superb tutorial about finding federal information on the Web. The page was created by two government documents librarians at the University of California.

Among other topics, the tutorial discusses how to use search engines and other resources to find government information, how to locate government agencies on the Web, how to locate government regulations and legislation, and how to find statistics such as demographic data. The tutorial is sprinkled with links to some of the best federal Web sites.

Vital Stats:

Access method:	WWW
To access:	http://www.library.ucsb.edu/universe/dedecker.html
E-mail:	webmaster@library.ucsb.edu

National Academy Press

The National Academy Press site claims that it offers a "virtual treasure trove of books, reports and publications that deal with all that is new and important in the worlds of science, technology, and health," and that's no hype. It has the full text of more than 1,000 books and other publications from the National Academy of Sciences, a private nonprofit organization that was chartered by Congress in 1863 to advise the federal government on scientific and technical matters.

The publications are arranged under such topics as agriculture sciences, behavioral and social sciences, computer sciences, education, environmental issues, food and nutrition, medical sciences and health care, science and ethics, and urban development, among many others.

Just a few of the titles available are *Preventing Reading Difficulties in Young Children; Resources for Teaching Middle School Science; Dying to Quit: Why We Smoke and How to Stop; Teaching about Evolution and the Nature of Science; Scientific Opportunities and Public Needs: Improving Priority Setting and Public Input at the National Institutes of Health; Health Data in the Information Age: Use, Disclosure, and Privacy; Voice Communication Between Humans and Machines; The Ozone Depletion Phenomenon; Pesticides in the Diets of Infants and Children; Eat for Life: The Food and Nutrition Board's Guide to Reducing Your Risk of Chronic Disease; Employment and Health Benefits: A Connection at Risk; Losing Generations: Adolescents in High-Risk Settings; Violence and the American Family; Dispelling the Manufacturing Myth: American Factories Can Compete in the Global Marketplace; Post–Cold War Conflict Deterrence;* and *Earthquake Prediction: The Scientific Challenge.*

Vital Stats:

Access method:	WWW
To access:	http://www.nap.edu
E-mail:	webmaster@nas.edu

Uncle Sam

The highlight of this site is a collection of research guides to federal government information on the Internet. Each guide contains annotated links to key Internet sites that have been selected by librarians. Uncle Sam is operated by the Government Publications Department at the University of Memphis Library.

The site offers guides to administrative law resources, education resources, Freedom of Information Act sites, federal forms, federal internship information, legislative resources, resources for medical professionals, small-business resources, statistical resources, and welfare reform information, among other topics.

It also provides links to federal Web sites arranged by topic and agency, links to federal databases, and links to government serials and periodicals that are now available on the Internet.

Vital Stats:

Access method:	WWW
To access:	http://www.lib.memphis.edu/gpo/unclesam.htm
E-mail:	willias@dewey.lib.memphis.edu

U.S. Government Documents Ready Reference Collection

This site provides links to dozens of the most requested federal government publications. It's operated by the Documents Service Center at Columbia University Libraries.

The site has links to electronic versions of the *Catalog of U.S. Government Publications, County and City Data Book, Statistical Abstract of the United States, Agriculture Fact Book, Census of Manufactures, Commerce Business Daily, Monthly Labor Review, Occupational Outlook Handbook, Social Security Handbook, State and Metropolitan Area Data Book, Compendium of Federal Justice Statistics, Hate Crime Statistics, Immigration to the United*

States, Sourcebook of Criminal Justice Statistics, Terrorism in the United States, Uniform Crime Reports of the United States, Digest of Education Statistics, Annual Energy Outlook, Code of Federal Regulations, Congressional Record, Federal Register, Where to Write for Vital Records, Arms Control and Disarmament Agreements, National Military Strategy of the United States, and *World Military Expenditures and Arms Transfers,* among many others.

Vital Stats:

Access method:	WWW
To access:	http://www.cc.columbia.edu/cu/libraries/indiv/dsc/readyref.html
E-mail:	www.dsc@libraries.cul.columbia.edu

U.S. Government Printing Office

The U.S. Government Printing Office (GPO) offers GPO Access, a collection of databases that provide the full text of bills introduced in Congress, the *Congressional Record,* the *Federal Register,* General Accounting Office reports, the U.S. Code, Supreme Court decisions from 1937 to 1975, and other documents.

Most users will find the basic search interface for the GPO Access databases sufficient. Power searchers, however, will want to check out the specialized search pages that are available for many of the databases. They provide many more options than the basic interface for targeting your search. To reach the specialized search pages directly, use the address http://www.access.gpo.gov/su_docs/aces/special.html.

To give you further help in using the databases, the site includes extensive descriptions of the databases and tips for searching them. It also has lists of federal depository libraries around the country that provide dial-in and Internet gateways into GPO Access.

Here are some highlights from among the dozens of databases provided by GPO Access:

Budget of the United States Government   This database contains the full text of the federal budget from 1997 to the present.

Code of Federal Regulations   This database contains the full text of the Code of Federal Regulations, which is the codification of rules established by federal agencies.

Congressional Bills   This database has the published versions of all bills introduced in Congress. It has bills dating back to the 103d Congress, which was in session from 1993 to 1994. The database is updated daily by 6 a.m. EST when bills are published and approved for release.

Congressional Calendars—House   The House calendar has a listing of daily House activities. It also contains a history of House and Senate bills and resolutions that have been reported or considered by either house. Every Monday issue of the House calendar contains a subject index.

Congressional Calendars—Senate   The Senate calendar is published daily when the Senate is in session, and contains a listing of daily Senate activities.

Congressional Directory   This database is an electronic version of the *Congressional*

Directory, which contains information about members of Congress and congressional committees.

Congressional Documents   This database contains selected House, Senate, and treaty documents dating back to January 1995. A "Catalog of Available Documents" is provided.

Congressional Record   The *Congressional Record* contains the full text of statements made in Congress, along with information about congressional activities. The database contains issues dating back to January 1994, the beginning of the second session of the 103d Congress. The database is updated between 9 a.m. and 11 a.m. EST each day that the *Congressional Record* is published.

Congressional Record Index   This database is an index of the *Congressional Record* dating back to 1992.

Congressional Reports   This database has selected House, Senate, and Executive reports dating back to January 1995. A "Catalog of Available Documents" is provided.

Constitution of the United States of America   This database contains the full text of the U.S. Constitution, along with annotations of cases decided by the U.S. Supreme Court.

Economic Indicators   This database has Economic Indicators dating back to April 1995. The reports, which are published monthly, are prepared for the Joint Economic Committee by the Council of Economic Advisors.

Economic Report of the President   This database contains the full text of the *Economic Report of the President*, an annual document that discusses trends and goals in such areas as employment, unemployment, production, income, and federal spending.

Federal Register   The *Federal Register* database contains proposed and final federal regulations, presidential documents, meeting and grant notices, and other official documents. The database contains daily issues of the *Federal Register* dating back to January 3, 1994. The database is updated at 6 a.m. EST each day that the *Federal Register* is published.

GAO Reports   This database contains the full text of reports issued by the General Accounting Office, the investigative arm of Congress. Reports are available dating back to October 1994. The database is updated daily, and reports are available within two business days after their public release.

GILS Records   The Government Information Locator Service (GILS) database has records about public information available from the federal government, along with directions for obtaining the information.

Government Manual   This database contains an electronic version of the most recent *United States Government Manual*.

History of Bills and Resolutions   This database is an index of every action taken on a bill as reported in the *Congressional Record*. For each bill, the database provides a short description and a list of *Congressional Record* citations where the action was reported. You can search the database by bill number. Records are available back to January 1994.

House Rules Manual   This database contains the full text of rules used in the House of Representatives.

Public Laws   This database contains the text of each law enacted by Congress. It contains laws back to January 1995.

Senate Manual   This database has the full text of the Senate Manual, which contains the standing rules, orders, laws, and resolutions of the U.S. Senate.

Supreme Court Decisions   This database has the full text of decisions by the U.S. Supreme Court from 1937 to 1975.

Unified Agenda   The Unified Agenda, also known as the Semi-Annual Regulatory Agenda, summarizes pending regulatory actions by federal agencies. The database is updated semiannually when the Unified Agenda is published in the *Federal Register*.

United States Code   This database contains the laws of the United States in effect as of January 1996.

The site also has the full text of the *Statistical Abstract of the United States;* a searchable database containing the *Monthly Catalog of United States Government Publications;* more than 150 subject bibliographies that list publications, periodicals, and electronic products available for sale by the GPO; a searchable database of federal depository libraries; and information about U.S. government bookstores around the country, including maps of their locations.

Vital Stats:

Access method:	WWW
To access:	http://www.access.gpo.gov
E-mail:	wwwadmin@www.access.gpo.gov

U.S. House of Representatives Internet Law Library

The U.S. House of Representatives Internet Law Library offers a searchable version of the U.S. Code, which is the text of all public laws passed by Congress. The site is operated by the Law Revision Counsel in the U.S. House of Representatives.

Besides the U.S. Code database, the site has extensive links to other Internet sites that have U.S. federal laws, U.S. state and territorial laws, laws of other nations, treaties and international laws, laws of all jurisdictions arranged by subject, and other legal information.

Vital Stats:

Access method:	WWW
To access:	http://law.house.gov
E-mail:	usc@mail.house.gov

LIBRARIES

Library of Congress Home Page

The Library of Congress Home Page provides text and images from LC exhibitions, a database related to Vietnam War POWs and MIAs, more than seventy Army Area Handbooks for countries around the world, an excellent collection of links to Internet sites operated by local, state, federal, and foreign governments, and lots, lots more.

Here are just a few highlights of what's available:

- A Web-based interface to the LC catalog.

- Text and images from online exhibits about the fiftieth anniversary of the Marshall Plan, Frank Lloyd Wright, the Russian church and native Alaskan cultures, the Vatican library, the Russian archives, African American culture and history, the drafting of the Declaration of Independence, the building of the Capitol, the Gettysburg Address, women journalists during World War II, and the Dead Sea scrolls.

- A database containing information about more than 131,000 records related to American soldiers who were prisoners of war or missing in action during the Vietnam War. You can search the database by last name, country name, service branch, keywords, and other variables. Copies of any documents identified through the database can be ordered from the LC.

- A database containing records from Task Force Russia, which attempted to locate American soldiers in Vietnam who were thought to have been captured and held in the former Soviet Union.

The site also has an online catalog and various publications from the National Library Service for the Blind and Physically Handicapped, a list of book fairs and literary festivals from the Center for the Book, a database with abstracts of national laws from countries around the world, extensive bibliographies for various science and technology topics, superb guides to resources available in various reading rooms at the LC, information about copyright from the U.S. Copyright Office, a book-length history of the library, a huge bibliography about Latin America, a calendar of LC events, and links to more than 200 online library catalogs around the world.

Vital Stats:

Access method:	WWW
To access:	http://lcweb.loc.gov
E-mail:	lcweb@loc.gov

Library of Congress Information System (LOCIS)

LOCIS allows you to search the Library of Congress (LC) catalog, track bills that have been introduced in Congress, and much more.

The catalog is separated into several databases. You can search most of the databases by author, title, subject, series, partial LC call number, Dewey number, ISBN, and LC record number. A separate database contains terms used as LC subject headings.

The legislative databases track and describe bills and resolutions introduced in Congress from 1973 to the present. Each database covers a separate Congress, although you also can search all bills from 1973 to the present.

For each bill, the database lists the official title, the bill number, the sponsor(s), the committee(s) where it was referred, the subcommittee(s) where it was referred, all actions taken regarding the bill, and a detailed summary of the legislation. The database does not include the full text of bills or information about how specific members of Congress voted.

Most information in the legislative databases is current. For example, bill numbers, official titles, sponsors, and status changes are added within forty-eight hours. However, indexing terms and digests are recorded later, sometimes several weeks after the bill is added to the database.

You can search the legislative databases by subject, member's name, keywords, bill number, public law number, and committee name.

LOCIS also has databases containing records of works registered with the LC Copyright Office since 1978, records of publications for people who are unable to read print publications, and abstracts of legislation of all Spanish- and Portuguese-speaking countries as reported by legal gazettes since 1976.

Vital Stats:

Access method:	Telnet
To access:	telnet://locis.loc.gov
E-mail:	lconline@loc.gov
Available:	Most parts of LOCIS are available twenty-four hours a day except from 5 p.m. Saturday to noon Sunday, EST. Some catalog commands are not available Sunday through Friday from 9:30 p.m. to 6:30 a.m. LOCIS is not available on national holidays.

LM_NET

Subscribers to the LM_NET mailing list exchange messages about school library media topics. The list is sponsored by the ERIC Clearinghouse on Information and Technology, which is funded by the U.S. Department of Education.

Vital Stats:

Access method:	E-mail
To access:	Send an e-mail message to listserv@listserv.syr.edu
Subject line:	
Message:	**SUBSCRIBE LM_NET** *firstname lastname*
E-mail (for questions):	LM_NET-request@listserv.syr.edu

National Institutes of Health Library Catalog

This site provides access to the online catalog at the National Institutes of Health Library. The catalog, which lists books and journals in the library's collection, can be searched by author, title, words in the title, subject, and call number.

Vital Stats:

Access method: Telnet
To access: telnet://nih-library.ncrr.nih.gov

NLM Locator

NLM Locator is the online catalog at the National Library of Medicine, which is the world's largest biomedical library. The library's collection includes 4.9 million items.

The site offers separate catalogs of the library's books, audiovisual materials, and journal titles; information about the library's hours and services; and a searchable database of organizations that provide health information.

Vital Stats

Access method:	Telnet
To access:	telnet://locator.nlm.nih.gov
Login:	**locator**
E-mail:	ref@nlm.nih.gov

Online Library System (OLS)

The Environmental Protection Agency's Online Library System (OLS) provides listings from *Access EPA,* a publication that has contact information for about 300 sources of environmental information.

The site also has several databases that offer bibliographic citations for books, reports, and journals held by EPA libraries around the country. The publications cover such topics as air quality, hazardous waste, laboratory methods, pollution prevention, toxic substances, water pollution, and the impact of pollution on health. You can search the databases by title, author, corporate source, keywords, call number, year of publication, and report number.

Vital Stats:

Access methods:	Telnet, dial-in
To access:	telnet://epaibm.rtpnc.epa.gov
Dial-in access:	919-549-0720
Note:	If you access by Telnet, select PUBLIC at the first menu. At the second menu, select OLS. If you access by dial-in, type **d** at the "Selection?" prompt.

AGRICULTURE

Agricultural Research Service

The Agricultural Research Service site has quarterly reports about current research projects, the monthly magazine *Agricultural Research,* the *Food and Nutrition Research Briefs* newsletter, and a directory of ARS experts that can be searched by keyword, broad subject area, and area of research.

The site also has background information about the agency, press releases, information about job openings, and dozens of images of lab research, plants, animals, crops, insects, fruits and vegetables, field research, and other subjects.

Vital Stats:

Access method:	WWW
To access:	http://www.ars.usda.gov
E-mail:	arsweb@nal.usda.gov

Alternative Farming Systems Information Center

This site has information about alternative cropping systems such as sustainable, organic, low-input, biodynamic, and regenerative agriculture. It also specializes in information about alternative crops, new uses for traditional crops, and crops grown for industrial production. It's operated by the Alternative Farming Systems Information Center, which is part of the National Agricultural Library.

The site's highlight is its collection of bibliographies and other publications about adopting sustainable alternatives, alternative crops, economic aspects of alternative farming systems, breeding and selecting crops for insect resistance, compost, conservation tillage, farmland preservation, growing for the medicinal herb market, herbicide tolerance and resistance in plants, herbs and herb gardening, integrated pest management, irrigation, organic gardening, small-scale farming, and raising emus and ostriches, among many other subjects.

The site also has lots of information about aquaculture and an excellent set of links to other Internet sites about alternative farming issues.

Vital Stats:

Access method:	WWW
To access:	http://www.nal.usda.gov/afsic
E-mail:	afsic@nal.usda.gov

Animal Welfare Information Center

This site specializes in information about using animals in research, although it also covers other animal welfare issues. The site is operated by the National Agricultural Library.

The site has a report from the National Institutes of Health titled *Plan for the Use of Animals in Research,* a National Agricultural Library document titled *Essentials for Animal Research: A Primer for Research Personnel,* a wide range of federal and international laws and regulations about caring for animals, bibliographies on numerous animal welfare topics, a newsletter, and links to other animal welfare sites.

Vital Stats:

Access method:	WWW
To access:	http://www.nal.usda.gov/awic
E-mail:	awic@nal.usda.gov

Current Research Information System (CRIS)

CRIS offers descriptions of more than 30,000 current and recently completed research projects in agriculture, forestry, and food and nutrition. CRIS is operated by the U.S. Department of Agriculture.

The projects listed in CRIS are conducted or sponsored by USDA research agencies, state agricultural experiment stations, the state land grant university system, other state institutions, and participants in USDA's National Research Initiative Competitive Grants Program. The database is updated weekly.

The research projects listed in CRIS cover such topics as management and conservation of soil, water, forest, and range resources; protection of crops and livestock from insects, diseases, pests, and other hazards; biological production management systems; farm and forest product development; marketing of crop, animal, and forest products; foreign trade and market development; food and human nutrition; rural and community development; and related topics.

Vital Stats:

Access method:	WWW
To access:	http://cristel.nal.usda.gov:8080
E-mail:	rbroome@cristel.nal.usda.gov

Economic Research Service

The Economic Research Service site has a fantastic collection of reports about agriculture, food, natural resources, and rural America. The service is part of the U.S. Department of Agriculture.

Some sample report titles are *The Taxpayer Relief Act of 1997: Provisions for Farmers and Rural Communities; USDA Agricultural Baseline Projections to 2007; Agricultural Adaptation to Climatic Change: Issues of Longrun Sustainability; The Benefits of Protecting Rural Water Quality; Voluntary Incentives for Reducing Agricultural Nonpoint Source Water Pollution; Benefits of Safer Drinking Water: The Value of Nitrate Reduction; Credit in Rural America; Issues in Agricultural and Rural Finance; The Future of China's Grain Market; Bacterial Foodborne Disease: Medical Costs and Productivity Losses; The Diets of America's Children; An Economic Assessment of Food Safety Regulations; The Structure of Dairy Markets;* and *Rural Economic Development: What Makes Rural Communities Grow?*

The site also has farm income estimates by state, telephone numbers and e-mail addresses for ERS subject specialists, and state fact sheets that contain information for each state about population, income, earnings, poverty, employment, farm and farm-related jobs, top export commodities, and farm characteristics, among other subjects.

Vital Stats:

Access method: WWW
To access: http://www.econ.ag.gov
E-mail: webadmin@econ.ag.gov

National Agricultural Library

The highlight of the National Agricultural Library (NAL) site is AGRICOLA, a database containing bibliographic records for more than two million items in the library's collection. Until recently, AGRICOLA was a fee-based system. However, the NAL now offers a free online version.

The bibliographic records cover a wide range of agricultural subjects, including plant and animal sciences, forestry, entomology, soil and water resources, agricultural economics, agricultural engineering, agricultural products, alternative farming practices, food and nutrition, agricultural trade and marketing, rural America, and animal welfare.

AGRICOLA is actually two databases that must be searched separately. The Online Public Access Catalog has citations for books, audiovisual materials, and serial publications. The Journal Article Citation Index has records for journal articles, book chapters, reports, and reprints. Both databases are updated daily.

Besides AGRICOLA, the site offers an NAL telephone directory, links to other sites with agricultural information, and links to Web sites operated by numerous NAL information centers, including the Food and Nutrition Information Center, the Rural Information Center, and the Technology Transfer Information Center. It also has a nice collection of images of homesteads, plant pests and diseases, forest fire fighters, forest insects, rare botanical prints, and other subjects.

Vital Stats:

Access method: WWW
To access: http://www.nal.usda.gov
E-mail: webmaster@nal.usda.gov

North Carolina Cooperative Extension Service

Although there are lots of Cooperative Extension Service Internet sites around the country, the North Carolina Cooperative Extension Service site is among the best. It specializes in information for both home gardeners and commercial farmers that is useful whether you live in North Carolina or elsewhere.

The site offers more than 100 leaflets about such horticultural topics as growing asparagus and home landscaping, publications about plant pathology, booklets about wildlife stewardship, extensive demographic data for every North Carolina county, detailed National Weather Service forecasts for North Carolina, an excellent set of links to information about food safety, and much more.

Vital Stats:

Access method:	WWW
To access:	http://www.ces.ncsu.edu
E-mail:	webmaster@www.ces.ncsu.edu

Rural Development

The Rural Development site provides information about business and economic development, housing programs, community facilities programs, services to cooperatives, utility programs, community development, and related subjects. It's operated by the rural development agencies of the U.S. Department of Agriculture.

The site has dozens of case studies of successful rural development programs, rural development regulations, rural highlights from the 1996 farm bill, links to other economic development sites on the Internet, and lots more.

Vital Stats:

Access method:	WWW
To access:	http://www.rurdev.usda.gov
E-mail:	webmaster@rurdev.usda.gov

Rural Information Center

This site has links to rural information sites on the Internet and a calendar of rural conferences. It's operated by the Rural Information Center, which is a cooperative project of the National Agricultural Library and the USDA Cooperative State Research, Education, and Extension Service.

The site's highlight is its bibliographies on issues affecting rural America. A few of the topics covered are agricultural safety and health, arts and humanities programs in rural America, crime in rural areas, downtown revitalization, financial management for local governments, health care in rural America, information access, rural education, managed care, population migration in rural America, poverty in rural areas, tourism, retirement communities, and rural youth employment.

Vital Stats:

Access method:	WWW
To access:	http://www.nal.usda.gov/ric/ricpage.htm
E-mail:	ric@nal.usda.gov

USDA Economics and Statistics System

The USDA Economics and Statistics System has hundreds of reports and data sets about agriculture. The system is a joint project of the U.S. Department of Agriculture's Economic Research Service and the Albert R. Mann Library at Cornell University.

There are more than 100 reports, including Economic Research Service Situation and Outlook Reports, National Agricultural Statistics Service reports, and World Agricultural Outlook Board reports. They cover such topics as agricultural income and finances, farm production expenses, dairy production, industrial uses of agricultural materials, agricultural trade, livestock inventories, world agricultural supply and demand, and the outlook for vegetables and specialty crops. Automatic subscriptions to new editions of the reports are available through the USDA Reports Electronic Mailing List (this page).

The system also provides more than 140 data sets, most of which are available in Lotus 1-2-3 format. Data are available about worldwide textile fiber production, farm production expenses, sales of milk and dairy products, food spending in American households, fertilizer use, weather in U.S. agriculture, and many other topics.

Vital Stats:

Access methods:	WWW, Gopher
To access:	http://usda.mannlib.cornell.edu *or* gopher://usda.mannlib.cornell.edu
E-mail:	help@usda.mannlib.cornell.edu

USDA Home Page

The USDA Home Page offers the full text of the *Agriculture Fact Book,* which has information about the structure of U.S. agriculture, rural America, rural economic and community development programs, food and nutrition, natural resources and the environment, and other subjects.

The site, which is operated by the U.S. Department of Agriculture, also has a calendar of agricultural events, details about the department's budget, information about the 1996 farm bill, and links to Internet sites operated by Agriculture Department agencies.

Vital Stats:

Access method:	WWW
To access:	http://www.usda.gov
E-mail:	vic.powell@usda.gov

USDA Reports Electronic Mailing List

The USDA Reports Electronic Mailing List offers subscriptions to more than fifty reports about agriculture. They include Economic Research Service Situation and Outlook Reports, National Agricultural Statistics Service reports, and World Agricultural Outlook Board reports. The mailing list is a joint project of the U.S. Department of Agriculture's Economic Research Service and the Albert R. Mann Library at Cornell University.

The reports cover such topics as agricultural income and finances, farm production expenses, dairy production, industrial uses of agricultural materials, agricultural trade, livestock inventories, world agricultural supply and demand, and the outlook for vegetables and specialty crops.

The same reports are also available through the USDA Economics and Statistics System (p. 36).

Vital Stats:

Access method:	E-mail
To access:	Send an e-mail message to usda-reports@jan.mannlib.cornell.edu
Subject line:	
Message:	**lists** (to get a list of available reports)
E-mail (questions):	help@usda.mannlib.cornell.edu

Water Quality Information Center

The effect of agriculture on water quality is the primary focus of this site, which is operated by the National Agricultural Library. The site has bibliographies, calendars of meetings, a list of Internet mailing lists about water issues, publications, links to more than two dozen water-related databases, and links to related sites.

Vital Stats:

Access method:	WWW
To access:	http://www.nal.usda.gov/wqic
E-mail:	jmakuch@nal.usda.gov

ARTS AND MUSEUMS

The First 150 Years: The Traveling Exhibition

This site celebrates the Smithsonian Institution's 150th birthday, which occurred in 1996. It has extensive information about the Smithsonian's early years and its evolution, in addition to hundreds of photographs of the museum's most popular artifacts.

Vital Stats:

Access method: WWW
To access: http://www.150.si.edu

The John F. Kennedy Center for the Performing Arts

This site provides calendars of upcoming concerts, plays, and other performances at the John F. Kennedy Center for the Performing Arts in Washington, D.C. It also has information about tours of the Kennedy Center and opportunities for young performers.

Vital Stats:

Access method: WWW
To access: http://kennedy-center.org
E-mail: comments@mail.kennedy-center.org

National Air and Space Museum

This site allows you to take a virtual tour of the National Air and Space Museum, the most popular attraction in Washington, D.C., from the comfort of your computer chair. It has extensive photographs and background information about exhibits at the museum, which traces the history of space flight from its beginnings to the present day. It even has information and photographs about many artifacts that aren't on display, such as the SR71 Blackbird spy plane and the space shuttle *Enterprise.*

Besides the exhibit information, the site has a map of the museum, press releases about new exhibits, alphabetical lists of all aircraft and space artifacts displayed at the museum, and information about touring the separate facility where aircraft are restored.

Vital Stats:

Access method: WWW
To access: http://www.nasm.edu
E-mail: web@www.nasm.edu

National Endowment for the Arts

The National Endowment for the Arts site has background information about the NEA, applications for funding, a list of free publications that can be ordered from the NEA, a staff directory, contact information for state arts agencies and related organizations, links to dozens of Web sites operated by other arts organizations, and *Arts.community,* a monthly online journal about the arts in America.

Vital Stats:

Access method: WWW
To access: http://arts.endow.gov
E-mail: webmgr@arts.endow.gov

National Gallery of Art

This beautifully designed site lets you browse through the collection of the National Gallery of Art in Washington, D.C. There are more than 3,000 images of paintings, sculptures, decorative arts, and works on paper from the gallery's collection, along with brief descriptions of the items. In addition, the site has a searchable database that contains information about all 100,000 items in the gallery's collection.

The site also offers information about visiting the gallery, brochures and teacher's guides for current exhibitions, information about upcoming exhibitions, details about research facilities, a catalog of posters and other items that can be ordered from the gallery, and a calendar of lectures, demonstrations, films, and concerts.

Vital Stats:

Access method: WWW
To access: http://www.nga.gov
E-mail: webfeedback@nga.gov

National Museum of American Art

The National Museum of American Art site offers hundreds of images of artworks in the museum's collection. The museum is part of the Smithsonian Institution.

The site's search feature is very helpful. You can search the whole site, or you can search by artwork or text references.

As well as the images, the site offers a list of current, upcoming, and traveling exhibitions; information about internships and fellowships; databases of American paintings executed before 1914 and American sculptures executed through the twentieth century; teacher's guides and student activity packets; directions to the museum and its hours of operation; and press releases.

Vital Stats:

Access methods: WWW
To access: http://www.nmaa.si.edu
E-mail: mbriggs@nmaa.si.edu

National Museum of Natural History

This site offers online exhibits from the National Museum of Natural History, which is part of the Smithsonian Institution. The exhibits available include "In Search of Giant Squid," "Ocean Planet," "Crossroads of Continents," "Hologlobe, " "Global Warming," and "Portraits of Smithsonian Science."

The site also has a calendar of events, information about visiting the museum, lists of Smithsonian scientists by department, and files and searchable databases about anthropology, botany, entomology, vertebrate zoology, invertebrate zoology, mineral sciences, and paleobiology.

Vital Stats:

Access method:	WWW
To access:	http://www.nmnh.si.edu
E-mail:	webmaster@www.nmnh.si.edu

National Portrait Gallery

The National Portrait Gallery site offers portraits of all the presidents, patriots and statesmen from America's revolutionary period, and prominent Native Americans. The gallery is part of the Smithsonian Institution.

The site also includes images from current exhibits, a calendar of events, a database containing information about all 10,000 items in the museum's collection, a database called the Catalog of American Portraits that contains images and information about 65,000 portraits, a list of gallery publications, and press releases.

Vital Stats:

Access method:	WWW
To access:	http://www.npg.si.edu
E-mail:	capnpg@sivm.si.edu

Smithsonian Institution

Like the Smithsonian Institution itself, the institution's Web site is a place where it's easy to lose yourself for hours. Whether you're planning a trip to the Smithsonian or just want to view some of its treasures from the comfort of your home, the site is a wonderful resource.

The site offers thousands of text files, maps, photographs, sound samples, and video clips. If you're looking for something specific, a search feature allows you to quickly find what you're seeking.

Among the highlights, the site has detailed information about each of the Smithsonian museums; information about visiting the National Zoo, which is part of the Smithsonian; continuously updated webcam pictures of various animal exhibits at the National Zoo; and online exhibits prepared by various Smithsonian facilities. You'll also find extensive information about planning a trip to Washington, D.C., and the Smithsonian, including details about attractions for children, where to stay and eat, sightseeing in Washington, visiting the Smithsonian, tourism information sources, and traveling to Washington.

The site also has a searchable directory of Smithsonian staff members, information about internship and volunteer opportunities, catalogs of items that can be ordered from Smithsonian shops, and links to Internet sites operated by Smithsonian museums.

Vital Stats:

Access method:	WWW
To access:	http://www.si.edu
E-mail:	webmaster@si.edu

Smithsonian Institution Research Information System (SIRIS)

The Smithsonian Institution Research Information System (SIRIS) consists of six databases that have records about items in the collections of the Smithsonian and other museums. The most interesting databases contain records describing American paintings completed before 1914, sculptures by artists born or active in the United States through the twentieth century, the approximately 1.2 million volumes in the Smithsonian's various libraries, and more than 100,000 manuscripts, photographs, sound recordings, and films in the Smithsonian's collection.

Vital Stats:

Access method:	WWW
To access:	http://www.siris.si.edu
E-mail:	siris@sivm.si.edu

BUSINESS, TRADE, AND ECONOMICS

BUSINESS

The Bureau of Export Administration

This site offers a huge amount of information for exporters. It's operated by the Bureau of Export Administration, which is part of the Commerce Department.

The site has details about trade sanctions against various countries, fact sheets about who needs an export license and what agencies have jurisdiction over exports, explanations of how to fill out various export license forms, a list of things to consider when hiring foreign nationals, and speeches and congressional testimony by export officials.

It also offers a calendar of seminars and conferences, a list of people and companies that have been denied export privileges, a list of foreign companies and individuals who are barred from buying certain products because of proliferation concerns, links to other federal export control sites, and much more.

Vital Stats:

Access method:	WWW
To access:	http://www.bxa.doc.gov
E-mail:	website@bxa.doc.gov

Federal Electronic Commerce Program Office

This site offers federal electronic commerce news and information about such topics as electronic benefits transfer, electronic funds transfer, electronic grants, interoperable electronic catalogs, and smart cards. The site, which is operated by the General Services Administration, also has links to other federal sites on electronic commerce.

Vital Stats:

Access method:	WWW
To access:	http://ec.fed.gov
E-mail:	electronic.commerce@gsa.gov

IBM Patent Server

The IBM Patent Server allows you to search more than two million patents filed with the U.S. Patent and Trademark Office from 1974 to the present. You can search the database by keyword, patent number, inventor, assignee, title, abstract, claims, and agent.

For selected patents issued from 1971 to 1973, the site provides bibliographic data and the text. For all patents issued from 1974 to the present, it also provides images.

Vital Stats:

Access method:	WWW
To access:	http://www.patents.ibm.com
E-mail:	patent_help@vnet.ibm.com

Office of Economic Conversion Information

This site is designed to help businesses, communities, and workers affected by defense conversion and other economic development issues. It's a joint project of the Commerce and Defense Departments.

The site has lists of contacts at military installations that are scheduled to close, military base closure and realignment status reports, civilian industry trend data, information about property available at closing and realigning military bases, community and industry case studies, information about financing strategies, details about government and private sector programs to help communities and workers, applicable federal laws and regulations, and much, much more.

Vital Stats:

Access method:	WWW
To access:	http://netsite.esa.doc.gov
E-mail:	jlavery@doc.gov

Office of the United States Trade Representative's Homepage

The Office of the United States Trade Representative's Homepage provides agreements negotiated by the trade representative, biographical information about senior officials in the office, speeches and congressional testimony, press releases, information about the North American Free Trade Agreement, and numerous reports, including *A Comprehensive Trade and Development Policy for the Countries of Africa* and *U.S. Regulation of Products Derived from Biotechnology.*

Vital Stats:

Access method:	WWW
To access:	http://www.ustr.gov

Online Women's Business Center

Although this site is targeted at women, it contains valuable information for anyone starting a small business. It's operated by the Small Business Administration in cooperation with private businesses.

The site has hundreds of articles and publications from various sources about starting, expanding, financing, and managing a business, in addition to marketing, procurement, and technology. Some of the available titles are *Business Plan Basics; Evaluating Start-up Costs;*

Trends in Home-Based Small Businesses; Matching Personal Interests with Marketplace Needs; Taking Risks: Your Attitude toward Business Growth; How to Form a Powerful Alliance; Common Roadblocks for Developing Businesses; Keeping Accounting Costs Down; and *What Type of Capital Does Your Business Need?*

Some additional titles are *Understanding the Types of Insurance; How to Measure Employee Effectiveness; Leasing Office Space; The Interview Process: How to Select the "Right" Person; Controlling Time Waste; How Much Is Your Time Worth?; Developing an Effective Media Campaign; Internet Marketing Ideas; Business Research on the Internet; Planning Your Business Web Site; Getting Your Company Mentioned in Publications; How to Work a Trade Fair; How to Register to Do Business with the Federal Government; Do I Really Need a PC?;* and *How a Techno-phobic Lives with Technology.*

The site also has a searchable database of local resources around the country for small businesses, message boards and chat rooms, a sample employee handbook, success stories, contact information for Women's Business Assistance Centers around the country, and links to dozens of Web sites that provide information for small businesses.

Vital Stats:

Access method:	WWW
To access:	http://pro-net.sba.gov
E-mail:	virtual@onramp.net

SBA PRO-Net

This site provides procurement information both for and about small businesses. It's operated by the Small Business Administration.

The site's highlight is a database that contains information about more than 171,000 small, disadvantaged, 8(a), and women-owned businesses. Government agencies and prime contractors can use it to find small-business contractors, subcontractors, or partnership opportunities. You can search the business listings by SIC codes, keywords, location, quality certifications, business type, ownership race and gender, and other factors.

The site also has links to lots of federal sites that offer procurement information.

Vital Stats:

Access method:	WWW
To access:	http://pro-net.sba.gov

Tourism

Subscribers to the Tourism mailing list exchange messages about tourism development for communities, regions, states, and businesses. Some of the topics discussed include public and private tourism development programs, educational and technical assistance needs, and the use of technology in tourism development. The list is operated by the Agriculture Department.

Vital Stats:

Access method:	E-mail
To access:	Send an e-mail message to majordomo@reeusda.gov
Subject line:	
Message:	**subscribe tourism**
E-mail (questions):	tourism-approval@reeusda.gov

U.S. Business Advisor

The U.S. Business Advisor has a remarkable feature that allows you to search more than 535,000 government Web pages at once. The database uses a fill-in-the-blanks form, which makes searching simple. To access the database directly, use the address http://www.business.gov/Search_Online.html.

The site, which is operated by the National Performance Review, bills itself as a "one-stop electronic link to government for business." It offers no original information, but has a conveniently arranged set of links to other government Web sites that have information about addressing and packaging mail, doing business with the General Services Administration, financing a business, getting leads from *Commerce Business Daily,* getting a passport, exporting goods, paying taxes, complying with regulations of the Occupational Safety and Health Administration, paying Social Security taxes, selling to the government, and related topics.

Vital Stats:

Access method:	WWW
To access:	http://www.business.gov
E-mail:	comment@www.npr.gov

U.S. Department of Commerce

The U.S. Department of Commerce site has remarkably little substantive information. That's surprising, given the huge role that the Commerce Department plays in the federal government and the vast number of documents it produces.

The site has the department's budget, information for contractors, links to government and nongovernmental sites about electronic commerce, and many documents about electronic commerce policy, including reports titled *The Emerging Digital Economy* and *A Framework for Global Electronic Commerce.*

The site also has transcripts of congressional testimony by Commerce officials and links to Internet sites operated by Commerce Department bureaus such as the Bureau of the Census, International Trade Administration, National Oceanic and Atmospheric Administration, National Telecommunications and Information Administration, Patent and Trademark Office, National Institute of Standards and Technology, and National Technical Information Service.

Vital Stats:

Access method:	WWW
To access:	http://www.doc.gov
E-mail:	webmaster@doc.gov

U.S. Department of the Treasury

The Treasury Department site has answers to frequently asked questions about coins, paper currency, savings bonds, taxes, and the federal budget and federal debt.

The site also provides information about auctions of seized property, details about touring the Treasury Building in Washington, D.C., procurement information, and sanctions and embargo information from the Office of Foreign Assets Control.

In addition, the site has information about how to submit Freedom of Information Act requests to the Treasury Department and its bureaus, details about redesigns of U.S. currency, biographies and photographs of top Treasury officials, and links to Internet sites operated by Treasury bureaus such as the Internal Revenue Service, U.S. Mint, Bureau of the Public Debt, and Comptroller of the Currency.

Vital Stats:

Access method:	WWW
To access:	http://www.ustreas.gov
E-mail:	wwwadmin@www.ustreas.gov

United States Government Electronic Commerce Policy

This site has reports titled *The Emerging Digital Economy* and *A Framework for Global Electronic Commerce,* a presidential directive about electronic commerce, and links to lots of other sites about electronic commerce policy. It's operated by the Commerce Department.

Vital Stats:

Access method:	WWW
To access:	http://www.ecommerce.gov
E-mail:	secretariat@doc.gov

U.S. International Trade Commission

Although the U.S. International Trade Commission site has some serious interface problems, it offers a valuable collection of information about foreign trade issues.

The first problem is that you cannot read many of the documents online—you have to download them to your computer before reading them. This is bad design, besides being a royal pain. In addition, some of the files have been compressed in a self-extracting format that makes them unusable on most Macintosh computers. One of the beauties of the Internet is that it's a cross-platform medium—except when webmasters screw up their files.

Those problems aside, the site has tables showing U.S. trade statistics, a list of USITC trade analysts by subject, the *Harmonized Tariff Schedule of the United States,* recent petitions and complaints filed with the USITC about trade practices, notices from the *Federal Register,* a bibliography of trade-related articles from law journals, links to other trade-related Internet sites, and press releases about imports, antidumping investigations, and other subjects.

Vital Stats:

Access method:	WWW
To access:	http://www.usitc.gov
E-mail:	webmaster@usitc.gov

U.S. Patent and Trademark Office

This site is in the midst of a major upgrade. When the improvements are completed, it will provide free access to the full text of the two million patents issued from 1976 to the present and the text and images of 800,000 trademarks and 300,000 pending registrations from the late 1800s to the present.

During the project's first phase, trademark text was placed online in the summer of 1998. The patent text and trademark images were scheduled to be online by November 1998, and patent images by March 1999.

Besides the new databases, the site offers a huge quantity of information about patents and trademarks. It has weekly compilations of bibliographic data and abstracts for new patents, a subject list that provides access to contact points for obtaining further information from the PTO, and basic information about registering patents and trademarks.

It also has various patent and trademark forms, including the patent application form; reports titled *A Guide to Filing a Design Patent Application, Intellectual Property and the National Information Infrastructure,* and *The Conference on Fair Use: An Interim Report to the Commissioner;* books titled *Manual of Patent Examining Procedures* and *Examination Guidelines for Computer-Related Inventions;* and transcripts of hearings about commercial security on the National Information Infrastructure, converting to a twenty-year patent term, the eighteen-month publication of patent applications, the patenting of biotechnological inventions, and software patent protection.

In addition, the site has a PTO telephone directory, proposed legislative changes to patent and trademark laws, a list of patent and trademark depository libraries, a database that has contact information for more than 16,000 attorneys who are licensed to practice before the PTO, speeches by PTO officials, press releases, acquisitions and procurement documents, links to dozens of other Internet sites around the world that offer patent and trademark information, and lots more.

Vital Stats:

Access method:	WWW
To access:	http://www1.uspto.gov
E-mail:	www@uspto.gov

USPTO Patent Databases

This site, which is operated by the U.S. Patent and Trademark Office, provides two databases with patent information.

The U.S. Patent Bibliographic Database provides the front page of all patents issued from 1976 to the present. The AIDS Patent Database provides the full text and images of AIDS-related patents issued by patent offices in the United States, Japan, and Europe.

Vital Stats:

Access method:	WWW
To access:	http://patents.uspto.gov
E-mail:	www@uspto.gov

United States Postal Service

The United States Postal Service site offers everything from a program for tracking express mail packages to information about how to detect mail bombs.

The site has domestic and international postal rates, information for business mailers, explanations of various types of postal fraud and scams, extensive moving tips, wanted posters from the Postal Inspection Service, publications about mail classification reform, information about new stamp releases, a Zip Code database, a database of postal facilities, information for contractors, speeches by USPS officials, press releases, links to other USPS Internet sites and Internet sites operated by foreign postal authorities, and much more.

Vital Stats:

Access method:	WWW
To access:	http://www.usps.gov
E-mail:	customer@email.usps.gov

U.S. Securities and Exchange Commission

The U.S. Securities and Exchange Commission site provides the full text of reports filed by public corporations with the SEC. Reports are added to the site twenty-four hours after they're processed at the SEC.

There are many ways to search the reports. You can search reports filed in the previous week; search prospectus forms; search all reports at once using keywords; and search by other variables. You also can look up a company's central index key and its stock exchange ticker symbol. Extensive information is provided about how to search the database.

Besides the reports, the site offers SEC publications about investing, reports about the securities industry, press releases, proposed and final rules, news about SEC enforcement actions, and the daily *SEC News Digest,* which provides information about enforcement proceedings, rule filings, policy statements, and upcoming commission meetings.

Vital Stats:

Access method:	WWW
To access:	http://www.sec.gov
E-mail:	webmaster@sec.gov

U.S. Small Business Administration

The U.S. Small Business Administration site offers a huge quantity of information for people who run small businesses and those who are thinking of doing so.

It has documents about developing a business, workbooks about developing a business plan and marketing a business, information for companies that want to become government contractors, hundreds of freeware and shareware software programs, and speeches and congressional testimony by SBA officials.

The site also has addresses and telephone numbers for all SBA offices, information for minority owners of small businesses, details about SBA disaster loan programs, press releases, information about assistance for veterans who are interested in starting a business, and much, much more.

Vital Stats:

Access method:	WWW
To access:	http://www.sba.gov
E-mail:	feedback@www2.sbaonline.sba.gov

WhoWhere? Edgar

WhoWhere? Edgar provides the full text of reports that public corporations file with the Securities and Exchange Commission. They're the same documents that are available through the U.S. Securities and Exchange Commission Web site (p. 52). WhoWhere? Edgar is operated by a private company.

One special feature of WhoWhere? Edgar allows you to sign up for e-mail notices when documents about a particular company are added to the site. Another feature lets you create a permanent list of your favorite companies so that you don't have to conduct a search every time you visit the site. You must register to use the two special features, but registration is free.

Vital Stats:

Access method:	WWW
To access:	http://www.whowhere.com/EDGAR

ECONOMIC DATA

Board of Governors of the Federal Reserve System

Although the Board of Governors of the Federal Reserve System site specializes in technical economic data, it also has a few consumer pamphlets. Some of the available titles are *How to File a Consumer Complaint about a Bank; Shop: The Card You Pick Can Save You Money; Keys to Vehicle Leasing;* and *Home Mortgages: Where to Shop and What to Look For.*

The site also has a searchable database of bank ratings under the Community Reinvestment Act, background information about the Federal Reserve System, biographies of members of the Board of Governors, information about the Federal Open Market Committee, congressional testimony and speeches by Federal Reserve officials, press releases, reports to Congress, a summary of Federal Reserve regulations, articles from the *Federal Reserve Bulletin,* links to Internet sites operated by Federal Reserve banks, and much more.

Vital Stats:

Access method:	WWW
To access:	www.bog.frb.fed.us

Bureau of the Public Debt on the Net

The Bureau of the Public Debt on the Net has information about the size of the federal debt from 1987 to the present, details about various investment opportunities available from the federal government, descriptions of scams and frauds involving government securities, several dozen files about savings bonds, and the results of auctions of T-bills, notes, and bonds.

Vital Stats:

Access method:	WWW
To access:	http://www.publicdebt.treas.gov
E-mail:	OAdmin@bpd.treas.gov

Federal Reserve Banks

All twelve Federal Reserve Banks operate Web sites. What's offered varies among the sites, but they frequently provide economic data for the region they cover, weekly and quarterly publications about economics, speeches by bank officials, research publications, and press releases.

Some of the sites also offer a wide range of federal statistics, including data regarding the consumer price index, savings deposits at commercial banks, prime rate changes, federal government debt, the gross national product, civilian employment, population, foreign exchange rates, and other economic indicators. Many of the sites also operate e-mail mailing lists that automatically deliver new data to subscribers' e-mail mailboxes.

One especially cool feature at the Federal Reserve Bank of Minneapolis site lets you compare what a given amount of money was worth in any two years between 1913 and the present. The feature is based on the consumer price index. To reach it directly, use the address http://woodrow.mpls.frb.fed.us/economy/calc/cpihome.html.

Vital Stats:

Access method: WWW
To access: See accompanying box

Federal Reserve Banks

Federal Reserve Bank of Atlanta
To access: http://www.frbatlanta.org

Federal Reserve Bank of Boston
To access:
http://www.bos.frb.org/index.shtml

Federal Reserve Bank of Chicago
To access: http://www.frbchi.org

Federal Reserve Bank of Cleveland
To access: http://www.clev.frb.org

Federal Reserve Bank of Dallas
To access: http://www.dallasfed.org

Federal Reserve Bank of Kansas City
To access: http://www.kc.frb.org

Federal Reserve Bank of Minneapolis
To access:
http://woodrow.mpls.frb.fed.us

Federal Reserve Bank of New York
To access: http://www.ny.frb.org

Federal Reserve Bank of Philadelphia
To access: http://www.phil.frb.org

Federal Reserve Bank of Richmond
To access: http://www.rich.frb.org

Federal Reserve Bank of St. Louis
To access: http://www.stls.frb.org

Federal Reserve Bank of San Francisco
To access: http://frbsf.org

GOVERNMENT CONTRACTS, GRANTS, AND SALES

Acquisition Reform Network (ARNet)

The Acquisition Reform Network (ARNet) provides the text of the Federal Acquisition Regulations. It also has a huge collection of links to federal Internet sites that offer information related to procurement, including regulations, policy papers, lists of procurement opportunities, and lots more.

The site, which is operated by the General Services Administration's Office of Federal Procurement Policy, also has a searchable database of companies and people who are barred from participating in federal procurement programs.

Vital Stats:

Access method:	WWW
To access:	http://www.arnet.gov
E-mail:	comments@www.arnet.gov

CBD Net

CBD Net provides free access to the full text of the *Commerce Business Daily*, which lists notices of proposed government procurement actions, contract awards, sales of government property, and other procurement information. The site is a joint project of the Department of Commerce and the Government Printing Office.

You can search or browse through the CBD, each edition of which typically contains 500 to 1,000 notices. A new edition is published every business day. The site has extensive information about how to use the CBD.

Vital Stats:

Access method:	WWW
To access:	http://cbdnet.access.gpo.gov
E-mail:	cbd-support@gpo.gov

daily-sales, gov.us.fed.doc.cbd.forsale

The daily-sales mailing list, which is mirrored to the newsgroup gov.us.fed.doc.cbd.forsale, sends summaries of all government asset sales and surplus listings from the *Commerce Business Daily*. Messages are sent each business day.

The list and newsgroup are operated by FinanceNet.

Vital Stats:

Access methods: E-mail, Usenet newsgroup
To access (mailing list): Send an e-mail message to listproc@financenet.gov
Subject line:
Message: **subscribe daily-sales** *firstname lastname*
To access (Usenet):   gov.us.fed.doc.cbd.forsale
E-mail (questions):   support@financenet.gov

Federal Acquisition Regulation

This site, which is operated by the General Services Administration, offers the full text of the Federal Acquisition Regulations. You can browse the regulations online or download them in zipped files or PDF format.

The site also has federal acquisition circulars, previous editions of the Federal Acquisition Regulations, and answers to frequently asked questions.

Vital Stats:

Access method: WWW
To access: http://www.arnet.gov/far
E-mail: comments@www.arnet.gov

Ginnie Mae: Government National Mortgage Association

The Ginnie Mae site has background information about the agency and the securities that it issues. It also provides information about contracting opportunities. Ginnie Mae is a wholly owned corporation within the Department of Housing and Urban Development.

Vital Stats:

Access method: WWW
To access: http://www.ginniemae.gov
E-mail: webmaster@ginniemae.gov

---

govsales, gov.topic.forsale.misc

The govsales mailing list, which is mirrored to the newsgroup gov.topic.forsale.misc., distributes announcements about sales of public property by federal, state, and local governments. It provides news about auctions and public sales of everything from loans to houses to cars.

The list and newsgroup are operated by FinanceNet.

Vital Stats:

Access methods:	E-mail, Usenet newsgroup
To access (mailing list):	Send an e-mail message to listproc@financenet.gov
Subject line:	
Message:	**subscribe govsales** *firstname lastname*
To access (Usenet):	gov.topic.forsale.misc
E-mail (questions):	support@financenet.gov

List of Defaulted Borrowers

This site lists doctors around the country who have defaulted on their student loans. According to the Health Resources and Services Administration, which runs the site, the doctors owe the government a total of about $120 million.

You can browse the list by amount due, discipline, name, school, and state of residence. You can also download the entire list to your computer. For each doctor, the list includes the full name, city and state of practice, school attended, year graduated, discipline, and amount owed.

Vital Stats:

Access method:	WWW
To access:	http://defaulteddocs.dhhs.gov
E-mail:	defaulteddocs@hrsa.dhhs.gov

Loren Data Corp.

This site provides free access to the *Commerce Business Daily,* which contains information about proposed government procurement actions and contract awards of more than $25,000. The site is operated by Loren Data Corp., which also provides various fee-based services involving the CBD.

A new, fully searchable edition of the CBD is posted each business day. Issues of the CBD back to January 1995 also are available.

Vital Stats:

Access method:	WWW
To access:	http://www.ld.com/cbd.html
E-mail:	info@ld.com

Marshall Space Flight Center Procurement Site

The most useful feature at this site is the Procurement Reference Library, which has links to government sites that provide the *Commerce Business Daily,* the Federal Acquisition Regulations, acquisition regulations for individual agencies, procurement information, and electronic commerce resources. To access the library directory, use the address http://ec.msfc.nasa.gov/msfc/procref.html.

The site also has information about doing business with the Marshall Space Flight Center, a directory of employees in Marshall's Procurement Office, and NASA's current *Acquisition Forecast* for its various facilities, which lists procurement opportunities valued at more than $100,000.

Vital Stats:

Access method: WWW
To access: http://ec.msfc.nasa.gov/msfc
E-mail: Rick.Glover@msfc.nasa.gov

NAIS Email Notification Service

This page lets you sign up to receive procurement announcements by e-mail from the NASA Acquisition Internet Service (NAIS). Subscribers receive pre-solicitation and post-award notices, notices of solicitation, and general procurement announcements.

Numerous mailing lists are available. You can sign up to receive all NASA procurement notices, all notices from selected NASA centers, or all notices from selected product service classifications.

Vital Stats:

Access method: WWW
To access: http://nais.nasa.gov/maillist.html
E-mail: Jim.Bradford@msfc.nasa.gov

NASA Acquisition Internet Service (NAIS) Home Page

The highlight of this site is the Federal Acquisition Jumpstation, which provides links to dozens of federal Internet sites that have procurement information. The sites offer acquisition forecasts, announcements, solicitations, how-to guides, small-business assistance information, federal acquisition regulations, and much more. To reach the jumpstation directly, use the address http://nais.nasa.gov/fedproc/home.html.

Another interesting feature is the Financial and Contractual Status (FACS) On-Line Query System, which has information about all NASA contracts, grants, space act agreements, and cooperative agreements valued at more than $25,000. The database can be searched by contractor, location, contract number, and other variables.

NAIS also has links to numerous NASA Internet sites that have procurement information.

Vital Stats:

Access method: WWW
To access: http://nais.nasa.gov
E-mail: Jim.Bradford@msfc.nasa.gov

National Endowment for the Humanities

This site has information about grants and programs of the National Endowment for the Humanities, an independent federal agency that awards grants for projects in history, literature, philosophy, and other areas of the humanities.

The site also has an NEH directory, a directory of state humanities councils, a list of recent grants, NEH publications, a guide to current exhibitions and catalogs funded by the NEH, links to NEH-supported projects that are available online, and information about humanities events in every state and territory.

Vital Stats:

Access method: WWW
To access: http://www.neh.fed.us
E-mail: info@neh.fed.us

National Science Foundation

The National Science Foundation site offers thousands of documents about science and engineering, including the *National Science Foundation Bulletin,* the *NSF Guide to Programs,* information about grants and awards, press releases, reports about various scientific subjects, a staff directory, NSF job vacancy announcements, and descriptions of research projects funded by the foundation.

Vital Stats:

Access method: WWW
To access: http://www.nsf.gov
E-mail: webmaster@nsf.gov

U.S. General Services Administration

The U.S. General Services Administration site specializes in information for government contractors. It offers publications titled *Contracting Opportunities with GSA* and *Forecast of GSA Contracting Opportunities,* in addition to contact information for regional GSA Small Business Centers around the country.

The site also has lots of information about buying federal real estate. Some of the highlights include a publication titled *How You Can Acquire Federal Real Property for Public or Private Use,* listings of federal properties that are for sale, and links to other federal agencies that sell property.

Finally, the site offers publications titled *Security Guidelines for Federal Employees* and *What You Should Know About Coping with Threats and Violence in the Federal Workplace,* a directory of federal government TDD/TTY numbers, and a searchable version of the Catalog of Federal Domestic Assistance, which has information about federal loans, grants, and technical assistance programs available to various levels of government, Indian tribes, private institutions, and individuals.

Vital Stats:

Access method:	WWW
To access:	http://www.gsa.gov
E-mail:	webmaster@gsa.gov

The U.S. Mint

The U.S. Mint site has information about new coins and their designs, production figures for current coins, details about commemorative coins produced by the mint, and press releases. It also has information about coins, coin jewelry, commemorative coins, holiday ornaments, and medals that you can order from the mint.

Vital Stats:

Access method:	WWW
To access:	http://www.usmint.gov

SPECIFIC BUSINESSES AND INDUSTRIES

Federal Communications Commission

The Federal Communications Commission site has information about taxes and other charges on your telephone bill, how to avoid improper charges on your local telephone bill, and what you can do about unsolicited telemarketing calls and faxes.

The site also has documents about such subjects as telecommunications services for people with disabilities, digital television, children's educational programming on television, local competition, and the V-chip. Of special interest to Internet users are documents about Internet bandwidth issues and universal service.

Other items available include the *FCC Daily Digest,* press releases, public notices, meeting notices, calendars of events, speeches by FCC officials, FCC orders, lists of FCC job vacancies, information about regulatory and processing fees, a phone directory for FCC staff members, and selected FCC forms.

Vital Stats:

Access method:	WWW
To access:	http://www.fcc.gov
E-mail:	fccinfo@fcc.gov

Federal Deposit Insurance Corporation

Anyone examining bank failures would do well to spend some time with the Federal Deposit Insurance Corporation (FDIC) site. It has reports that summarize the financial condition of insured commercial banks and savings institutions in each state, lists of private agencies and government agencies that rate and analyze the financial health of banks and thrift institutions, and publications with titles like *Is Your Bank Healthy?*

The site also has consumer publications such as *Mortgage Loan Prequalifications, A Guide to Fair Lending,* and *Consumer Rights;* information about commercial buildings, private residences, and loans that the FDIC has available for sale; warnings about suspicious Internet banking sites; technical statistics on banking; lists of publications available from the FDIC, many for free; a list of the nation's major banking laws; press releases; and lots more.

Vital Stats:

Access method:	WWW
To access:	http://www.fdic.gov
E-mail:	webmaster@fdic.gov

Federal Financial Institutions Examination Council

The highlight of this site is its collection of extensive financial data for each bank, savings and loan association, and credit union in the country. It's operated by the Federal Financial Institutions Examination Council.

The site also has databases listing foreign branches of U.S. banks and U.S. branches of foreign banks, a database containing information about bank mergers and acquisitions, lists of the top 100 banks and bank holding companies by total assets, and a database containing information about bank holding companies.

Other highlights include reports about the performance of lending institutions under the Home Mortgage Disclosure Act, data reported under the Community Reinvestment Act, dozens of documents about the Year 2000 problem, and links to other sites with bank data.

Vital Stats:

Access method:	WWW
To access:	http://www.ffiec.gov
E-mail:	ffiec-suggest@frb.gov

HomePath

HomePath provides information about buying and refinancing a home. It's operated by Fannie Mae, a private corporation that's sponsored by the federal government.

The site has documents about the pros and cons of homeownership, the types of mortgage loans, determining how much home loan you can afford, shopping for the best mortgage deal, applying for a mortgage, closing on the home, refinancing, and other subjects. It also has a glossary of mortgage and financial terms and several mortgage calculators.

Vital Stats:

Access method:	WWW
To access:	http://www.homepath.com

National Credit Union Administration

The National Credit Union Administration site offers a searchable database that contains extensive data about individual credit unions, including statements about each credit union's financial condition. The NCUA supervises and insures more than 6,900 federal credit unions and insures more than 4,200 state-chartered credit unions.

The site also has background information for consumers about credit unions, the *Federal Credit Union Handbook,* legislation, proposed and final rules, regulatory alerts, legal opinion letters, newsletters, links to hundreds of Internet sites operated by credit unions and financial regulators, and lots more.

Vital Stats:

Access method: WWW
To access: http://www.ncua.gov
E-mail: webmaster@ncua.gov

National Gambling Impact Study Commission

This site includes the law that created the National Gambling Impact Study Commission, a fact sheet about the commission, a report about lotteries, the commission's research agenda, a calendar of meetings, transcripts of testimony at public meetings, and press releases.

Vital Stats:

Access method: WWW
To access: http://www.ngisc.gov
E-mail: cstaff@btgcinema.com

TAXES AND SOCIAL SECURITY

The Digital Daily

The Digital Daily, which is operated by the Internal Revenue Service, is the premier Internet site for federal tax information. To help you find what you're seeking, the site has a search feature and a site tree that provides a detailed table of contents.

The site offers tax forms and publications, tax regulations, information about how to obtain tax forms and instructions by fax, details about important changes in the tax law, extensive tax information for businesses, answers to frequently asked tax questions, press releases, tax statistics, links to other Internet sites that have state tax forms, and much more.

Vital Stats:

Access method:	WWW
To access:	http://www.irs.ustreas.gov
E-mail:	helpdesk@fedworld.gov

Digital Dispatch

Subscribers to the Digital Dispatch mailing list receive occasional messages from the Internal Revenue Service. The messages provide IRS press releases, announcements, news about new items on the IRS Web site, reminders about upcoming tax dates, and related information.

Vital Stats:

Access method:	E-mail
To access:	Send an e-mail message to lstsrvr@io.fedworld.gov
Subject line:	**SUBSCRIBE**
Message:	
E-mail:	helpdesk@fedworld.gov

IRIS (Internal Revenue Information Services)

IRIS offers more than 500 tax forms, instructions, and publications from the Internal Revenue Service for individuals, businesses, and other organizations. You can download the tax forms, print them, fill them out, and send them to the IRS, but you cannot fill out the forms online and file electronically.

The site also offers free Adobe Acrobat Reader software that lets you read and print many of the files it offers. The software is available for Windows and Macintosh computers.

Vital Stats:

Access methods:	Telnet, dial-in
To access:	telnet://fedworld.gov
Dial-in access:	703-321-8020
Note:	If you use Telnet access, you must register and then choose item 2, *IRS - IRS Tax forms, Publications and Information.* The login is **guest** if you use dial-in access.

Social Security Online

Social Security Online provides extensive information about your Social Security number and card, Supplemental Security Income, your rights to appeal, Medicare, and retirement, survivors, and disability benefits. Many of the documents are available in Spanish versions.

Some of the available publications are *Social Security: What Every Woman Should Know; Financing Social Security; Social Security: What You Need to Know When You Get Retirement or Survivors Benefits; How Your Retirement Benefit Is Figured; Medicare; Social Security Disability Programs; Social Security Benefits for People Living with HIV/AIDS; Household Workers;* and *If You Are Self-Employed.*

The site also has the Social Security Administration's budget and its annual report to Congress; *Social Security Programs Throughout the World,* a publication that summarizes social security legislation in 165 countries; the *Social Security Handbook,* which has detailed information about Social Security Administration programs; numerous Social Security forms; and much more.

Vital Stats:

Access method:	WWW
To access:	http://www.ssa.gov

Taxing Times

Taxing Times offers a huge collection of federal income tax forms and instructions. It's operated by Maxwell Technologies Inc., with the cooperation of the Internal Revenue Service. The forms and instructions are in Adobe Portable Document Format (PDF).

Besides tax forms, the site offers instructions for forms and schedules, general guides, specialized publications, Spanish-language publications, a list of IRS Tele-Tax telephone numbers for recorded tax information, details about how to call the IRS with tax questions, and links to other Internet sites that have state tax forms.

Vital Stats:

Access method:	WWW
To access:	http://www.maxwell.com/tax
E-mail:	webmaster@maxwell.com

CHILDREN AND FAMILIES

The Administration for Children and Families

This site has reports, press releases, and background information about the dozens of programs operated by the Administration for Children and Families. These include Aid to Families with Dependent Children, Child Support Enforcement, Community Services Block Grants, Head Start, and Low Income Home Energy Assistance, among many others. The site also has information about the administration's welfare reform initiative.

Vital Stats:

Access method:	WWW
To access:	http://www.acf.dhhs.gov
E-mail:	WebMaster@acf.dhhs.gov

ChildStats.gov

The highlight of this site is an annual report titled *America's Children: Key National Indicators of Child Well-Being*. The site is operated by the Federal Interagency Forum on Child and Family Statistics, which publishes the report.

The site also has a long list of e-mail contacts from whom you can obtain federal statistics about children and families, links to reports and Web sites about children and families, and a report titled *Nurturing Fatherhood: Improving Data and Research on Male Fertility, Family Formation, and Fatherhood*.

Vital Stats:

Access method:	WWW
To access:	http://www.childstats.gov
E-mail:	childstats@ed.gov

Coming Up Taller: Arts and Humanities Programs for Children and Youth at Risk

This site's highlight is a report that describes more than 200 after-school, weekend, and summer arts and humanities programs for children around the country. The report also has contact information for each program. It is operated by the President's Committee on the Arts and the Humanities.

The site also has information about awards given to outstanding arts and humanities programs for children, background information about the Coming Up Taller initiative, and links to related sites.

Vital Stats:

Access method:	WWW
To access:	http://www.cominguptaller.org

National Child Care Information Center (NCCIC)

The National Child Care Information Center (NCCIC) site offers research publications from various sources. Some of the available titles are *Child Care for Low Income Families, Long Term Outcomes of Early Childhood Programs, Results of the NICHD Study of Early Child Care,* and *Child Care and Early Education Program Participation of Infants, Toddlers, and Preschoolers.* The center is funded by the Department of Health and Human Services.

The site also has a guide to finding child care information on the Internet, issues of the *Child Care Bulletin,* a list of organizations active on child care issues, information about President Bill Clinton's child care initiative, a conference calendar, and links to dozens of related sites.

Vital Stats:

Access method:	WWW
To access:	http://ericps.crc.uiuc.edu/nccic
E-mail:	nccicweb@ericps.crc.uiuc.edu

National Clearinghouse on Child Abuse and Neglect Information

The National Clearinghouse on Child Abuse and Neglect Information site includes profiles of effective community-based prevention programs around the country, a national directory of child abuse and neglect treatment programs, and a database containing bibliographic information about more than 24,000 documents concerning child abuse and neglect. The clearinghouse is funded by the Department of Health and Human Services.

The site also has information about services and publications available from the clearinghouse, a conference calendar, statistics on child abuse and neglect, answers to frequently asked questions about child abuse and neglect, information about preventing child abuse, and state civil and criminal statutes concerning child maltreatment.

Vital Stats:

Access method:	WWW
To access:	http://www.calib.com/nccanch
E-mail:	nccanch@calib.com

National Parent Information Network (NPIN)

The National Parent Information Network (NPIN) site has dozens of publications for parents from many sources. Some sample titles are *Ten Signs of a Great Preschool, Busy Parent's Guide to Child Care, Children's Illnesses and Child Care, Child Safety on the Information Highway, Monitoring TV Time, Video Games and Children, Nurturing Giftedness in Young Children, Books for Children, Encouraging Young Children's Writing, The Single Parent,* and *Working Parents' Survival Guide.* The site is a joint project of the ERIC Clearinghouse on Elementary and Early Childhood Education and the ERIC Clearinghouse on Urban Education, both of which are funded by the U.S. Department of Education.

The site also has a list of books for parents from various publishers, a monthly magazine titled *Parent News,* links to other Internet sites that offer dozens of newsletters and magazines for parents, and links to dozens of Internet sites related to children, education, and parenting.

In addition, the site has lots of publications for people who work with parents. Sample titles include *A Community Guide to Multicultural Education Programs, Connecting Families and Schools to Help Our Children Succeed,* and *A Guide to Communicating with Asian American Families.*

Vital Stats:

Access method: WWW
To access: http://ericps.crc.uiuc.edu/npin
E-mail: npinweb@ericps.crc.uiuc.edu

Office of the Assistant Secretary for Planning and Evaluation

This site has numerous reports about children and youth policy. It's operated by the Office of the Assistant Secretary for Planning and Evaluation in the Department of Health and Human Services.

The reports cover such subjects as community responses to domestic violence, trends in the well-being of children and youths, preventing teen pregnancy, adolescent sex and child-bearing, child care prices, services for migrant children, intensive family reunification programs, teaching preschool children affected by substance abuse, designing welfare-to-work programs, child support, and welfare reform.

The site also has the federal poverty guidelines and the *Catalog of Federal Domestic Assistance,* which provides details about more than 1,300 federal programs, projects, and services that provide assistance or benefits to the American public.

Vital Stats:

Access method: WWW
To access: http://aspe.os.dhhs.gov
E-mail: aspeinfo@osaspe.dhhs.gov

PARENTING-L

Subscribers to the PARENTING-L mailing list exchange messages about parenting children from birth through adolescence. Some of the topics discussed are child development, day care, education, family leave, and parental rights. The list is operated by the ERIC Clearinghouse on Elementary and Early Childhood Education, which is funded by the U.S. Department of Education.

Vital Stats:

Access method: E-mail
To access: Send an e-mail message to listserv@postoffice.cso.uiuc.edu
Subject line:
Message: **subscribe PARENTING-L** *firstname lastname*
E-mail (questions):   listadmn@ericps.crc.uiuc.edu

Safe Places to Play

This page offers an excellent collection of annotated links to thirty Web pages for kids operated by a variety of federal agencies and departments. The pages are provided by the Justice Department, Labor Department, Environmental Protection Agency, Forest Service, White House, NASA, National Science Foundation, FBI, U.S. Geological Survey, and other agencies. The Department of Housing and Urban Development sponsors the link page.

Vital Stats:

Access method: WWW
To access: http://www.hud.gov/kids/safeplay.html

Web Pages for Kids around the Federal Government

This page provides links to Web pages for kids operated by twenty federal agencies and departments. There are links to pages operated by the White House, Consumer Product Safety Commission, Environmental Protection Agency, FBI, Federal Emergency Management Agency, Interior Department, National Science Foundation, Social Security Administration, NASA, and National Institute of Environmental Health Sciences, among other agencies. The link page is provided by the U.S. Department of Health and Human Services.

Vital Stats:

Access method: WWW
To access: http://www.hhs.gov/families/kids.htm

YouthInfo

The YouthInfo site offers little original information, but it has an excellent collection of links to other Internet sites that have reports and publications about adolescents, speeches by federal officials on youth topics, and other types of information about youths. It's operated by the U.S. Department of Health and Human Services.

Vital Stats:

Access method: WWW
To access: http://youth.os.dhhs.gov
E-mail: youth@osaspe.dhhs.gov

COMPUTERS

CIAC-Bulletin

The CIAC-Bulletin mailing list distributes urgent notices about new computer security problems. It's operated by the Computer Incident Advisory Capability, an Energy Department agency that also operates a Web site (next entry).

Vital Stats:

Access method:	E-mail
To access:	Send an e-mail message to majordomo@tholia.llnl.gov
Subject line:	
Message:	**subscribe ciac-bulletin**
E-mail (questions):	owner-majordomo@tholia.llnl.gov

Computer Incident Advisory Capability

The Computer Incident Advisory Capability site has a vast collection of resources about computer viruses and security. It's operated by the Energy Department.

The site has bulletins about new computer security vulnerabilities and recommended solutions, detailed descriptions of hundreds of computer viruses, information about anti-virus products for various types of computers, and links to other Internet sites that provide information about computer security and viruses.

Of particular interest are several files about virus hoaxes. The files describe the most common hoaxes, the history behind virus hoaxes, and how to identify a hoax.

The CIAC also operates the CIAC-Bulletin mailing list (previous entry).

Vital Stats:

Access method:	WWW
To access:	http://ciac.llnl.gov
E-mail:	webmaster@ciac.gov

Computer Security Resource Clearinghouse

Virtually anyone who uses a computer will find interesting and valuable information at the Computer Security Resource Clearinghouse, which is operated by the National Institute of Standards and Technology. The site contains hundreds of files about computer security—everything from detailed information about computer viruses to a calendar of security-related seminars and conferences.

The site also has alerts that describe new computer viruses, a list of computer security publications published by the National Institute of Standards and Technology, federal computer security policy documents, links to other Internet sites worldwide that offer computer security information, and lots more.

Vital Stats:

Access method:	WWW
To access:	http://csrc.nist.gov
E-mail:	webmaster-csrc@nist.gov

FedCIRC

The FedCIRC (Federal Computer Incident Response Capability) site has a searchable database that contains descriptions of hundreds of computer viruses. The agency, which is a joint project of the National Institute of Standards and Technology, the Energy Department's Computer Incident Advisory Capability, and the Carnegie Mellon Software Engineering Institute, provides civilian federal agencies with guidance in handling computer security incidents.

Besides the database, the site includes advisories about new computer security problems, links to Internet sites that offer computer security tools, and an excellent collection of links to Internet sites that provide computer security information.

Vital Stats:

Access method:	WWW
To access:	http://fedcirc.llnl.gov
E-mail:	fedcirc-web@fedcirc.nist.gov

Federal Y2K Commercial Off-the-Shelf (COTS) Product Database

This database provides information about computer products that are Year 2000 compliant—commonly abbreviated as Y2K compliant. It contains vendor information, notations by federal agencies about their experiences with specific products, and details of Year 2000 code compliance. The system was jointly developed by the Social Security Administration and the General Services Administration.

The site also has links to Web sites operated by vendors and others involved in the Year 2000 computer problem.

Vital Stats:

Access method:	WWW
To access:	http://y2k.policyworks.gov

IT Policy On-Ramp

Just about anything you might want to know about federal information technology (IT) policy is available at this site. It's operated by the Office of Information Technology in the General Services Administration.

The site includes IT strategic plans, a calendar of IT conferences and other events, information about the Year 2000 problem, details about the development and use of performance measures, information about making technology accessible for people with disabilities, a list of vendors of ergonomic products, best practices guidelines, legislation and regulations, and much more.

Vital Stats:

Access method:	WWW
To access:	http://www.itpolicy.gsa.gov
E-mail:	tokey.bradfield@gsa.gov

President's Council on Year 2000 Conversion

This site provides a large collection of links to articles, reports, and Web sites about the Year 2000 problem. It's operated by the President's Council on Year 2000 Conversion.

There are links to Y2K Web resources and information grouped by economic sector, other federal Web sites that provide Y2K guides and reports, Y2K pages operated by states around the country, and a Y2K job bank. The site also has the text of the Year 2000 Information and Readiness Disclosure Act.

Vital Stats:

Access method:	WWW
To access:	http://www.y2k.gov
E-mail:	theresa.noll@gsa.gov

DEFENSE

CHEMICAL AND BIOLOGICAL WEAPONS

The Nuclear, Biological, and Chemical Medical Defense Information Server

This site, which covers medical aspects of nuclear, biological, and chemical weapons, is operated by the U.S. Army Medical Department.

Its highlights include a book titled *Medical Management of Biological Casualties Handbook*, a document titled *What Every Person Needs to Know About the Anthrax Vaccine*, and links to news articles at other sites about nuclear, biological, and chemical weapons.

The site also has a calendar of conferences, links to related sites, and video tutorials about blister agents, chemical defense, cyanide agents, lung agents, nerve agents, and riot agents.

Finally, through original documents and links to other sites, it provides field manuals, government documents, White House documents, Defense Department reports, and newsletters.

Vital Stats:

Access method:	WWW
To access:	http://www.nbc-med.org
E-mail:	LTC_Carl_Curling@OTSG-AMEDD.ARMY.MIL

U.S. Army Chemical and Biological Defense Command

This site has fact sheets about chemical weapons stored at specific U.S. facilities, press releases about incidents and inspections at the facilities, and reports about environmental remediation efforts at the Rocky Mountain Arsenal.

It also offers background about the domestic preparedness program, including information about the chemical-biological rapid response team and the chemical-biological hotline. The site is operated by the U.S. Army Chemical and Biological Defense Command.

Vital Stats:

Access method:	WWW
To access:	http://www.cbdcom.apgea.army.mil
E-mail:	webmaster@cbdcom.apgea.army.mil

The United States Army Medical Research Institute of Chemical Defense

This site's highlight is its excellent collection of links to other Web sites about chemical and biological weapons. It's operated by the United States Army Medical Research Institute of Chemical Defense.

The site also has the full text of publications about treating chemical warfare casualties. Two of the most interesting publications are *Medical Management of Chemical Casualties Handbook* and *Treatment of Chemical Agent Casualties and Conventional Military Chemical Injuries,* which have chapters about nerve agents, cyanide, riot control agents, decontamination, chemical defense equipment, and other topics. The site also has a list of papers published since 1981 by institute researchers.

Vital Stats:

Access method:	WWW
To access:	http://chemdef.apgea.army.mil
E-mail:	roberts@asia.apgea.army.mil

United States Army Medical Research Institute of Infectious Diseases

This site's highlights are two books about biological weapons. *Defense against Toxin Weapons* provides basic information about various biological weapons, while *Medical Management of Biological Casualties* discusses bacterial agents such as anthrax, viral agents, biological toxins, personal protection, decontamination, and related issues.

The site is operated by the United States Army Medical Research Institute of Infectious Diseases, which conducts research about biological warfare threats and infectious diseases.

Vital Stats:

Access method:	WWW
To access:	http://140.139.42.105
E-mail:	bio@detrick.army.mil

GENERAL

ACQWeb

ACQWeb offers a fascinating hodgepodge of defense information—everything from grant announcements to videos of tests of ballistic missile defense systems. It's operated by the Office of the Under Secretary of Defense for Acquisition and Technology.

The site specializes in acquisition information, including grant announcements, documents about privatization of military housing, transportation policies, testimony before Congress about acquisition reform, and related information.

It also has data on Defense Department aircraft losses, policy documents, congressional testimony about technical issues such as ballistic missile defense, speeches, and other bits and pieces of defense information. Fortunately, the site has a search engine that helps you quickly find what you're seeking.

Vital Stats:

Access method:	WWW
To access:	http://www.acq.osd.mil
E-mail:	Webmaster@acq.osd.mil

Air Force Link

Air Force Link has all kinds of information related to the Air Force—everything from hundreds of photographs to a report about the July 1947 "Roswell Incident" where, according to some people, the Army Air Force found remains from a flying saucer.

The site includes press releases, papers about information warfare and the Air Force in the twenty-first century, a directory of Air Force facilities, news about Air Force reunions, biographies of Air Force leaders, fact sheets about Air Force organizations and weapons systems, answers to frequently asked questions, details about Air Force careers, information about Air Force bands and music, speeches, and links to hundreds of other Air Force Web sites.

Vital Stats:

Access method:	WWW
To access:	http://www.af.mil

Air Force News Service

Users can sign up at this page to receive mailings to their e-mail account from the Air Force News Service. News items are mailed daily.

Vital Stats:

Access method: WWW
To access: http://www.af.mil/news/afnssub.html

BosniaLINK

BosniaLINK is the official Defense Department Web site about U.S. military activities in connection with the NATO peacekeeping mission in Bosnia. The site has archival information from the start of the operation through October 1, 1997. Through links to other sites, it provides current news, photos, briefings, and related information.

Vital Stats:

Access method: WWW
To access: http://www.dtic.mil/bosnia
E-mail: dpcintrn@osd.pentagon.mil

Critical Infrastructure Assurance Office

This site is operated by the Critical Infrastructure Assurance Office. The office was announced by President Bill Clinton in May 1998 and charged with creating a national plan to protect critical services such as telecommunications, banking and finance, electric power, transportation, gas and oil, emergency services, and government services.

The site has presidential directives about combating terrorism and protecting America's critical infrastructure, speeches and congressional testimony, meeting announcements, biographical information about CIAO officials, and press releases.

Vital Stats:

Access method: WWW
To access: http://www.ciao.gov
E-mail: webtech@ciao.gov

Defense Intelligence Agency

The Defense Intelligence Agency site provides congressional testimony by DIA officials about global threats to the United States and its interests abroad, a history of the agency, the agency's strategic plan, answers to frequently asked questions, employment information, and information for contractors.

Vital Stats:

Access method: WWW
To access: http://140.47.5.4

Defense Technical Information Center (DTIC) Home Page

The Defense Technical Information Center (DTIC) Home Page offers an incredible collection of defense information, either directly or through links to hundreds of other defense-related sites around the world. It offers everything from information for contractors to translations of a long list of military acronyms to explanations of weapons systems.

On the home page, much of the most interesting information is available by selecting *Web Links* and then clicking on *Joint Resources*. You also can use the address http://www.dtic.mil/dtic/joint-inet.html to reach the page directly.

Vital Stats:

Access method: WWW
To access: http://www.dtic.mil
E-mail: bcporder@dtic.mil

DefenseLINK

DefenseLINK, the home page for the Department of Defense, offers a huge amount of information about defense issues.

Of particular interest is its collection of reports, including several reports about base closures and realignments, a 1997 report to Congress titled *Domestic Preparedness Program in the Defense against Weapons of Mass Destruction,* a 1998 report about Defense Department policy on homosexuals, a report by the National Defense Panel titled *Transforming Defense: National Security in the Twenty-first Century,* and a 1998 report on military requirements and costs of NATO enlargement, among others.

The site also offers papers analyzing the biological warfare threat and the anthrax vaccine, news articles from the American Forces Press Service, transcripts of news briefings, news photos, speeches by DOD leaders, information about touring the Pentagon, and much, much more.

Vital Stats:

Access method: WWW
To access: http://www.defenselink.mil
E-mail: dpcintrn@osd.pentagon.mil

DefenseLINK News by Email

This page lets users sign up to automatically receive news items from the Defense Department by e-mail. Users can subscribe to seven different lists: news articles from the American Forces Press Service, news releases, contract announcements, memoranda for correspondents, press advisories, transcripts of news and background briefings, and Marine Corps news.

Vital Stats:

Access method:	WWW
To access:	http://www.defenselink.mil/news/subscribe.html
E-mail:	dpcintrn@osd.pentagon.mil

Department of Defense Inspector General

This site offers thorough information about reporting fraud, waste, and abuse to the Defense Department's inspector general. The site has a form that can be used to file a report online, information about protection for whistleblowers, and answers to frequently asked questions.

The site also has lists of reports prepared by the inspector general's office, congressional testimony by the inspector general, information about recent indictments and convictions for various fraudulent activities, and job listings.

Vital Stats:

Access method:	WWW
To access:	http://www.dodig.osd.mil
E-mail:	webmaster@dodig.osd.mil

Department of Veterans Affairs

The Department of Veterans Affairs site has a broad range of information for veterans and their families, in addition to documents for businesses that wish to sell goods or services to the VA.

The site offers information about benefits for veterans and their families, VA benefit and medical forms, a database of veterans service organizations, numerous documents and links related to Persian Gulf illness, information about how to contact the VA, a list of VA facilities around the country, information about the National Cemetery System, details about how to get military records for veterans, information about VA job openings, congressional testimony, press releases, and links to other Internet sites of interest to veterans.

Vital Stats:

Access method:	WWW
To access:	http://www.va.gov

Intelligence Reform Program

The Intelligence Reform Program site offers a huge assortment of government documents related to intelligence agencies and activities. It's operated by the Federation of American Scientists.

The site has transcripts of congressional hearings on intelligence reform, presidential directives and executive orders on intelligence, the text of intelligence laws and regulations, General Accounting Office reports on intelligence, directives from the Central Intelligence Agency and the Defense Department, statements at hearings of the Commission on the Roles and Capabilities of the U.S. Intelligence Community, speeches by CIA officials and others on intelligence threat assessments, statements at congressional hearings on security in cyber-space, and much more.

Vital Stats:

Access method:	WWW
To access:	http://www.fas.org/irp
E-mail:	johnpike@fas.org

MarineLINK

MarineLINK offers an exhaustive collection of materials about the Marine Corps—everything from historical information to details about joining the corps.

The site also has a recording of the Marines' Hymn, hundreds of images, information about Marine Corps aircraft and equipment, information about Medal of Honor recipients, biographies of Marine Corps officers, uniform regulations, press releases, articles from *Marines* magazine, information about reunions, a list of public affairs contacts, links to Internet sites operated by Marine Corps commands around the world, and lots more.

Vital Stats:

Access method:	WWW
To access:	http://www.usmc.mil

National Security Agency

The National Security Agency site offers declassified documents from the Cuban missile crisis, documents about the Kennedy assassination and UFOs released under the Freedom of Information Act, background information about the agency and its role in the intelligence community, a sampling of exhibits from the National Cryptologic Museum, and information about how to submit a Freedom of Information Act request.

One of the site's most interesting sections concerns the VENONA project, which collected and decrypted messages from the Soviet KGB during the 1940s. The site has scanned images of hundreds of declassified VENONA documents, background information about the project, and a chronology of the effort.

The site also has an index to more than 1.3 million pages of declassified historic crypto-logic documents that the NSA turned over to the National Archives in 1996. The documents date from before World War I to the end of World War II.

Vital Stats:

Access method: WWW
To access: http://www.nsa.gov:8080

National Security Council

This site has background information about the National Security Council, speeches by NSC officials, reports titled *A National Security Strategy for a New Century* and *History of the National Security Council 1947–1997,* and documents about the administration's policy regarding controlling international crime, protecting critical infrastructure, reforming multi-lateral peace operations, and managing complex contingency operations.

Vital Stats:

Access method: WWW
To access: http://www.whitehouse.gov/WH/EOP/NSC/html/nschome.html

---

The Pentagon Book Store Online

Few people can visit the Pentagon bookstore in person (since it's located inside the Pentagon), but anyone can visit the store's Web site to read lists of new military and political books and learn about signed editions that can be ordered from the store. The store and Web site are operated by a private company.

Vital Stats:

Access method: WWW
To access: http://www.booksdc.com
E-mail: pmccord@booksdc.com

President's Commission on Critical Infrastructure Protection

The highlight of this site is a report titled *Critical Foundations: Protecting America's Infrastructures,* which the President's Commission on Critical Infrastructure Protection released in early 1998. The panel was created by an executive order in 1996.

The site also has the text of the executive order creating the commission, speeches by com-missioners, information about commission members, and press releases.

Vital Stats:

Access method: WWW
To access: http://www.pccip.gov
E-mail: comments@pccip.gov

Selective Service System

This site provides information about who must register with the Selective Service, an application for a registration form, answers to frequently asked questions, and information about conscientious objection and alternative service.

It also has the system's annual report to Congress, induction statistics since the beginning of the Selective Service, details about how to obtain classification records for individuals, and results of draft lotteries during the Vietnam War.

Vital Stats:

Access method:	WWW
To access:	http://www.sss.gov
E-mail:	Information@sss.gov

U.S. Arms Control and Disarmament Agency

The U.S. Arms Control and Disarmament Agency site has the full text of dozens of treaties and agreements, including the Limited Test Ban Treaty, the Anti-Ballistic Missile Protocol, the Non-Proliferation Treaty, the Biological Weapons Convention, the Open Skies Treaty, the Charter of Paris for a New Europe, the Comprehensive Nuclear Test Ban Treaty, and the Strategic Arms Reduction Treaty, among others. Background documents are available for many of the treaties.

The site also has extensive information about the Chemical Weapons Convention, including the full text of the treaty, statements by U.S. officials, a list of signatories and ratifiers, endorsements, and fact sheets.

In addition, it offers reports titled *World Military Expenditures and Arms Transfers* and *Adherence and Compliance with Arms Control Agreements,* speeches by agency officials, background information about the agency, and fact sheets about nuclear weapons–free zones, conventional weapons, export controls, missile defense, and nuclear, biological, and chemical weapons.

Vital Stats:

Access method:	WWW
To access:	http://www.acda.gov
E-mail:	webmaster@acda.gov

U.S. Army Homepage

The U.S. Army Homepage is a gateway into army resources on the Internet. It has links to hundreds of army and army-related Internet home pages, arranged alphabetically and by subject.

The site also offers information about how to locate an active duty soldier in the army, details about benefits for army retirees and their survivors, a newsletter for retirees, news releases, photographs, a huge list of army alumni organizations and associations, publications from the U.S. Army Center of Military History, and much more.

Access method: WWW
To access: http://www.army.mil
E-mail: webmaster@hqda.army.mil

United States Army Recruiting Web Site

The United States Army Recruiting Web Site has information about joining the army. It provides details about training and pay, and also features information about joining special army units such as the Special Forces, Golden Knights, Judge Advocate General's Corps, Army Band, and Chaplain Corps.

Vital Stats:

Access method: WWW
To access: http://www.goarmy.com
E-mail: martinm@emh1.usarec.army.mil

U.S. Coast Guard

This site provides exhaustive information about marine safety and environmental protection for both recreational boaters and commercial shippers.

It offers selected marine accident reports, photos from marine accidents, summaries of rescue statistics, technical publications about marine safety, safety alerts, and a large number of documents about oil spill response. It also has data sheets about Coast Guard vessels and careers, information about Coast Guard careers, links to other marine safety sites, and lots more.

Vital Stats:

Access method: WWW
To access: http://www.uscg.mil
E-mail: webmaster@www.uscg.mil

U.S. Navy

This site is a one-stop source for information about the U.S. Navy. It provides little original information, but offers an excellent set of links to hundreds of Navy sites on the Internet. The sites provide press releases, speeches, policies, images, briefing transcripts, fact sheets about everything from aircraft to ships, and much more.

Vital Stats:

Access method: WWW
To access: http://www.navy.mil

NUCLEAR WEAPONS

Defense Nuclear Facilities Safety Board Server

The Defense Nuclear Facilities Safety Board Server has documents related to the oversight of nuclear weapons plants operated by the U.S. Department of Energy. The board reviews operations and accidents at DOE nuclear facilities and makes recommendations aimed at protecting public health and safety.

The site includes board recommendations, technical reports, a list of documents received by the board, reports about inspection trips to various nuclear facilities by staff members, notices of public hearings, the text of legislation creating the board, press releases, and links to other Energy Department Web sites.

Vital Stats:

Access method:	WWW
To access:	http://www.dnfsb.gov
E-mail:	mailbox@dnfsb.gov

Department of Energy Nevada Operations Office

This Department of Energy site has information about the Nevada Test Site, where the United States tested nuclear weapons for more than four decades. It has dozens of photos of nuclear tests and the test site, clips from recently declassified movies of nuclear tests, a list of all nuclear weapons tests conducted by the United States from July 1945 through September 1992, and information about all nuclear weapons tests conducted from September 1961 through September 1992 in which radioactive effluents were released.

Vital Stats:

Access method:	WWW
To access:	http://www.nv.doe.gov
E-mail:	webmaster@nv.doe.gov

Environment, Safety, and Health Technical Information Services

Reports about accidents and other problems at U.S. Department of Energy nuclear weapons plants are available on the Environment, Safety, and Health Technical Information Services site. The accident reports are provided in a newsletter titled *Operating Experience Weekly Summary*. Each issue has numerous reports.

The site, which is operated by DOE's Office of Environment, Safety, and Health, also has summaries of radiation exposure data for the Energy Department and its contractors, extensive information from the Advisory Committee on Human Radiation Experiments, reports about occupational injuries and property damage that occurred at DOE facilities, hundreds of files about worker health and safety, and much more.

Vital Stats:

Access method:	WWW
To access:	http://tis.eh.doe.gov
E-mail:	support@tis.eh.doe.gov

Explorer

The Explorer site provides numerous directives and orders relating to operation of the Department of Energy's nuclear weapons plants. Some sample titles are "Nuclear Explosive and Weapons Surety," "Identification and Protection of Unclassified Controlled Nuclear Information," "Startup and Restart of Nuclear Facilities," "Safeguards and Security Program," and "Radiological Control."

Vital Stats:

Access method:	WWW
To access:	http://www.explorer.doe.gov
E-mail:	Explorer@lanl.gov

DEMOGRAPHIC DATA

Bureau of Labor Statistics

The Bureau of Labor Statistics site offers the full text of the *Occupational Outlook Handbook,* which provides highlights of the job outlook through 2006, a list of sources of career information, information about finding a job and evaluating a job offer, and much more. The bureau is part of the U.S. Department of Labor.

The site also has a huge quantity of national and regional economic and labor statistics about the consumer price index (CPI), producer price index (PPI), employment cost trends, worker safety and health, the labor force, local area unemployment, labor productivity, foreign labor, international price indexes, and many other subjects.

In addition, the site provides press releases and links to other Internet sites that offer statistics from the federal government and foreign governments.

Vital Stats:

Access method: WWW
To access: http://stats.bls.gov
E-mail: labstat.helpdesk@bls.gov

---

censusandyou, i-net-bulletin, press-release, *and* product-announce

The Census Bureau operates four mailing lists that provide information about its products and services:

- censusandyou is an electronic version of the monthly newsletter *Census and You,* which has articles about new Census Bureau products and tips about how to use them.

- i-net-bulletin is a biweekly list of new data files, reports, and features on the Census Bureau's World Wide Web site.

- press-release distributes Census Bureau press releases, most of which provide news about new reports.

- product-announce has news about new printed reports, CD-ROMs, computer tapes, floppy disks, and other products available from the Census Bureau.

Vital Stats:

Access method: E-mail
To access: Send an e-mail message to majordomo@census.gov
Subject line:
Message: **subscribe** *listname*
E-mail (questions):   majordomo-owner@census.gov

Current Population Survey

This site has data and press releases related to the Current Population Survey, a monthly survey of about 50,000 households that is the primary source of information about the U.S. labor force. The site, which is a joint project of the Bureau of Labor Statistics and the Census Bureau, also has statements by BLS officials and provides links to other Internet sites that have labor statistics.

Vital Stats:

Access method:	WWW
To access:	http://www.bls.census.gov/cps
E-mail:	cpshelp@info.census.gov

FERRET

FERRET provides data from the Current Population Survey, the Survey of Income and Program Participation, and the National Health Interview Survey. The site is a joint project of the Census Bureau and the Bureau of Labor Statistics.

FERRET also offers data about employment and unemployment, displaced workers, job tenure, race and ethnicity, school enrollment, income, doctor visits, teenage attitudes about health, access to health care, health insurance, AIDS knowledge and attitudes, and many other topics.

The strength of this site is the power it gives users to manipulate the data. Users can get specific tabulations, make comparisons between different data sets, create simple tables, and download huge amounts of data for further analysis.

Vital Stats:

Access method:	WWW
To access:	http://ferret.bls.census.gov
E-mail:	ccapps@census.gov

Geospatial and Statistical Data Center

The Geospatial and Statistical Data Center site offers numerous searchable databases containing data from the Census Bureau, Bureau of Economic Analysis, FBI, and other agencies. It is operated by the University of Virginia.

The site includes various editions of the Census Bureau's *County and City Data Book,* a database containing data from the Census Bureau's *County Business Patterns* reports, a database containing historical and forecasted levels for population and income for each state from 1969 to 2045 from the Bureau of Economic Analysis, the National Income and Products Accounts database from the Bureau of Economic Analysis, the 1987 *Standard Industrial Classification Manual,* and several editions of the FBI's *Uniform Crime Report,* among other databases.

Vital Stats:

Access method: WWW
To access: http://fisher.lib.virginia.edu
E-mail: ssdc@fisher.virginia.edu

U.S. Census Bureau

The U.S. Census Bureau site offers a wealth of statistical information about the nation's people and economy. It has data about housing, health insurance coverage, income, poverty, the labor force, industrial production, international trade, agriculture, population, and county business patterns, among other subjects.

The biggest challenge at the Web site is simply sorting through all the information to find what you're seeking. Fortunately, you can search all the files on the site at once. You also can use the site's subject index, which has links to all the files on particular topics.

Information on the site is presented in text files and databases. One of the coolest features is Map Stats, an interactive system that presents statistical profiles of states, congressional districts, and counties, as well as detailed maps for counties.

Another cool feature provides up-to-the-second projections of the current population of the United States and the world. The site also has the full text of the *Statistical Abstract of the United States,* software for analyzing Census Bureau data, press releases, links to other Internet sites that offer Census data, and lots, lots more.

Vital Stats:

Access method: WWW
To access: http://www.census.gov
E-mail: webmaster@census.gov

United States Historical Census Data Browser

This site provides U.S. Census data from 1790 to 1970. Data are available about the people and economy of each state and county. The site is a cooperative effort of the Instructional Computing Group at Harvard University and the Inter-University Consortium for Political and Social Research.

The types of data vary with each census, but frequently there are data on agriculture, churches, manufacturing, population, slave ownership, and real estate and personal property.

Vital Stats:

Access method: WWW
To access: http://icg.fas.harvard.edu/census
E-mail: bergen@fas.harvard.edu

EDUCATION

ARTSEDGE

ARTSEDGE offers an incredible collection of resources about arts education in grades K–12. The arts covered include dance, design arts, folk arts, literary arts, media and film, music, theater, and visual arts. The site is a joint project of the John F. Kennedy Center for the Performing Arts, the National Endowment for the Arts, and the U.S. Department of Education.

ARTSEDGE has lesson plans for teachers, guidelines for designing curriculums, articles about the arts and arts education, information about grants and contests, a huge collection of links to Web sites related to arts education, another huge collection of links to sites that have information about how to use the Internet, and lots more.

Vital Stats:

Access method:	WWW
To access:	http://artsedge.kennedy-center.org
E-mail:	editor@artsedge.kennedy-center.org

AskERIC

AskERIC is an extraordinary resource for educators and anyone else interested in education issues. It's operated by the ERIC Clearinghouse on Information and Technology, with funding from the Office of Educational Research and Improvement at the U.S. Department of Education.

The site has AskERIC InfoGuides that list resources about dozens of topics, more than 1,000 lesson plans, a calendar of hundreds of education-related conferences, links to other Internet sites that have education information, and many other resources.

The site also has an online form that teachers, librarians, administrators, and others interested in education can use to submit requests to AskERIC for education information.

Vital Stats:

Access method:	WWW
To access:	http://www.askeric.org
E-mail:	askeric@askeric.org

Civnet

Civnet, which is managed by the U.S. Information Agency, offers extensive information about civic education from various nongovernmental sources such as the Center for Civic Education and the American Federation of Teachers.

It has numerous lesson plans for teachers on civics issues, bibliographies about civics education, a directory of hundreds of civic education organizations and programs around the world, a calendar of events, and more than a dozen historical documents, including the Magna Carta, the Virginia Declaration of Rights, the Declaration of Independence, and the United Nations Charter.

Vital Stats:

Access method: WWW
To access: http://civnet.org
E-mail: klehrman@usia.gov

Computers for Learning

This site provides information about the donation of surplus federal computer equipment to schools. All public, private, parochial, and home schools and nonprofit educational groups serving students in pre-kindergarten through grade 12 are eligible to participate. The program was created by Vice President Al Gore and is funded by the Energy Department.

Schools and nonprofit educational groups can register at the site and list the equipment they need. Federal agencies then browse the listings when they have surplus equipment to donate. Special consideration is given to schools and nonprofits located within an empowerment zone or enterprise community.

The site also has listings of National Tech Corps volunteers in each state who have technical computer knowledge.

Vital Stats:

Access method: WWW
To access: http://www.computers.fed.gov

ECENET-L

Subscribers to the ECENET-L mailing list exchange messages about early childhood education. The list is sponsored by the ERIC Clearinghouse on Elementary and Early Childhood Education, which is funded by the U.S. Department of Education.

Vital Stats:

Access method: E-mail
To access: Send an e-mail message to listserv@postoffice.cso.uiuc.edu
Subject line:
Message: **subscribe ECENET-L** *firstname lastname*
E-mail (questions):   ECENET-L-request@postoffice.cso.uiuc.edu

ECPOLICY-L

Subscribers to the ECPOLICY-L mailing list discuss policy issues related to young children. The list's purpose is to raise the awareness of policy makers, educators, the media, and parents about issues that are important to the future of young children. It's sponsored by the National Association for the Education of Young Children and the ERIC Clearinghouse on Elementary and Early Childhood Education, which is funded by the U.S. Department of Education.

Vital Stats:

Access method:	E-mail
To access:	Send an e-mail message to listserv@postoffice.cso.uiuc.edu
Subject line:	
Message:	**subscribe ECPOLICY-L** *firstname lastname*
E-mail (questions):	ECPOLICY-L-request@postoffice.cso.uiuc.edu

EDInfo

Subscribers to the EDInfo mailing list receive reports and information from the U.S. Department of Education. EDInfo distributes findings from education research, statistics, highlights from new reports, news about department initiatives and programs, legislative updates, and information about updates to the department's Web site.

Vital Stats:

Access method:	E-mail
To access:	Send an e-mail message to listproc@inet.ed.gov
Subject line:	
Message:	**subscribe edinfo** *firstname lastname*
E-mail (questions):	kirk_winters@ed.gov

EDSITEment

EDSITEment is a gateway to humanities education resources on the Internet. EDSITEment is a joint project of the National Endowment for the Humanities, the Council of the Great City Schools, MCI Communications Corp., and the National Trust for the Humanities.

The site's highlight is its links to dozens of the top humanities sites on the Web. The links are arranged under four major topics: literature, art history, foreign language, and history. EDSITEment also has lesson plans that use materials from the linked sites.

Vital Stats:

Access method:	WWW
To access:	http://edsitement.neh.gov

Educational Resources Information Center (ERIC)

The Educational Resources Information Center (ERIC) offers dozens of brief publications for parents about the development of preschoolers, children's reading, children's self-esteem, teachers' qualifications, the rights and responsibilities of parents of children with disabilities, gifted children, home schooling, and teaching children second languages, among other subjects. ERIC is funded by the U.S. Department of Education.

The site also has a searchable calendar of education-related conferences, links to Internet sites operated by ERIC clearinghouses, information about mailing lists operated by the clearinghouses, and a brochure titled *Getting Online: A Friendly Guide for Teachers, Students, and Parents.*

Vital Stats:

Access method:	WWW
To access:	http://www.aspensys.com/eric
E-mail:	acceric@inet.ed.gov

ERIC Clearinghouse for Community Colleges

The ERIC Clearinghouse for Community Colleges offers dozens of publications about community colleges. Some of the available titles are *Advantages and Disadvantages of Employing Part-Time Faculty in Community Colleges, Addressing Sexual Harassment on Campus, Technology in Community Colleges, Creating and Maintaining a Diverse Faculty,* and *Community Colleges as Facilitators of School-to-Work.* The clearinghouse is operated by the University of California at Los Angeles and funded by the U.S. Department of Education.

The site also has information about recent books related to community college education, bibliographies about community college subjects, brief summaries of current trends and practices, and links to other Internet sites about community colleges.

Vital Stats:

Access method:	WWW
To access:	http://www.gseis.ucla.edu/ERIC/eric.html
E-mail:	ericcc@ucla.edu

ERIC Clearinghouse for Social Studies/Social Science Education

The ERIC Clearinghouse for Social Studies/Social Science Education has numerous brief publications about social studies topics. Some of the available titles are *Trends in Peace Education; Global Education: Internet Resources; Using Literature to Teach Geography in High Schools; Oral History in the Teaching of U.S. History;* and *Teaching About Africa.*

The site also has a list of publications that can be ordered from the clearinghouse and links to other Internet resources for social studies education. The clearinghouse is operated by Indiana University and funded by the U.S. Department of Education.

Vital Stats:

Access method:	WWW
To access:	http://www.indiana.edu/~ssdc/eric_chess.htm
E-mail:	lpinhey@indiana.edu

ERIC Clearinghouse on Adult, Career, and Vocational Education

The ERIC Clearinghouse on Adult, Career, and Vocational Education site has brief publications about adult career counseling, learning in the workplace, using the Internet in vocational education, prison literacy programs, workplace literacy, distance learning, and many other subjects. The clearinghouse is operated by Ohio State University, with funding from the U.S. Department of Education.

The site also has links to lots of other education-related Internet sites.

Vital Stats:

Access method: WWW
To access: http://ericacve.org
E-mail: ericacve@postbox.acs.ohio-state.edu

ERIC Clearinghouse on Assessment and Evaluation

The ERIC Clearinghouse on Assessment and Evaluation site provides two databases that are superb resources for anyone interested in education. The ERIC Digest database has the full text of more than 1,600 brief reports about research and issues in education. The ERIC Database has more than 850,000 abstracts of conference papers, reports, journal articles, and other documents about education research and practice.

The site also offers a huge collection of publications about fair testing practices, how to select a test, how to study for tests, writing multiple-choice test items, and lots of other issues related to educational testing and evaluation. In addition, it has annotated links to dozens of other Internet sites that offer materials about assessment and evaluation.

The clearinghouse is operated by the Catholic University of America, with funding from the U.S. Department of Education.

Vital Stats:

Access method: WWW
To access: http://ericae.net
E-mail: feedback@ericae.net

ERIC Clearinghouse on Disabilities and Gifted Education

The ERIC Clearinghouse on Disabilities and Gifted Education has tips for teachers and parents on helping children learn to read, announcements about upcoming conferences, and a list of state, national, and international associations devoted to gifted education. The clearinghouse is operated by the Council for Exceptional Children and funded by the U.S. Department of Education.

The site also has bibliographies of resources about attention deficit disorders, autism, learning disabilities, the use of technology for people with disabilities, deafness and hearing impairments, gifted students and educational reform, identifying gifted children, mainstreaming, and the social and emotional needs of gifted children, among many other subjects.

In addition, it has information about Internet mailing lists about disabilities or gifted education and links to other Internet sites devoted to the subjects.

Vital Stats:

Access method:	WWW
To access:	http://www.cec.sped.org/ericec.htm

ERIC Clearinghouse on Educational Management

The ERIC Clearinghouse on Educational Management site has brief publications about teacher morale, charter schools, student dress codes, school size, block scheduling, multi-age classrooms, home schooling, school violence prevention, poverty and learning, substance abuse policy, and school discipline, among other subjects. The clearinghouse is operated by the University of Oregon with funding from the U.S. Department of Education.

The site also has a directory of nearly 200 service and research organizations in the field of educational management, a catalog of books and other publications that can be ordered from the clearinghouse, and links to other Internet sites about education.

Vital Stats:

Access method:	WWW
To access:	http://eric.uoregon.edu

ERIC Clearinghouse on Elementary and Early Childhood Education

The ERIC Clearinghouse on Elementary and Early Childhood Education has dozens of brief publications about such topics as spanking, the learning style of Hispanic American students, improving students' socialization skills, working with perfectionist students, preventing and resolving teacher-parent differences, working with shy or withdrawn students, fostering resilience in children, and advertising in the schools, among others. The clearinghouse, which is funded by the U.S. Department of Education, is operated by the University of Illinois at Urbana–Champaign.

The site also has information about the Reggio Emilia approach to early childhood education, links to dozens of other education-related Internet sites, and the *MAGnet Newsletter,* which provides information about the use of mixed-age groups in elementary classrooms.

Vital Stats:

Access method:	WWW
To access:	http://ericeece.org
E-mail:	eeceweb@ericps.crc.uiuc.edu

ERIC Clearinghouse on Higher Education

More than eighty brief reports about academic freedom, budgeting for higher education at the state level, diversity, college alcohol and drug abuse prevention programs, fund raising, faculty evaluation, high risk students and higher education, balancing academics and athletics, reducing stress among students, sexual harassment, and other subjects are available from the ERIC Clearinghouse on Higher Education site. The clearinghouse is operated by George Washington University and funded by the U.S. Department of Education.

The site also has information concerning new books about higher education, links to other Internet sites devoted to higher education, and more than two dozen bibliographies about such topics as affirmative action, alcohol on campus, collective bargaining in higher education, community service learning, crime on campus, distance learning, faculty tenure, multiculturalism, part-time and adjunct faculty, students with disabilities, and technology.

Vital Stats:

Access method:	WWW
To access:	http://www.gwu.edu/~eriche
E-mail:	mkozi@eric-he.edu

ERIC Clearinghouse on Information and Technology

The ERIC Clearinghouse on Information and Technology offers information about educational technology and library and information science. The clearinghouse is operated by Syracuse University, with funding from the U.S. Department of Education.

The site's highlight is a collection of brief publications about Internet resources for K–12 educators, copyright issues in the electronic age, K–12 technology planning, library collection development in the electronic age, local area networks for K–12 schools, and choosing software, among other subjects.

The site also has a catalog of books and other publications that can be ordered from the clearinghouse, and it provides links to other educational technology and library and information science sites on the Internet.

Vital Stats:

Access method:	WWW
To access:	http://ericir.syr.edu/ithome
E-mail:	eric@ericir.syr.edu

ERIC Clearinghouse on Languages and Linguistics

The ERIC Clearinghouse on Languages and Linguistics site offers several dozen brief publications about computer-assisted language learning, African languages at the K–12 level, cross-age tutoring, foreign language immersion programs, fostering second language development in young children, teaching grammar, starting an elementary school foreign language program, and Internet resources for language teachers, among other subjects. The clearinghouse is operated by the Center for Applied Linguistics and funded by the U.S. Department of Education.

The site also has bibliographies of materials about such subjects as bilingual education, self-guided second language learning, foreign language study by African American students, foreign languages and careers, and games and activities for teaching foreign languages to young children.

Vital Stats:

Access method:	WWW
To access:	http://www.cal.org/ericcll
E-mail:	eric@cal.org

ERIC Clearinghouse on Reading, English, and Communication

The ERIC Clearinghouse on Reading, English, and Communication has brief publications about teaching expressive writing, motivating low-performing adolescent readers, political correctness on campus, revision in the writing process, teaching English to gifted students, home schooling and socialization of children, publishing children's writing, teaching minority students to write effectively, helping children overcome reading difficulties, and dozens of other topics. The clearinghouse is operated by Indiana University and funded by the U.S. Department of Education.

The site also has dozens of bibliographies of materials (including Web sites) about adolescent literature, at-risk learners, class size, creative writing in elementary schools, Dr. Seuss, ebonics, extended school years, home schooling, integrating the Internet into schools, multicultural literature, Shakespeare, spelling instruction, tech-prep education, school violence, and many other subjects.

In addition, it offers numerous lesson plans, a list of books that can be ordered from the clearinghouse, links to other education-related Internet sites, a list of Internet mailing lists and Usenet newsgroups about education, information about language arts courses offered through Indiana University's Distance Education program, and *Parents and Children Together*, a magazine that features stories and articles for children that are suitable for reading out loud and articles for parents about reading and writing.

Vital Stats:

Access method:	WWW
To access:	http://www.indiana.edu/~eric_rec
E-mail:	sstroup@indiana.edu

ERIC Clearinghouse on Rural Education and Small Schools

The ERIC Clearinghouse on Rural Education and Small Schools site has more than two dozen brief publications about the academic effectiveness of small schools, Indian education, private schools, migrant farmworkers and their children, the role of rural schools in rural community development, rural school consolidation and student learning, instructional strategies for migrant students, rural child care, and child labor in agriculture, among other topics. The clearinghouse is operated by the Appalachia Educational Laboratory and funded by the U.S. Department of Education.

The site also has links to other Internet sites that provide information about American Indians and Alaska Natives, outdoor education, Mexican Americans, rural education, migrant education, and small schools.

Vital Stats:

Access method:	WWW
To access:	http://www.ael.org/eric
E-mail:	aelinfo@ael.org

ERIC Clearinghouse on Teaching and Teacher Education

The ERIC Clearinghouse on Teaching and Teacher Education site has brief publications about teaching in elementary and secondary schools, finding a teaching job, choosing a teacher education college, financial aid for teacher education students, international teaching opportunities, and related subjects. The clearinghouse is operated by the American Association of Colleges for Teacher Education and is funded by the U.S. Department of Education.

The site also has short documents about adolescents and AIDS, childhood obesity, comprehensive school health education, teaching culturally diverse children, drug and alcohol prevention education, national standards for school health education, safer playgrounds for young children, and other topics.

In addition, it has links to lots of other K–12 education sites on the Internet, including sites offering lesson plans.

Vital Stats:

Access method:	WWW
To access:	http://www.ericsp.org

ERICNews

ERICNews is a one-way mailing list that distributes news about the Educational Resources Information Center (ERIC), which is part of the National Library of Education. Bimonthly mailings describe new ERIC publications and products, changes to the ERIC Web site, and new ERIC document delivery systems.

Vital Stats:

Access method: E-mail
To access: Send an e-mail message to listproc@aspensys.com
Subject line:
Message: **subscribe ERICNews** *firstname lastname*
E-mail (questions):   kmitchell@aspensys.com

FAFSA on the Web

Students can use this site to complete and submit an online version of the Free Application for Federal Student Aid (FAFSA). The site is operated by the Education Department.

FAFSA is used to determine a student's eligibility for Pell Grants, Supplemental Educational Opportunity Grants, Stafford Loans, Perkins Loans, Federal Work Study, and Title VII and Public Health Act Programs.

You also can use the site to check the status of your application once it's submitted and to obtain more information about federal student aid programs.

Vital Stats:

Access method: WWW
To access: http://www.fafsa.ed.gov

FCCsend, FCCshare, *and* edtech

FCCsend, FCCshare, and edtech are three mailing lists about technology in schools and libraries. The lists are operated by the Federal Communications Commission.

FCCsend is a one-way list that distributes information about preparing schools and libraries to get the most out of communications technology. FCCshare is a list where students, teachers, librarians, administrators, parents, and others exchange messages about using technology. And edtech is a one-way list that distributes speeches by FCC commissioners about universal service.

Vital Stats:

Access method: E-mail
To access: Send an e-mail message to subscribe@info.fcc.gov
Subject line:
Message: **sub** *listname firstname lastname*
E-mail (questions):   learnet@fcc.gov

Federal Resources for Educational Excellence (FREE)

FREE is a fantastic resource for teachers, parents, and others involved in education. The site, which is operated by the U.S. Department of Education, offers links to hundreds of teaching and learning resources developed by more than thirty federal agencies.

FREE has links to materials in the broad areas of the arts, educational technology, foreign languages, health and safety, language arts, mathematics, physical education, science, social studies, and vocational education. Some of the specific subjects covered are American painters, folklife, world languages, the human genome project, nutrition, space, dinosaurs, global change, stamps, black soldiers in the Civil War, trains, Africa, and the U.S. Constitution, among many, many others.

A special page has links to federal materials created especially for kids. To reach the page directly, use the address http://www.ed.gov/free/kids.html.

Vital Stats:

Access method:	WWW
To access:	http://www.ed.gov/free
E-mail:	FREE@ed.gov

LingNet

LingNet offers an incredible collection of computer programs and files to help you learn foreign languages—everything from Chinese to Russian to Urdu to Vietnamese. The system also offers basic information about some foreign countries. It's run by the Foreign Language Center at the Defense Language Institute.

You must register to receive access to most of LingNet's features. It typically takes twenty-four hours for your registration to be processed.

LingNet's files area offers an amazing selection of resources. It has foreign language dictionaries, drills and tutorials, flashcards, games, maps, translating programs, and word processors. It also offers lots of more esoteric items, like the Russian criminal code, the Macedonian constitution, a list of bulletin board systems in Russia, and a list of Internet mailing lists about foreign languages.

LingNet also has a set of active message forums, mostly about specific languages. There are forums about Arabic, Chinese, Farsi, French, German, Korean, Russian, Spanish, Thai, and other languages.

Finally, LingNet has a huge set of links to other Internet sites that offer language resources.

Vital Stats:

Access method:	WWW
To access:	http://lingnet.army.mil
E-mail:	admin@lingnet.army.mil

MIDDLE-L

MIDDLE-L is a mailing list for the discussion of issues related to middle school education and early adolescence. It's aimed at teachers, administrators, researchers, parents, school librarians, and others interested in middle schools. The list is operated by the ERIC Clearinghouse on Elementary and Early Childhood Education, which is funded by the U.S. Department of Education.

Vital Stats:

Access method:	E-mail
To access:	Send an e-mail message to listserv@postoffice.cso.uiuc.edu
Subject line:	
Message:	**subscribe MIDDLE-L** *firstname lastname*
E-mail (questions):	MIDDLE-L-request@postoffice.cso.uiuc.edu

National Center for Education Statistics

This site offers a huge collection of technical data, publications, and databases about education.

Some of the major publications available include an annual report to Congress titled *The Condition of Education, Projections of Education Statistics to 2008, The Digest of Education Statistics, Youth Indicators,* and *Education in States and Nations: Indicators Comparing U.S. States with the Other Industrialized Countries in 1991.*

Some of the other publications available are *Student Strategies to Avoid Harm at School; Arts Education in Public Elementary and Secondary Schools; Distance Education in Higher Education Institutions; Dropout Rates in the United States; Public School Kindergarten Teachers' Views on Children's Readiness for School; Status of Education Reform in Public Elementary and Secondary Schools: Principals' Perspectives; Federal Support for Education: Fiscal Years 1980 to 1998; School Policies and Practices Affecting Instruction in Mathematics; High School Students Ten Years after a Nation at Risk; Educational Progress of Black Students; The Cost of Higher Education; Minorities in Higher Education;* and *Teachers' Working Conditions,* among many others.

One especially noteworthy feature is the National Public School Locator Search, a database that lets you find detailed information about every public school in the nation. The database is particularly useful if you're planning to move and want to check out the schools in your new community.

For each school, the database provides the address, phone number, numbers of teachers and students, student-teacher ratio, grades included, number of students in each grade, number of students eligible for free lunches, and number of students by race or ethnicity.

Vital Stats:

Access method:	WWW
To access:	http://nces.ed.gov
E-mail:	NCESwebmaster@ed.gov

National Clearinghouse for ESL Literacy Education (NCLE)

The National Clearinghouse for ESL Literacy Education (NCLE) has dozens of brief publications about teaching English as a second language, answers to frequently asked questions about adult ESL literacy, and a list of books and other publications that can be ordered from the clearinghouse. The clearinghouse is operated by the Center for Applied Linguistics, with funding from the U.S. Department of Education.

Vital Stats:

Access method:	WWW
To access:	http://www.cal.org/ncle
E-mail:	ncle@cal.org

National Education Goals

This site is operated by the National Education Goals Panel, a federal agency devoted to improving the education system. The site has annual reports about progress toward achieving the National Education Goals, state education scorecards, searchable databases containing the annual reports and other National Education Goals Panel publications, and a list of the eight goals.

Vital Stats:

Access method:	WWW
To access:	http://www.negp.gov
E-mail:	negp@goalline.org

National Institute for Literacy Home Page

The National Institute for Literacy Home Page offers fact sheets about adult literacy, correctional education, English for speakers of other languages, literacy and health, literacy and learning disabilities, literacy and welfare, workforce literacy, and related topics.

It also has information about literacy-related legislation, links to Internet sites operated by regional and state literacy centers, links to dozens of other Internet sites devoted to literacy and adult education, publications from the National Adult Literacy and Learning Disabilities Center, resource directories for adults with literacy and learning disabilities, grant notices, a calendar of events, and press releases.

The institute also operates the National Literacy Advocacy mailing list (next entry).

Vital Stats:

Access method:	WWW
To access:	http://www.nifl.gov
E-mail:	webmaster@novel.nifl.gov

National Literacy Advocacy

Subscribers to the National Literacy Advocacy mailing list exchange messages about legislative, policy, and funding issues affecting adult literacy, basic skills, and English as a second language programs. The list is operated by the National Institute for Literacy, which also has a Web site (previous entry)

Vital Stats:

Access method:	E-mail
To access:	Send an e-mail message to majordomo@world.std.com
Subject line:	
Message:	**subscribe nla**
E-mail (questions):	DJRosen@world.std.com

Project EASI (Easy Access for Students and Institutions)

Project EASI is designed to be a one-stop source of information about financial aid for college students. It provides little original information but has links to lots of other Internet sites with financial aid information. The site has links to numerous publications about planning for college, federal financial aid programs, student financial aid resources in individual states, tests for postsecondary school admission, individual colleges and universities, and more. It's operated by the U.S. Department of Education.

Vital Stats:

Access method:	WWW
To access:	http://easi.ed.gov
E-mail:	Project_EASI@ed.gov

Quest

Teachers are the primary audience for Quest, which is aimed at helping them use the Internet as an educational resource. The site, which is operated by NASA, has information about how to bring the Internet into the classroom; curriculum materials for classes that can be taught using the Internet; online interactive projects and virtual conferences with NASA scientists, researchers, and engineers; links to sites that provide lists of schools that are online; links to numerous Internet sites that have K–12 education materials; and links to lots of other NASA Internet sites.

Vital Stats:

Access method:	WWW
To access:	http://quest.arc.nasa.gov
E-mail:	feedback@quest.arc.nasa.gov

READPRO

READPRO is a mailing list aimed at reading specialists, elementary and secondary teachers, college professors, librarians, and others involved in teaching reading. Some of the subjects discussed include methods of teaching language arts, phonics instruction, Internet resources for language arts, and conferences on reading-related topics. The list is operated by the ERIC Clearinghouse on Reading, English, and Communication, which is operated by Indiana University and funded by the U.S. Department of Education.

Vital Stats:

Access method:	E-mail
To access:	Send an e-mail message to majordomo@indiana.edu
Subject line:	**SUBSCRIBE READPRO**
Message:	**subscribe disted_readpro**
	end
E-mail (questions):	disted@indiana.edu

ReadyWeb

ReadyWeb offers numerous publications about getting children ready for school. Some sample titles are *Helping Children Learn about Reading, Helping Your Child Get Ready for School, Helping Your Child Be Healthy and Fit, Helping Your Child Learn Responsible Behavior,* and *Helping Your Child Succeed in School.* ReadyWeb is operated by the ERIC Clearinghouse on Elementary and Early Childhood Education, which is funded by the U.S. Department of Education.

It also has ERIC digests titled *Preparing Children with Disabilities for School* and *Protecting Children from Inappropriate Practices,* a report from the National Association for the Education of Young Children titled *Back to School Time—Tips to Help Children Adjust,* a report from the Southern Regional Education Board titled *Getting Schools Ready for Children: The Other Side of the Readiness Goal,* and bibliographies of publications about school readiness.

Vital Stats:

Access method:	WWW
To access:	http://readyweb.crc.uiuc.edu
E-mail:	readyweb@ericps.crc.uiuc.edu

Smithsonian Education

The Smithsonian Education site has several lesson plans on topics ranging from presidential elections to ocean ecology to landscape painting. The lessons are aimed at upper elementary and middle school students.

The site also has extensive details about school tours of the Smithsonian Institution, information about summer seminars for teachers, and a list of nearly 500 teaching guides, posters, resource lists, study guides, slides, and other educational products available from the Smithsonian.

Vital Stats:

Access method:	WWW
To access:	http://educate.si.edu
E-mail:	smigiela@soe.si.edu

This is MEGA Mathematics!

The MEGA Mathematics site has lesson plans, activities, and stories related to the math involved in map coloring, graph theory, knots, algorithms, finite state machines, logic, and infinity. The site, which is designed for elementary school children and their teachers, is a project of the Computer Research and Applications Group at Los Alamos National Laboratory.

Vital Stats:

Access method:	WWW
To access:	http://www.c3.lanl.gov/mega-math

U.S. Department of Education

The U.S. Department of Education site offers thousands of documents about education—everything from extensive reports about education reform to information about grants, loans, and work study programs available for college students.

Of particular interest are a series of publications about how to help your children do better in school. Available titles include *Helping Your Child Learn Math, Helping Your Child Learn to Read, Helping Your Child Learn History, Helping Your Child Get Ready for School, Help Your Child Improve in Test Taking, Help Your Child Learn to Write Well, Helping Your Child Use the Library, Helping Your Child Learn Geography, Helping Your Child Learn Science, Helping Your Child Learn Responsible Behavior, Helping Your Child with Homework,* and *Helping Your Child Succeed in School.*

The site also has an interesting collection of reports, studies, and other publications. Some of the available titles are *Parents Guide to the Internet; Getting Ready for College Early; Preparing Your Child for College; Funding Your Education; Museums and Learning: A Guide for Family Visits; Summer Home Learning Recipes; Guide to U.S. Department of Education Programs; New Teacher's Guide to the U.S. Department of Education; Arts Education and School Improvement Resources for Local and State Leaders;* and *Creating Safe and Drug-Free Schools: An Action Guide.*

Some of the other reports available are *Read with Me: A Guide for Student Volunteers Starting Early Childhood Literacy Programs; Educational Programs That Work; Computer Accessibility Technology Packet; Reaching All Families: Creating Family-Friendly Schools; Transforming Ideas for Teaching and Learning the Arts; Education Reform and Students at Risk:*

A Review of the Current State of the Art; A Study of Charter Schools: First-Year Report; Reducing Class Size: What Do We Know?; Diverse Forms of Tech-Prep: Implementation Approaches in Ten Local Consortia; State of the Art: Transforming Ideas for Teaching and Learning to Read; Catalog of School Reform Models; and *Safe and Smart: Making After-School Hours Work for Kids.*

A few of the site's other highlights are an online version of the Free Application for Federal Student Aid (FAFSA), a bibliographic database containing information about the more than 23,000 publications produced or funded by the Education Department since its creation in 1980, a directory of more than 2,000 education organizations, a database containing information about hundreds of education conferences, details about administrative education initiatives, and speeches and congressional testimony by Education Department officials.

Vital Stats:

Access method:	WWW
To access:	http://www.ed.gov
E-mail:	CustomerService@inet.ed.gov

U.S. Department of Education Search Page

This site has two databases that let you search Web sites either funded or operated by the Education Department.

The first database, called the Cross-Site Indexing Project, lets you search more than 150 Web sites funded by the Education Department. You can search the entire database or only certain types of sites, such as Educational Resources Information Centers (ERIC), regional educational laboratories, special education and rehabilitation services, and foreign language resource centers, among others.

The second database lets you search across all the Web sites operated by the Education Department. You can search the entire database or only certain types of documents, such as legislative texts, *Federal Register* documents, press releases, and *Eric Digests,* among others.

The site also offers links to other Internet sites that have large education-related databases.

Vital Stats:

Access method:	WWW
To access:	http://search.ed.gov
E-mail:	CustomerService@inet.ed.gov

Urban Education Web

The Urban Education Web has numerous publications for parents, including *How to Help Your Child Avoid Violent Conflicts, What Parents and Guardians Can Do about Learning Disabilities, Working with the School and Community to Keep Your Children Drug Free, How to Recognize and Develop Your Children's Special Talents, How to Prepare Your Children for Work, A Guide to Computer Learning in Your Child's School,* and *A Community Guide to Multicultural Education Programs,* among other. The ERIC Clearinghouse on Urban Education at Columbia University operates the site, with funding from the U.S. Department of Education.

The site also has the full text of publications about urban education from various sources. Some of the available titles are *Principals' Best Ten Tips to Increase Parental Involvement in Schools; The "Hard-To-Reach" Parent: Old Challenges, New Insights;* and *Hand in Hand: How Nine Urban Schools Work With Families and Community Services.*

In addition, the site has dozens of brief publications about the educational attainment of immigrants, strategies to reduce school violence, after-school programs for urban youth, school dropouts, overcrowding in urban schools, homeless students, year-round education, gangs in schools, and retaining good teachers in urban schools; bibliographies about single-sex education, urban school finances, mentoring programs, refugee education, the importance of minority teachers, and other subjects; *A Directory of Anti-Bias Education Resources and Services;* publications about historically black colleges and universities; and links to numerous other education sites on the Internet.

Vital Stats:

Access method: WWW
To access: http://eric-web.tc.columbia.edu
E-mail: lry2@columbia.edu

EMERGENCY RESPONSE AND FIRE SAFETY

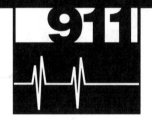

Federal Emergency Management Agency

The Federal Emergency Management Agency site has a wide range of information about how to prepare for disasters and how to cope once they've struck.

The site has weather warnings, an explanation of the La Nina weather pattern, and U.S. weather forecast maps; details about how to prepare for earthquakes, floods, hurricanes, winter storms, and other disasters; information about types of assistance that are available to disaster victims; guidelines about how the public can help disaster victims; publications about helping children cope with disaster, family disaster plans, and emergency food and water supplies; photos from various disasters, including the Oklahoma City bombing and Hurricane Bonnie; and press releases about disasters.

The FEMA site also has links to Internet sites around the world operated by emergency management agencies, fire fighting agencies, search and rescue organizations, state emergency management agencies, and other organizations involved in emergency management.

The site also features a special section for kids.

Vital Stats:

Access method:	WWW
To access:	http://www.fema.gov
E-mail:	eipa@fema.gov

National Interagency Fire Center

The National Interagency Fire Center provides information about current wildfires, an outlook for the coming fire season, a link to a National Weather Service site that provides forecasts of fire weather, and links to other sites that have information about wildfires. The center is a cooperative project of several federal agencies.

Vital Stats:

Access method:	WWW
To access:	http://www.nifc.gov

U.S. Fire Administration

This site offers numerous publications for consumers about fire safety. Some of the available titles are *After the Fire: Returning to Normal; Curious Children and Fire: What Every Parent Should Know; During or after a Disaster: Factsheets on Fire Safety; Protecting Your Family from Fire; Safe at Home: Fire Do's and Don'ts;* and *Wildfire: Are You Prepared?* The site is operated by the U.S. Fire Administration, which is part of the Federal Emergency Management Agency.

Another highlight is a collection of technical reports about fires. Some of the available documents are *The Rural Fire Problem in the United States; Firefighter Fatalities in the United States; The Aftermath of Firefighter Fatality Incidents: Preparing for the Worst; Fire in the United States; Arson and Juveniles: Responding to the Violence; Arson in the United States;*

Children and Fire: The Experiences of Children and Fire in the United States; Guide to Federal Resources for Emergency Services Departments; Guide to Funding Alternatives for Fire and EMS Departments; and *Operational Considerations for High-Rise Firefighting.*

The site also has a self-study course titled *Emergency Response to Terrorism,* case studies of specific fires, a database that lists hotels and motels that meet the requirements of the Hotel and Motel Fire Safety Act of 1990, hotel and motel fire safety tips, a list of firefighters who have been killed in the line of duty, and a special page of materials for children.

Vital Stats:

Access method: WWW
To access: http://www.usfa.fema.gov

ENERGY

Alternative Fuels Data Center

The Alternative Fuels Data Center has information about demonstration and evaluation programs, news about alternative fuel vehicles available from various manufacturers, a directory of alternative fuel refueling stations across the country, and brochures and reports about alternative fuels. The site is operated by the National Renewable Energy Laboratory, with funding from the U.S. Department of Energy.

The site also has press releases related to alternative fuel vehicles from various organizations, legislative documents, a calendar of conferences and events, links to other Internet sites that provide information about alternative fuels, and much more.

Vital Stats:

Access method:	WWW
To access:	http://www.afdc.doe.gov
E-mail:	hotline@afdc.nrel.gov

Bioenergy Information Network

The Bioenergy Information Network has information about converting trees and grasses for fuel and power generation. It features reports about biofuels and biomass crops, background information about biopower, a list of U.S. ethanol producers and the capacities of their plants, a calendar of conferences and meetings, links to related Internet sites, and lots more. It's sponsored by the U.S. Department of Energy.

Vital Stats:

Access method:	WWW
To access:	http://www.esd.ornl.gov/bfdp
E-mail:	are@ornl.gov

Biofuels Information Center

The Biofuels Information Center site has reports about ethanol, methanol, global warming and biofuels emissions, converting wastes to biogas and compost, and related subjects. The center is operated by the National Renewable Energy Laboratory, with funding from the U.S. Department of Energy.

The site also has news about research projects at the NREL's Biotechnology Center, a searchable database of documents about biofuels technologies, a newsletter titled *Biofuels UPDATE*, a calendar of events, and links to other Internet sites that provide information about biofuels.

Vital Stats:

Access method:	WWW
To access:	http://www.biofuels.nrel.gov
E-mail:	neufelds@tcplink.nrel.gov

Clean Cities

This site provides information about the U.S. Department of Energy's Clean Cities program, which seeks to expand the use of alternatives to gasoline and diesel fuel. The site has the *Clean Cities Guide to Alternative Fuel Vehicle Incentives and Laws,* a list of contacts, grant information, a calendar of events, and links to other Internet sites that provide information about alternative fuel vehicles.

Vital Stats:

Access method:	WWW
To access:	http://www.ccities.doe.gov
E-mail:	ccities@afdc.nrel.gov

DOE Information Bridge

This incredible site offers more than two million pages of full-text scientific and technical reports produced by the Energy Department and its contractors. The documents cover such topics as physics, chemistry, materials, biology, environmental sciences, energy technologies, engineering, computer and information science, and renewable energy, among others. The site is a joint project of the Energy Department and the Government Printing Office.

The growing site boasts 27,000 reports that have been produced since January 1996. You can search the reports database by author, title, laboratory, sponsoring organization, subject, keywords, date, and other variables.

Vital Stats:

Access method:	WWW
To access:	http://www.doe.gov/bridge/home.html
E-mail:	kathy.chambers@ccmail.osti.gov

DR-NRR, GC-NRR, *and* PR-OPA

DR-NRR, GC-NRR, and PR-OPA are mailing lists that distribute information from the Nuclear Regulatory Commission. Here are descriptions of each list:

- DR-NRR distributes daily reports from the Nuclear Regulatory Commission about the operating status of nuclear reactors and unusual events at the plants.

- GC-NRR distributes Generic Communications, which usually alert plant operators to new NRC policies or to problems at nuclear plants that the NRC believes may be widespread.

- PR-OPA distributes NRC press releases about fines levied against owners of nuclear plants, schedules of upcoming NRC meetings, and speeches by NRC officials.

Vital Stats:

Access method:	E-mail
To access:	Send an e-mail message to listproc@nrc.gov
Subject line:	
Message:	**subscribe** *listname firstname lastname*
E-mail (questions):	tgd@nrc.gov

EIA Email Lists

The Energy Information Administration operates thirty-one electronic mailing lists that distribute a huge array of energy information. The lists provide information about energy issues in seventy countries, crude oil production and prices, electric power generation and consumption, gasoline stocks and prices, natural gas prices, significant events in the international oil market, events in the petroleum market, coal production, retail gasoline prices, and other topics.

To sign up, simply provide your e-mail address at the Web site and check which lists you want:

- Country Analysis Briefs—All available countries
- Country Analysis Briefs —Americas
- Country Analysis Briefs—East Asia, South Asia, and Australia
- Country Analysis Briefs—Europe and the former Soviet Union republics
- Country Analysis Briefs—Middle East and North Africa
- Country Analysis Briefs—Special topics
- Country Analysis Briefs—Sub-Saharan Africa
- Crude Oil Watch Data
- Crude Oil Watch Summary
- Distillate Watch Data
- Distillate Watch Summary
- EIA New Releases
- EIA Press Releases
- Electric Power Monthly Summary
- Gasoline Watch Data
- Gasoline Watch Summary
- Monthly Electric Power Industry Developments
- Monthly Natural Gas Consumption
- Monthly Natural Gas Prices
- Monthly Natural Gas Supply and Disposition
- Monthly Oil Market Chronology
- Monthly Underground Natural Gas Storage
- Natural Gas Weekly Market Update
- Petroleum Market Report
- Propane Watch Data
- Propane Watch Summary

- Short-Term Energy Outlook Summary
- Weekly Coal Production
- Weekly On-Highway Diesel Prices
- Weekly Retail Gasoline Prices
- What's New at the Energy Information Administration Internet Site

Vital Stats:

Access method:	WWW
To access:	http://tonto.eia.doe.gov/email/index.htm
E-mail:	wmaster@eia.doe.gov

Energy Efficiency and Renewable Energy Network (EREN)

The Energy Efficiency and Renewable Energy Network (EREN) site has dozens of consumer publications, including *Cooling Your Home Naturally, Energy Efficient Lighting, Energy Efficient Windows, Energy-Saving Tips for Small Businesses, Landscaping for Energy Efficiency, Selecting a New Water Heater,* and *Solar Water Heating,* among others. The site also has a calendar of events, links to lots of related Internet sites, and technical information about building, industrial, transportation, and utility technologies.

Vital Stats:

Access method:	WWW
To access:	http://www.eren.doe.gov
E-mail:	webmaster.eren@nrel.gov

Energy Information Administration

Virtually anything you want to know about energy supply, demand, and prices is available at this site, which is operated by the Energy Information Administration. The site offers statistics on the cost of electricity nationwide, the number of offshore oil and gas wells, natural gas production, retail gasoline prices, the amount of electricity generated by nuclear power plants, U.S. energy supply and demand, and lots of other subjects.

It also has a calendar of events, a list of contacts at the Energy Information Administration, hundreds of links to energy related Internet sites, and much more.

Vital Stats:

Access method:	WWW
To access:	http://www.eia.doe.gov
E-mail:	infoctr@eia.doe.gov

International Nuclear Safety Center

The International Nuclear Safety Center offers basic information about nuclear reactors, research reactors, and fuel processing facilities around the world. It also has links to other government and industry Internet sites that have nuclear power information. The site is operated by the International Nuclear Safety Center at Argonne National Laboratory.

Vital Stats:

Access method:	WWW
To access:	http://www.insc.anl.gov
E-mail:	inscdb@anl.gov

International Nuclear Safety Program

This site provides extensive information from the International Nuclear Safety Program, a U.S. Department of Energy initiative to improve the safety of Soviet-designed nuclear power plants.

The highlights of this site are the detailed profiles of Soviet-designed nuclear power plants in Russia, Ukraine, Armenia, Bulgaria, the Czech Republic, Hungary, Kazakhstan, Lithuania, and Slovakia. For each plant, the site provides an operating history, summary of unusual events, organization charts, photographs, and list of safety upgrade projects that have been planned, completed, or are ongoing.

The site also features articles about the strengths and weaknesses of various Soviet plant designs, a brochure about the 1986 disaster and subsequent events at the Chernobyl nuclear power plant, biweekly reports about activities at Chernobyl, biweekly reports about recent efforts to improve international nuclear safety, links to dozens of related Web sites, and a searchable database containing bibliographic information about technical reports, periodicals, fact sheets, articles, press releases, presentations, videos, and photographs.

Vital Stats:

Access method:	WWW
To access:	http://insp.pnl.gov:2080
E-mail:	insp@pnl.gov

National Renewable Energy Laboratory

This site is operated by the National Renewable Energy Laboratory (NREL), which is the primary federal laboratory for renewable energy research. Its research focuses on such topics as alternative fuels, wind technology, and photovoltaics, among others. NREL is part of the U.S. Department of Energy.

The site has more than two hundred NREL reports about everything from traffic flow to energy-efficient windows, information about NREL technologies that are available for licensing, details about research at NREL, press releases, and documents for contractors.

Office of Scientific and Technical Information

The Office of Scientific and Technical Information (OSTI) offers several searchable databases. The most notable is the DOE Reports Bibliographic Database, which provides citations for all Department of Energy reports prepared from January 1994 to the present.

Other databases provide testimony by DOE officials before congressional committees, information about software funded by DOE or the Nuclear Regulatory Commission that can be ordered from OSTI, and bibliographic information for reports about energy efficiency and renewable energy.

Tennessee Valley Authority

The Tennessee Valley Authority site has financial reports, background information, congressional testimony and speeches, economic development information, lists of job openings, press releases, and biographical information about members of the TVA board of directors. The TVA is a federal corporation that is the nation's largest producer of electric power.

U.S. Department of Energy Home Page

The U.S. Department of Energy Home Page provides links to dozens of Internet sites operated by DOE laboratories and field offices around the country.

Besides the links, the site offers access to the OpenNet database, which contains bibliographic references to more than 250,000 declassified documents about human radiation experiments, nuclear testing, radiation releases, fallout, and related topics. Each reference includes information about how to obtain the paper document.

The site also provides speeches by the secretary of energy, congressional testimony, budget information, limited information about human radiation experiments, DOE press releases, a list of new publications, a calendar of conferences and workshops, historical information about the department and its predecessor agencies, links to Web sites operated by science museums and centers, and links to science pages for kids.

Vital Stats:

Access method: WWW
To access: http://www.doe.gov
E-mail: webmaster@apollo.osti.gov

United States Nuclear Regulatory Commission

This site has a huge amount of information about facilities—primarily nuclear power plants—that are regulated by the Nuclear Regulatory Commission. It offers a list of troubled nuclear plants on the NRC's special "watchlist," daily reports about problems at nuclear plants, a map showing the location of commercial nuclear power plants in the United States, information about the disposal of low-level and high-level radioactive waste, and Systematic Assessment of Licensee Performance (SALP) reports, which are detailed reviews of the performance of individual nuclear plants.

One of the site's highlights is a collection of plant information books for every operating nuclear reactor in the United States. The books have information about emergency response facilities, the plant site, evacuation routes, and the nuclear reactor and its various systems. There are even diagrams of some plant systems, such as the reactor coolant system, the emergency core cooling systems, and reactor containment.

Vital Stats:

Access method: WWW
To access: http://www.nrc.gov
E-mail: nrcweb@nrc.gov

ENVIRONMENT

GENERAL

Agency for Toxic Substances and Disease Registry

If you're looking for information about hazardous substances and public health, the Agency for Toxic Substances and Disease Registry site is the place to check. The agency is part of the U.S. Department of Health and Human Services.

The site's highlight is the HazDat database, which provides data about releases of hazardous substances from about 2,000 Superfund sites or spills and the effects of the substances on human health. The database provides information about site characteristics, contaminants found, maximum contaminant concentration levels, impact on population, community concerns, public health threat categorization, and physical hazards at the site, among other subjects.

There are several ways to search the database. Perhaps the easiest is to use the national map and click on the state you want. Doing so will produce a list of all contaminated sites in that state and lead to further details about individual locations.

The site also has fact sheets about individual toxic chemicals, a guide to communicating health risk information to the public, congressional testimony by agency staff, DOS software for researchers who are examining disease clusters, information about what levels of specific toxic substances pose a health risk, a list of the top twenty hazardous substances, information about child health programs, links to other Internet sites that provide information about toxic substances and health, and lots more.

Vital Stats:

Access method:	WWW
To access:	http://atsdr1.atsdr.cdc.gov:8080
E-mail:	ATSDRIC@cdc.gov

Biological Resources Division

The Biological Resources Division, which is part of the U.S. Geological Survey, offers more than a dozen images of animals and birds, research bulletins, documents for children about endangered species, and drawings of endangered species that kids can print out and then color.

It also has information about fish kills and amphibian research, press releases, links to biology education materials at other Internet sites, a report titled *Endangered Ecosystems of the United States: A Preliminary Assessment of Loss and Degradation,* and much more.

Vital Stats:

Access method:	WWW
To access:	http://biology.usgs.gov
E-mail:	webmaster@ttc.nbs.gov

The Chemical Scorecard

This extremely interesting site lets you find out which manufacturing plants are releasing toxic chemicals into your community. The site, which is based on the Environmental Protection Agency's Toxic Release Inventory, is operated by the Environmental Defense Fund.

To get information for your county, you simply type in your Zip Code. The database returns detailed information about which facilities release toxic chemicals, what chemicals they release, and how much of each chemical they release.

Vital Stats:

Access method:	WWW
To access:	http://www.scorecard.org
E-mail:	Bill_Pease@edf.org

Congressional Research Service Reports

This site offers the full text of hundreds of Congressional Research Service reports about the environment, agriculture, and natural resources. CRS is a division of the Library of Congress. Some of the topics covered are biodiversity, forestry, mining, wetlands, air quality, climate, pesticides, pollution, waste management, water quality, and public lands, among others.

Previously, the reports were available primarily to members of Congress and their staffs. The site is operated by the Committee for the National Institute for the Environment, a non-profit organization.

Vital Stats:

Access method:	WWW
To access:	http://www.cnie.org/nle/crs_main.html
E-mail:	khutton@cnie.org

Envirofacts Warehouse

This amazing site provides access to eight of the most important environmental databases maintained by the Environmental Protection Agency (EPA). You can search a single database or all the databases simultaneously. The databases are updated monthly.

The following databases are available:

- Superfund Data: Information about Superfund sites from the Comprehensive Environmental Response, Compensation, and Liability Information System (CERCLIS).

- Safe Drinking Water Info: Information about public water systems and their violations of EPA's regulations for safe drinking water.

- Hazardous Waste Data: Information about the activities of firms that generate, transport, treat, store, and dispose of hazardous waste, as reported to the Resource Conservation and Recovery Information System (RCRIS).

- Biennial Reporting System: Information about the activities of hazardous waste handlers, as reported to the Biennial Reporting System (BRS).

- Toxics Release Inventory: Information about releases and transfers of more than 650 toxic chemicals to the environment by various facilities, as reported to the Toxics Release Inventory (TRI).

- Water Discharge Permits: Information about permit limits and monitoring data for more than 75,000 wastewater treatment facilities nationwide, as reported to the Permit Compliance System (PCS).

- Air Releases: Information about the compliance of facilities with air pollution regulations, as reported to the Aerometric Information Retrieval System (AIRS).

- Grants Information: Information about grants awarded by EPA's Federal Grant Programs, as reported to the Grants Information and Control System (GICS).

The site also has links to news articles about Envirofacts and links to other environmental search engines and sources.

Vital Stats:

Access method:	WWW
To access:	http://www.epa.gov/enviro/index_java.html

---

environb-l, epa-press, internetnb-l, *and* oppt-newsbreak

The U.S. Environmental Protection Agency operates four mailing lists that distribute environmental news and information:

- environb-l distributes the *Enviro-Newsbrief,* a daily publication produced by the EPA Headquarters Library. The publication summarizes news about appointments to the EPA, regulatory reform, the Council on Environmental Quality, changes to the Office of Management and Budget's regulatory review process, reinventing government, environmental legislation, and other issues.

- epa-press distributes EPA press releases. It's primarily aimed at the news media, although anyone can subscribe.

- internetnb-l distributes the *Internet Newsbrief,* a weekly publication produced by the EPA Headquarters Library. The publication has items about new Internet sites that offer environmental information.

- oppt-newsbreak is a daily summary of newspaper articles about pollution prevention, toxic substances, and information dissemination. It's published by the EPA's Office of Pollution Prevention and Toxics Library.

Vital Stats:

Access method:	E-mail
To access:	Send an e-mail message to listserver@valley.rtpnc.epa.gov
Subject line:	
Message:	**subscribe** *listname firstname lastname*
E-mail (questions):	library-hq@epamail.epa.gov

EPA Federal Register Mailing Lists

The Environmental Protection Agency operates twelve mailing lists that provide information published in the *Federal Register*. You must subscribe to each list separately:

- epafr-contents2   The entire table of contents for the *Federal Register*.
- epa-meetings2   EPA meeting notices.
- epa-sab2   Material related to EPA's Science Advisory Board.
- epa-impact2   Environmental impact statements.
- epa-species2   Documents about endangered species.
- epa-general2   General EPA documents, presidential documents related to environmental issues, and other environmental documents.
- epa-air2   Documents from the Office of Air and Radiation.
- epa-pest2   Documents from the Office of Pesticide Programs.
- epa-tox2   Documents from the Office of Pollution Prevention and Toxic Substances.
- epa-tri2   Documents about the Community Right-to-Know program.
- epa-waste2   Documents about hazardous and solid waste.
- epa-water2   Documents from the Office of Water.

Vital Stats:

Access method:	E-mail
To access:	Send an e-mail message to listserver@valley.rtpnc.epa.gov
Subject line:	
Message:	**subscribe** *listname firstname lastname*

EPA Sector Notebooks

This site provides comprehensive environmental reports about more than two dozen industries. It's operated by the Environmental Protection Agency's Office of Enforcement and Compliance Assurance.

Each report, which runs from just under 100 pages to nearly 200 pages, provides an environmental profile, industrial process information, details about pollution prevention techniques, pollutant release data, lists of regulations, a history of compliance and enforcement, descriptions of innovative programs, contact names, and bibliographic references.

Reports are available for the following industries: air transportation, dry cleaning, electronics and computers, fossil fuel electric power generation, ground transportation, inorganic chemicals, iron and steel, lumber and wood products, metal casting, metal fabrication, metal mining, motor vehicle assembly, nonferrous metals, nonfuel nonmetal mining, organic chemistry, petroleum refining, pharmaceuticals, plastic resins and manmade fibers, printing, pulp and paper, rubber and plastics, shipbuilding and repair, stone and clay and glass and concrete, textiles, transportation equipment cleaning, water transportation, and wood furniture and fixtures.

Reports for the following areas should be added to the site soon: aerospace, agricultural chemicals, agricultural crop production, agricultural stock production, coal mining, local government, and oil and gas exploration and production.

Vital Stats:

Access method:	WWW
To access:	http://es.epa.gov/oeca/sector
E-mail:	heminway.seth@epamail.epa.gov

fws-news

The fws-news mailing list distributes press releases, bulletins, and other information from the U.S. Fish and Wildlife Service. The one-way list does not provide for discussion.

Vital Stats:

Access method:	E-mail
To access:	Send an e-mail message to listserv@www.fws.gov
Subject line:	
Message:	**subscribe fws-news** *firstname lastname*
E-mail (questions):	craig_rieben@mail.fws.gov

National Marine Fisheries Service

The National Marine Fisheries Service site has recordings of whale songs and cries, extensive information about threatened and endangered species, documents about protecting marine mammals, a computer-generated model of the pollution flow from Boston Harbor, drawings of fish found in the southeastern United States, information about the Sustainable Fisheries Act of 1996, links to lots of related Internet sites, and much more.

Vital Stats:

Access method:	WWW
To access:	http://www.nmfs.gov
E-mail:	Thomas.McIntyre@noaa.gov

National Wetlands Inventory

This site has a disappointingly small amount of information about wetlands in the United States. It's operated by the U.S. Fish and Wildlife Service.

It has reports titled *Classification of Wetlands and Deepwater Habitats of the United States* and *Southeast Wetlands Status and Trends Report,* national and regional lists of plant species that occur in wetlands, technical data, links to wetlands materials for educators, links to Web sites operated by state natural resources departments, and links to lots of other wetlands information sources.

NOAA Web Sites

This gateway provides links to Web sites operated by the National Oceanic and Atmospheric Administration. You can search the links or browse them by dozens of topics, including air temperature, Antarctica, blizzards, climate, clouds, commercial fisheries, coral reefs, dolphins, El Niño, endangered species, fire weather, glaciology, greenhouse effect, habitat protection, hurricanes, marine mammals, ocean drilling, rainfall prediction, sea turtles, severe weather watches and warnings, ship wrecks, ski reports, turbulence, volcanoes, weather models, and wetlands, among many others.

Vital Stats:

Access method: WWW
To access: http://www.websites.noaa.gov
E-mail: ward@hpcc.noaa.gov

North American Reporting Center for Amphibian Malformations

Information about research into what's causing malformations in frogs and other amphibians is featured at this site. It's operated by the Northern Prairie Wildlife Research Center, which is part of the U.S. Geological Survey.

The site has background information about malformed amphibians, a clickable map showing where amphibian malformations have been reported in the United States and Canada, photos of various types of malformations, and an online amphibian identification guide.

It also has articles and news releases about malformations, online forms for reporting amphibian malformations, a bibliography that provides citations to scientific papers about amphibian malformations and related issues, technical information for researchers, and links to related Web sites.

Vital Stats:

Access method: WWW
To access: http://www.npwrc.usgs.gov/narcam
E-mail: narcam@usgs.gov

RTK NET

RTK NET provides more than a dozen federal databases that contain information about the environment, housing, campaign finance, and other subjects. This is a tremendous service, since obtaining some of these databases from the federal government can cost hundreds or thousands of dollars. RTK NET is a joint project of OMB Watch and the Unison Institute, two public interest organizations in Washington, D.C.

The databases offer reports by companies that generate, ship, or receive hazardous waste; information about 38,000 sites that have been declared Superfund sites or that are potential Superfund sites; data about amounts of hazardous chemicals produced by 25,000 facilities; information about releases and transfers of toxic chemicals from manufacturing facilities; data about home purchase and home improvement loans made by banks, savings associations, credit unions, and other mortgage lenders; records about contributions to congressional candidates in the 1992 and 1994 election cycles; and much more.

You can access most of the databases through the Web site. However, access to a few databases and some advanced database manipulation tools is only available through the Telnet and dial-in systems. You must register before you can access the Telnet or dial-in systems.

RTK NET provides extensive online documentation about how to use each of the databases. The databases are quite sophisticated, but if you run into problems you can call the voice number for assistance.

Vital Stats:

Access methods:	WWW, Telnet, dial-in
To access:	http://www.rtk.net *or* telnet://rtk.net
User ID (first call only):	**public**
E-mail:	webmaster@rtk.net
Dial-in access:	202-234-8570
Voice:	202-234-8494

Sector Facility Indexing Project

This site provides detailed environmental compliance information for facilities in five industrial sectors: petroleum refining, iron and steel production, primary nonferrous metal refining and smelting, pulp manufacturing, and automobile assembly. It's operated by the Environmental Protection Agency's Office of Enforcement and Compliance Assurance.

You can search the database by facility name, city, state, and EPA region. For each facility, the reports provide information about the number and results of inspections, the number of times the facility violated its permit under the Clean Water Act, closed administrative or civil enforcement actions that have been taken against the facility for violating environmental laws, production capacity, total pounds of Toxic Release Inventory chemicals discharged, total pounds of known carcinogens released, on-site pollutant spills, and much more.

The site also has links to sites with related environmental information.

Vital Stats:

Access method: WWW
To access: http://es.epa.gov/oeca/sfi

State of the Coast

This site is designed to be a continuing report in progress about the state of coastal areas in the United States. It's operated by the National Oceanic and Atmospheric Administration.

The "report" is presented in more than a dozen essays about such topics as population density and growth, ecological effects of fishing, the extent and condition of U.S. coral reefs, oxygen depletion in coastal waters, restoring coastal habits, managing oil and chemical spills, and managing coastal resources, among others. New essays are added to the site periodically.

Vital Stats:

Access method: WWW
To access: http://state-of-coast.noaa.gov
E-mail: Sotc.Editors@noaa.gov

United States Environmental Protection Agency

This site offers an immense assortment of environmental information about everything from acid rain to pollution prevention. It has thousands of documents and databases—some of them extremely valuable—but it's designed so badly that finding anything is a good trick.

Ignore the interface on the home page—it's a total loss. There are two better options for accessing the site. If you know exactly what you're seeking, the best choice is to use the site's search engine. If your quest is more general, select "Browse" on the home page. It arranges the site's information by subject.

One of the site's highlights is a selection of searchable databases. They provide information about Superfund sites, sites that produce hazardous waste, releases of toxic chemicals, releases of airborne contaminants, and other topics.

Another cool feature is "Search by Zip Code." By simply typing in your Zip Code, you can get a list of facilities in your county that release pollutants or handle hazardous materials, details about where Superfund sites are located and the status of their cleanup efforts, and much more.

The site also has the full text of *Access EPA,* a directory of hundreds of environmental information resources provided by the EPA and other organizations; publications about pesticides, air quality, pollution prevention, hazardous waste, solid waste, water quality, wetlands, and other topics; *Federal Register* documents that deal with the environment or environment-related issues; technical reports and publications; and information about how to protect children from various pollutants.

Finally, it offers links to EPA laboratories and research centers, statistics about environmental quality and trends, extensive details about Superfund sites, lists of EPA clearinghouses and hotlines, lots of documents about acid rain, a catalog of more than 5,000 EPA documents that can be ordered free, speeches by EPA officials, guides and curricula for teachers, special sections with materials for kids, and lots, lots more.

Vital Stats:

Access method:	WWW
To access:	http://www.epa.gov
E-mail:	internet_support@epamail.epa.gov

United States Fish and Wildlife Service

The United States Fish and Wildlife Service site offers extensive information about everything from endangered species to the Federal Duck Stamp program.

The site has lists of all endangered and threatened species, the full text of the Endangered Species Act of 1973, images of selected endangered species, national policy directives, the full text of the *U.S. Fish and Wildlife Service Manual,* text and images about wildlife species ranging from the American black bear to the rhinoceros, a booklet about careers with the Fish and Wildlife Service, guides to biological and environmental resources on the Internet, and links to other Fish and Wildlife Service Internet sites that provide information about the national wildlife refuge system, wetlands protection, and other topics.

Vital Stats:

Access method:	WWW
To access:	http://www.fws.gov
E-mail:	web_reply@fws.gov

NUCLEAR WASTE

Office of Civilian Radioactive Waste Management

The Office of Civilian Radioactive Waste Management site contains information about efforts to build a permanent repository for high-level radioactive waste from nuclear power plants and other facilities. The office is part of the U.S. Department of Energy.

The site has background information about the office, abstracts of technical reports prepared by the office, the text of the Nuclear Waste Policy Act of 1982, budget information, congressional testimony and speeches by DOE officials, a calendar of events, a newsletter, *Federal Register* notices, information about nuclear waste disposal programs in other countries, links to other Internet sites related to civilian radioactive waste management, and fact sheets about radiation, storage and disposal of spent nuclear fuel, transportation of spent nuclear fuel, and related subjects.

The office also operates the Yucca Mountain Project site (this page).

Vital Stats:

Access method:	WWW
To access:	http://www.rw.doe.gov
E-mail:	tommy.smith@rw.doe.gov

U.S. Nuclear Waste Technical Review Board

This site provides information about the U.S. Nuclear Waste Technical Review Board, an independent agency that oversees the federal program for disposing of high-level radioactive waste from nuclear power plants. It includes reports by the board, congressional testimony, press releases, meeting announcements, the board's five-year strategic plan, and links to other nuclear-related Web sites.

Vital Stats:

Access method:	WWW
To access:	http://www.nwtrb.gov
E-mail:	info@nwtrb.gov

Yucca Mountain Site Characterization Project

The Yucca Mountain Site Characterization Project has background information about efforts to determine whether Yucca Mountain in Nevada would be a suitable place to bury high-level radioactive waste from nuclear power plants and other facilities. The site is operated by the Office of Civilian Radioactive Waste Management, which also operates a site about the office (this page).

The site has maps and photographs of the project location, maps of possible routes for transporting radioactive waste to it, transcripts of public meetings about the siting guidelines, and information about touring the project.

Vital Stats:

Access method:	WWW
To access:	http://www.ymp.gov
E-mail:	webmaster@notes.ymp.gov

PARKS AND PUBLIC LANDS

Alaska Public Lands Information Centers

This site, which is a project of eight federal and state agencies that manage public lands in Alaska, offers limited information about visiting the Land of the Midnight Sun.

The site has answers to frequently asked questions about visiting Alaska, information about renting wilderness cabins, schedules of special events in major cities, and clickable maps of Alaska showing national parks and preserves, national wildlife refuges, and state parks.

Vital Stats:

Access method: WWW
To access: http://www.nps.gov/aplic/center/index.html
E-mail: John_Morris@nps.gov

America's National Parks Electronic Bookstore

This site provides a large catalog of books, videos, maps, and other items either about or related to the national parks. The site also has a special page for books and videos about the Civil War. It's operated by an association that runs stores in many national parks.

You can search the catalog by national park, category, title, author, or keywords, and you can place an order online or by telephone.

Vital Stats:

Access method: WWW
To access: http://www.nationalparkbooks.org
E-mail: EastNatl@ix.netcom.com

Bureau of Land Management National Homepage

The homepage of the Bureau of Land Management (BLM) has information about visiting public lands managed by the bureau, background information about BLM, congressional testimony by agency officials, proposed rules, a calendar of events, information about adopting wild horses and burros, the bureau's budget and strategic plan, information about how to file a Freedom of Information Act request with BLM, and a link to a publication titled *Public Lands Statistics.*

The site also has an extensive collection of education materials on ecosystems, fire ecology, minerals, noxious weeds, riparian areas, water, wildlife, wild horses and burros, and other subjects.

Vital Stats:

Access method: WWW
To access: http://www.blm.gov
E-mail: webmaster@blm.gov

Grand Canyon National Park

This site has extensive information about visiting Grand Canyon National Park. It has suggested hiking itineraries, details about river trips, information about lodging, maps, answers to dozens of frequently asked questions, climate information, and much more. The site is a joint project of the National Park Service, the Grand Canyon Association, and Canyon WebWorks.

Vital Stats:

Access method: WWW
To access: http://www.thecanyon.com/nps/index.htm
E-mail: info@canyon.com

National Wildlife Refuge System

The National Wildlife Refuge System site provides searchable databases that provide information about individual refuges, threatened and endangered species in national wildlife refuges, and phone numbers for refuge system employees.

The site also has images of endangered animals and plants, a history of the National Wildlife Refuge System, and information about current legislation and hearings related to the refuge system.

In addition, it offers details about exhibits, festivals, and tours at refuges; information about specific birds, crustaceans, fish, insects, mammals, plants, and reptiles found in refuges; and lists of birds found in specific refuges.

Vital Stats:

Access method: WWW
To access: http://refuges.fws.gov
E-mail: Sean_Furniss@fws.gov

NatureNet

The National Park Service operates this site, which provides a huge quantity of information about air quality, wildlife, plants, biological diversity, threatened and endangered species, geology, water quality, wetlands, and wild and scenic rivers in the national parks.

One of the site's highlights is its collection of brochures and fact sheets. Some of the available titles are *Animals and Plants in the National Park System; Insects: Masters of Survival;*

Management of White-Tailed Deer in National Parks; Watchable Wildlife in the National Parks; Preserving Our Natural Heritage: A Strategic Plan for Managing Invasive Nonnative Plants on National Park System Lands; and *Exotic Species in the National Park System.*

It also has the National Park Service's quarterly publication *Park Science* and provides links to environmental education resources for students and teachers.

Vital Stats:

Access method:	WWW
To access:	http://www.nature.nps.gov
E-mail:	NatureNet@nps.gov

ParkNet

The National Park Service's ParkNet site is extremely helpful if you're planning a trip to a national park, battlefield, or other historic site managed by the service.

The site's most interesting feature allows you to access information about specific parks by name, state, region, or theme. The information available for each park varies somewhat, but it often includes the location, address, telephone number, hours, and an address to write to for further information. In addition, you'll frequently find details about recommended clothing, directions, transportation, fees, facilities and services, accessibility, special events, recommended activities, and adjacent visitor attractions. Some parks also offer "virtual visitors centers," which have park updates, guides for educators, historical images, maps and trail guides, and other information.

Vital Stats:

Access method:	WWW
To access:	http://www.nps.gov
E-mail:	nps_webmaster@nps.gov

Park Search

Park Search provides basic information about facilities and activities available at nearly 1,500 national parks, national wildlife refuges, national forests, state parks, and areas operated by the Bureau of Land Management. You can search the listings by park name, state, and activity. The site, which is operated by L. L. Bean, also has nearly 2,000 photos from the parks.

Vital Stats:

Access method:	WWW
To access:	http://www.llbean.com/parksearch

Recreation.GOV

This site is a one-stop source for information about recreational opportunities on federal lands. It's a joint effort of the National Park Service, Bureau of Land Management, U.S. Forest Service, Fish and Wildlife Service, Bureau of Reclamation, and U.S. Army Corps of Engineers.

The site's highlight is a database you can search for recreation opportunities. To conduct a search, you simply select a state and one or more activities from a long list. The database returns detailed information about facilities that meet your criteria, including links to any Web sites they operate.

Vital Stats:

Access method:	WWW
To access:	http://www.recreation.gov

USDA Forest Service Home Page

The USDA Forest Service Home Page has descriptions of national forests listed by state and name, lesson plans for teachers, information about how to volunteer in the national forests, congressional testimony and speeches by Forest Service officials, employee directories, a calendar of conferences and meetings, press releases, and information about wildlife, fish, and rare plants.

Vital Stats:

Access method:	WWW
To access:	http://www.fs.fed.us
E-mail:	comments@www.fs.fed.us

U.S. Fish and Wildlife Service Region 7—Alaska

This site provides a map of National Wildlife Refuges in Alaska, information about individual refuges in the state, a map of Alaska's ecosystems, a list of endangered and threatened species in Alaska, and pictures of Alaskan birds. It's operated by the U.S. Fish and Wildlife Service's Region 7 office in Alaska.

Vital Stats:

Access method:	WWW
To access:	http://www.r7.fws.gov
E-mail:	mary_mccormick@fws.gov

FOREIGN AFFAIRS

Bosnia Report

The Bosnia Report mailing list distributes a weekly newsletter containing news items about events in Bosnia. The newsletter is published by Radio Free Europe/Radio Liberty, a nonprofit corporation funded by the U.S. government.

Radio Free Europe/Radio Liberty also operates a Web site (p. 149).

Vital Stats:

Access method:	E-mail
To access:	Send an e-mail message to bosnia-report-request@list.rferl.org
Subject line:	
Message:	**subscribe**
E-mail (questions):	listmanager@list.rferl.org

Bureau of Consular Affairs Home Page

The Bureau of Consular Affairs Home Page is a one-stop source for an incredible amount of information about traveling to foreign countries. The State Department site has everything from details about how to get a passport to background information about countries worldwide.

One of the site's highlights is its collection of consular information sheets for every country in the world. Each one provides information about the location of U.S. embassies or consulates in the country, immigration practices, health conditions, minor political disturbances, currency and entry requirements, crime and security information, and drug penalties. Any areas of instability in the country are also listed.

The site also offers information about replacing a lost or stolen passport, acquiring U.S. citizenship, marriages abroad, international adoptions, how to have a safe trip, living abroad, travel for older Americans, foreign entry requirements, and many other topics. It also has links to Web sites operated by dozens of U.S. embassies and consulates around the world.

Vital Stats:

Access method:	WWW
To access:	http://travel.state.gov
E-mail:	ca@his.com

Bureau of Diplomatic Security

This State Department site has contact information for key U.S. foreign service officers at posts around the world, information about terrorists wanted by the United States and the counterterrorism rewards program, news reports about terrorist attacks, and a report titled *Significant Incidents of Political Violence against Americans.*

The site also offers background about programs that investigate passport and visa fraud, a brief history of diplomatic security, and links to other sites about terrorism and security.

Vital Stats:

Access method:	WWW
To access:	http://www.heroes.net/indexorigin.html
E-mail:	bsmith@heroes.net

Caucasus Report

The Caucasus Report mailing list distributes a weekly newsletter about political developments in the North Caucasus and Transcaucasia regions. The newsletter is published by
Radio Free Europe/Radio Liberty, a nonprofit corporation funded by the U.S. government.

Radio Free Europe/Radio Liberty also operates a Web site (p. 149).

Vital Stats:

Access method:	E-mail
To access:	Send an e-mail message to caucasus-report-request@list.rferl.org
Subject line:	
Message:	**subscribe**
E-mail (questions):	listmanager@list.rferl.org

Center for the Study of Intelligence

This site provides books, reports, and articles published by the Center for the Study of
Intelligence, which is part of the Central Intelligence Agency.

The highlight of the site is a collection of books that are provided in full text. Some of the
available titles are *CIA and the Vietnam Policymakers: Three Episodes, 1962–1968; Assessing the
Soviet Threat: The Early Cold War Years; Declassified National Intelligence Estimates on the
Soviet Union and International Communism, 1946–1984; Venona: Soviet Espionage and the
American Response, 1939–1957;* and *CIA Briefings of Presidential Candidates.*

The site also has selected articles from the magazine *Studies in Intelligence* and several
reports, including *CIA Assessments of the Soviet Union* and *Sharing Secrets with Lawmakers:
Congress as a User of Intelligence.*

Vital Stats:

Access method:	WWW
To access:	http://www.odci.gov/csi/index.html

The Central Intelligence Agency

You won't find any spy secrets on the Central Intelligence Agency site, but you will find extensive background information about foreign countries and about the CIA.

The site's most useful offering is the latest edition of the *World Factbook,* which has information about every country in the world. For each country, the book provides details about
geography, climate, terrain, natural resources, environment, population, ethnic divisions, reli-

gions, languages, labor force, government, legal system, political parties and leaders, international disputes, embassies and consulates, economy, communications, and defense forces, among many other topics.

The site also has a virtual tour of the CIA, pictures of spy gear, a book about the CIA and its history, a publication titled *Intelligence in the War for Independence,* a directory of chiefs of state and cabinet members of foreign governments, and detailed maps of the Balkans region. These maps provide information about political boundaries, ethnic populations, minerals and resources, energy, economic activity, and land use.

In addition, the site includes the *Handbook of International Economic Statistics,* transcripts of speeches and congressional testimony by CIA officials, reports from the CIA's Persian Gulf War Illnesses Task Force, and a catalog of CIA publications and maps that are for sale to the public.

Vital Stats:

Access method:	WWW
To access:	http://www.odci.gov/cia/ciahome.html

CIA Electronic Document Release Center

This site offers numerous collections of previously secret documents that are frequently requested from the Central Intelligence Agency under the Freedom of Information Act (FOIA).

There are separate document collections about Francis Gary Powers, the U-2 spy pilot who was shot down by the Soviet Union; UFOs; atomic spies Ethel and Julius Rosenberg; Lt. Col. Oleg Penkovsky, a Soviet military intelligence officer who spied for the United States and the United Kingdom; the Bay of Pigs invasion; and American soldiers who were prisoners of war or missing in action during the Vietnam war.

The site also has extensive information about how to request records from the CIA under the Freedom of Information Act, including the full text of the law; regulations that govern the CIA's administration of FOIA requests; a sample request letter; tips for requesters; and explanations of fees and fee waivers, exemptions, appeals of decisions, and the CIA's response process.

Finally, the site offers detailed information about requesting records under the Privacy Act; details about Executive Order 12958, which provides for the review of classified documents; links to other sources of CIA documents; news items about public access to government information; and important court decisions involving the CIA's administration of the Privacy Act, the Freedom of Information Act, and related laws.

Vital Stats:

Access method:	WWW
To access:	http://www.foia.ucia.gov

Foreign Affairs Network Listservs

The State Department distributes the full text of documents and publications by e-mail through six mailing lists. The lists are a joint project of the department and the libraries at the University of Illinois at Chicago. The lists include:

- DOSSEC—Speeches and congressional testimony by the secretary of state.
- DOSSDO—Speeches and congressional testimony by other senior State Department officials.
- DOSBRIEF—Transcripts of daily State Department press briefings.
- DOSDISP—Monthly notifications about the availability of new issues of the State Department magazine *Dispatch.*
- DOSBACK—Newly released Background Notes about individual foreign countries.
- DOSPDIEM—News about changes in State Department per diem rates for foreign travel.

Vital Stats:

Access method:	E-mail
To access:	Send an e-mail message to listserv@listserv.uic.edu
Subject line:	
Message:	**subscribe** *listname firstname lastname*
E-mail (questions):	doswork@uic.edu

International Broadcasting Bureau Servers

The International Broadcasting Bureau Servers have information about the Voice of America, Radio and TV Marti, and the WORLDNET Television and Film Service. All the services are operated by the U.S. Information Agency.

The Voice of America broadcasts programs overseas on shortwave and medium wave radio in more than fifty languages. The servers have the full text of the VOA English-language broadcast wire for the previous seven days, audio files from selected VOA broadcasts in AU and WAV formats, the VOA journalistic code, the VOA program schedule for broadcasts in dozens of languages, the VOA frequencies schedule, and the scripts of programs in Chinese, Croatian, and Serbian.

Radio and TV Marti broadcast to Cuba. The servers have program schedules for the two services, the full text of laws about broadcasting to Cuba, and detailed chronologies of events in Cuba back to 1993.

The WORLDNET Television and Film Service broadcasts television programs about American cultural, business, scientific, and technological developments. The servers have basic background materials about the service.

Vital Stats:

Access methods:	WWW, Gopher
To access:	http://www.voa.gov *or* gopher://gopher.voa.gov
E-mail:	pubaff@voa.gov

Overseas Security Advisory Council

The Overseas Security Advisory Council, which is part of the State Department, offers a wide range of news reports and publications of interest to people traveling overseas. The site is aimed primarily at security managers for U.S. corporations, although it's useful to anyone traveling abroad.

One of the highlights is a collection of publications about the security of Americans abroad. Some of the available titles are *Security Guidelines for American Families Living Abroad; Security Guidelines for American Enterprises Abroad; Emergency Planning Guidelines for American Businesses Abroad; Security Awareness Overseas: An Overview;* and *Personal Security Guidelines for the American Business Traveler Overseas.*

Another highlight is the OSAC Electronic Database. Anyone can access its daily reports, which provide information about events overseas that may affect travel safety and links to news headlines from around the world. American businesses that operate overseas can register for free access to restricted sections of the database. These provide profiles of terrorist groups, crime information for cities and countries, and security contacts at U.S. facilities overseas.

Vital Stats:

Access method:	WWW
To access:	http://ds.state.gov/osacmenu.cfm
E-mail:	osac@dsmail.state.gov

Peace Corps

This site offers detailed information about becoming a Peace Corps volunteer, descriptions of Peace Corps activities in individual countries, and dozens of lesson plans for teachers about countries around the world.

The site also has essays by current and former Peace Corps volunteers, letters from volunteers overseas to students in the United States, information for returned volunteers, press releases, and background information about the Peace Corps.

Vital Stats:

Access method:	WWW
To access:	http://www.peacecorps.gov
E-mail:	webmaster@peacecorps.gov

Radio Free Asia

When it's completed, the Radio Free Asia site will offer broadcast schedules and transcripts of daily broadcasts. Radio Free Asia broadcasts programs in local languages to Burma, Cambodia, China, Laos, North Korea, Tibet, and Vietnam. Radio Free Asia is a nonprofit corporation funded by the Broadcasting Board of Governors, which is part of the U.S. government.

Access method:	WWW
To access:	http://www.rfa.org
E-mail:	info@rfa.org

Radio Free Europe/Radio Liberty

The Radio Free Europe/Radio Liberty site has extensive news reports from Eastern and Southeastern Europe, Russia, the Caucasus, and Central Asia in both text and audio formats. It also provides background information about the countries it covers.

Radio Free Europe/Radio Liberty is a nonprofit corporation funded by the Broadcasting Board of Governors, which is part of the U.S. government. It broadcasts in twenty-four languages.

Radio Free Europe/Radio Liberty also distributes news briefs through the mailing lists called Bosnia Report (p. 144), Caucasus Report (p. 145), and RFE/RL Newsline (next entry).

Vital Stats:

Access method:	WWW
To access:	http://www.rferl.org
E-mail:	webmaster@rferl.org

RFE/RL Newsline

The RFE/RL Newsline mailing list distributes a daily newsletter containing news briefs about events in the former Soviet Union and Eastern Europe. The newsletter is published by Radio Free Europe/Radio Liberty, a nonprofit corporation funded by the U.S. government.

Radio Free Europe/Radio Liberty also operates a Web site (previous entry).

Vital Stats:

Access method:	E-mail
To access:	Send an e-mail message to newsline-request@list.rferl.org
Subject line:	
Message:	**subscribe**
E-mail (questions):	listmanager@list.rferl.org

Secretary of State

This site has transcripts of speeches and news interviews by the secretary of state; background information about the incumbent secretary, Madeleine K. Albright; information about the secretary's trips overseas; and a schedule of State Department town meetings.

Vital Stats:

Access method:	WWW
To access:	http://secretary.state.gov
E-mail:	publicaffairs@panet.us-state.gov

Travel-Advisories Mailing List

Subscribers to the Travel-Advisories Mailing List receive travel advisories by e-mail as they're issued by the State Department. The travel advisories consist of Consular Information Sheets, which provide background information about every country in the world, and Travel Warnings, which the State Department issues when it determines that a threat to Americans exists in a particular country.

State Department travel advisories are also available through the Bureau of Consular Affairs Home Page (p. 144).

Vital Stats:

Access method:	E-mail
To access:	Send an e-mail message to travel-advisories-request@stolaf.edu
Subject line:	
Message:	**subscribe**
E-mail (questions):	cdr@stolaf.edu

U.S. Agency for International Development

This site provides information about the U.S. Agency for International Development (USAID), which administers aid programs in developing nations. It has overviews of USAID programs in individual countries, reports about U.S. population assistance, facts and figures about foreign aid, procurement information, and a link to a searchable USAID telephone directory.

Vital Stats:

Access method:	WWW
To access:	http://www.info.usaid.gov
E-mail:	webmaster@info.usaid.gov

U.S. Department of State Electronic Reading Room

The highlight of this State Department site is six collections of declassified documents, some of which were released under the Freedom of Information Act. Each collection can be searched or browsed.

The collections include the following:

• More than 6,500 documents frequently requested by the public through the Freedom of Information Act. The documents cover a huge range of foreign policy subjects.

- More than 400 documents about the creation of the Central Intelligence Agency.

- Sixty documents created from 1974 to 1976 regarding the 1937 disappearance of Amelia Earhart.

- Documents about the murders of four American churchwomen in 1980 by Salvadoran National Guardsmen.

- More than 4,800 documents about human rights abuses against American citizens in Guatemala from 1984 to 1995.

- Some 1,200 documents, dated from 1944 to 1993, about diplomatic efforts to establish the fate of Raoul Wallenberg, a Swedish diplomat who rescued Jews from deportation by the Nazis during World War II. Wallenberg disappeared shortly after the war ended.

The site also offers numerous documents about the Freedom of Information Act and the Privacy Act. The documents include the full text of both laws, instructions for making a FOIA request, explanations of fees and how to appeal a FOIA or Privacy Act rejection, and the State Department's annual FOIA report.

Finally, it provides the full text of the *Foreign Affairs Manual,* a list of records transferred to the National Archives, a list of the types of records created by State Department bureaus and offices, and a June 1985 State Department report on embassy security overseas.

Vital Stats:

Access method:	WWW
To access:	http://foia.state.gov
E-mail:	ips@ms1239wpo.us-state.gov

U.S. Embassies and Consulates

More than 100 U.S. embassies and consulates in countries around the world operate Internet sites. What's available varies from site to site, but you'll often find information about services provided by the embassy or consulate, a list of key officers at the facility, speeches by the ambassador, and the State Department's *Country Report on Human Rights Practices* for the host country.

The sites also frequently offer information about traveling to the host country and to the United States, files for American exporters from the Commerce Department's Foreign Commercial Service, links to Internet sites operated by federal government agencies, and news reports, transcripts, and analyses of events around the world prepared by the U.S. Information Agency.

Vital Stats:

Access method:	WWW
To access:	See accompanying box

Foreign Embassies

Armenia
U.S. Embassy in Yerevan
To access:
   http://www.arminco.com/embusa

Australia
U.S. Embassy in Canberra
To access:
   http://www.ozemail.com.au/~usaemb

Austria
U.S. Embassy in Vienna
To access:
   http://www.usia.gov/posts/vienna.html

Azerbaijan
U.S. Embassy in Baku
To access:
   http://www.usia.gov/posts/baku.html

Bahrain
U.S. Embassy in Manama
To access: http://www.usembassy.com.bh

Bangladesh
U.S. Embassy in Dhaka
To access: http://www.citechco.net/
   usdhaka

Barbados
U.S. Embassy in Bridgetown
To access:
   http://www.usia.gov/abtusia/posts/
   BB1/wwwhemb1.html

Belgium
U.S. Embassy in Brussels
To access: http://ibase054.eunet.be/first/
   embassy.htm

Bolivia
U.S. Embassy in La Paz
To access:
   http://www.megalink.com/usemblapaz

Botswana
U.S. Embassy in Gaborone
To access: http://www.usia.gov/abtusia/
   posts/BC1/wwwhmain.html

Brazil
U.S. Embassy in Brasilia
To access: http://www.embaixada-
   americana.org.br

U.S. Consulate in Rio de Janeiro
To access: http://www.consulado-
   americano-rio.org.br/rio.htm

Bulgaria
U.S. Embassy in Sofia
To access: http://www.usis.bg

Canada
U.S. Embassy in Ottawa
To access:
   http://www.usembassycanada.gov

Chile
U.S. Embassy in Santiago
To access: http://www.rdc.cl/~usemb

China
U.S. Embassy in Beijing
To access: http://www.redfish.com/
   usembassy-china

Columbia
U.S. Embassy in Bogota
To access:
   http://www.usia.gov/posts/bogota.html

Costa Rica
U.S. Embassy in San Jose
To access: http://usembassy.or.cr

Côte d'Ivoire
U.S. Embassy in Abidjan
To access: http://www.usia.gov/posts/
   abidjan

Foreign Embassies *(Continued)*

Croatia
U.S. Embassy in Zagreb
To access: http://www.usembassy.hr

Cuba
U.S. Interests Section in Havana
To access: http://www.usia.gov/abtusia/
   posts/CU1/wwwhmain.html#5

Cyprus
U.S. Embassy in Nicosia
To access: http://www.americanembassy.
   org.cy

Czech Republic
U.S. Embassy in Prague
To access: http://www.usis.cz

Denmark
U.S. Embassy in Copenhagen
To access: http://www.usis.dk

Dominican Republic
U.S. Embassy in Santo Domingo
To access: http://www.usia.gov/abtusia.
   posts/DR1/wwwhemb.html

Ecuador
U.S. Embassy in Quito
To access: http://www.usis.org.ec

Egypt
U.S. Embassy in Cairo
To access: http://www.usis.egnet.net

El Salvador
U.S. Embassy in San Salvador
To access: http://www.usinfo.org.sv

Estonia
U.S. Embassy in Tallinn
To access:
   http://www.estnet.ee/usislib/cons.html

Finland
U.S. Embassy in Helsinki
To access: http://www.usis.fi/consul/
   conshome.htm

France
U.S. Embassy in Paris
To access: http://www.amb-usa.fr

Georgia
U.S. Embassy in Tbilisi
To access: http://georgia.net.ge/usis/
   about_mission.html

Germany
U.S. Embassy in Bonn
To access: http://www.usembassy.de

U.S. Consulate General in Hamburg
To access: http://ourworld.compuserve.
   com/homepages/acghamburg/
   enghp.htm

Greece
U.S. Embassy in Athens
To access: http://www.usisathens.gr

Guinea
U.S. Embassy in Conakry
To access: http://www.eti-bull.net/
   usembassy

Honduras
U.S. Embassy in Tegucigalpa
To access: http://www.usia.gov/abtusia/
   posts/HO1/wwwhmain.html

Hong Kong
U.S. Consulate General in Hong Kong
To access: http://www.usia.gov/abtusia/
   posts/HK1/wwwhcons.html

Foreign Embassies *(Continued)*

Hungary
U.S. Embassy in Budapest
To access: http://www.usis.hu

Iceland
U.S. Embassy in Reykjavik
To access: http://www.itn.is/america/
  mainemb.html

India
U.S. Embassy in New Delhi
To access: http://www.usia.gov/abtusia/
  posts/IN1/wwwhmain.html

U.S. Consulate General in Chennai
  (Madras)
To access:
  http://www.sphynx.com/madrasus

Indonesia
U.S. Embassy in Jakarta
To access:
  http://www.usembassyjakarta.org

Ireland
U.S. Embassy in Dublin
To access: http://www.indigo.ie/
  usembassy-usis

Israel
U.S. Embassy in Tel Aviv
To access: http://www.usis-
  israel.org.il/publish/consular.htm

U.S. Consulate General in Jerusalem
To access: http://www.usis-jerusalem.org

Italy
U.S. Embassy in Rome
To access: http://www.usis.it

Japan
U.S. Embassy in Tokyo
To access:
  http://www.usia.gov/posts/japan

U.S. Consulate in Fukuoka
To access: http://www.city.kitakyushu.jp/
  amconsul

U.S. Consulate General in Osaka-Kobe
To access: http://www.senri-
  i.or.jp/amcon/usa_01.htm

Jordan
U.S. Embassy in Amman
To access: http://www.usembassy-
  amman.org.jo

Korea (Republic of)
U.S. Embassy in Seoul
To access:
  http://www.usia.gov/posts/seoul

Kuwait
U.S. Embassy in Kuwait City
To access: http://www.kuwait.net/
  ~usiskwt/wwwhusis.htm

Laos
U.S. Embassy in Vientiane
To access: http://www.inet.co.th/org/
  usis/laos.htm

Latvia
U.S. Embassy in Riga
To access: http://www.usis.bkc.lv/embassy

Lebanon
U.S. Embassy in Beirut
To access: http://www.usembassy.com.lb

Lithuania
U.S. Embassy in Vilnius
To access: http://www.usis.lt/us_mission

Foreign Embassies *(Continued)*

Luxembourg
U.S. Embassy in Luxembourg
To access: http://www.usia.gov/abtusia/
posts/LU1/wwwhmain.html

Malaysia
U.S. Embassy in Kuala Lumpur
To access: http://www.jaring.my/usiskl

Malta
U.S. Embassy in Valletta
To access: http://www.usia.gov/abtusia/
posts/MT1/wwwhmain.html

Mauritius
U.S. Embassy in Port Louis
To access: http://usis.intnet.mu/
indexmu.htm

Mexico
U.S. Embassy in Mexico City
To access: http://www.usembassy.org.mx

U.S. Consulate General in Ciudad Juarez
To access: http://www.usia.gov/abtusia/
posts/MX2/wwwhmain.html

Morocco
U.S. Embassy in Rabat
To access: http://www.USEmbassy-
Morocco.org.ma

Nepal
U.S. Embassy in Kathmandu
To access: http://www.south-
asia.com/USA

Netherlands
U.S. Embassy in The Hague
To access: http://www.usemb.nl

U.S. Consulate General in Amsterdam
To access: http://www.usemb.nl/
consul.htm

New Zealand
U.S. Consulate General in Auckland
To access: http://homepages.ihug.co.nz/
~amcongen

Nicaragua
U.S. Embassy in Managua
To access: http://www.usia.gov/posts/
managua.html

Norway
U.S. Embassy in Oslo
To access: http://www.usembassy.no

Oman
U.S. Embassy in Muscat
To access: http://www.usia.gov/posts/
muscat

Pakistan
U.S. Consulate in Karachi
To access: http://www.usia.gov/abtusia/
posts/PK2/wwwhamcn.html

U.S. Consulate in Lahore
To access: http://www.usconsulate-
lahore.org.pk

Panama
U.S. Embassy in Panama City
To access: http://www.pty.com/usispan/
consular.htm

Peru
U.S. Embassy in Lima
To access: http://ekeko.rcp.net.pe/usa

Philippines
U.S. Embassy in Manila
To access:
http://www.usia.gov/abtusia/posts/
RP1/wwwh3007.html

Foreign Embassies *(Continued)*

Poland
U.S. Embassy in Warsaw
To access: http://www.usaemb.pl

U.S. Consulate General in Krakow
To access: http://www.polished.net/usis

Portugal
U.S. Embassy in Lisbon
To access: http://www.usia.gov/abtusia/
posts/PO1/wwwhmain.html

Qatar
U.S. Embassy in Doha
To access: http://qatar.net.qa/usisdoha/
wwwhemb.htm

Romania
U.S. Embassy in Bucharest
To access: http://usis.kappa.ro

Russia
U.S. Embassy in Moscow
To access: http://www.usia.gov/posts/
moscow.html

Senegal
U.S. Embassy in Dakar
To access: http://www.usia.gov/abtusia/
posts/SG1/wwwhemb.html

Serbia and Montenegro
U.S. Embassy in Belgrade
To access: http://www.amembbg.co.yu/
state.html

Singapore
U.S. Embassy in Singapore
To access: http://sunsite.nus.sg/usis/
Embassy/Consular/first.html

Slovakia
U.S. Embassy in Bratislava
To access: http://www.usis.sk

South Africa
U.S. Embassy in Pretoria
To access: http://www.usia.gov/abtusia/
posts/SF1/wwwhmain.html

Spain
U.S. Embassy in Madrid
To access: http://www.embusa.es/cons/
indexen.html

Sri Lanka
U.S. Embassy in Colombo
To access: http://www.usia.gov/posts/
sri_lanka

Sweden
U.S. Embassy in Stockholm
To access: http://www.usis.usemb.se/
cons.html

Switzerland
U.S. Embassy in Bern
To access: http://www3.itu.ch/
EMBASSY/US-embassy

Tanzania
U.S. Embassy in Dar Es Salaam
To access: http://www.cats-
net.com/Amemb

Thailand
U.S. Embassy in Bangkok
To access: http://www.inet.co.th/org/usis/
embindex.htm

U.S. Consulate General in Chiang Mai
To access: http://www.inet.co.th/org/usis/
chiang.htm

Turkey
U.S. Embassy in Ankara
To access: http://www.usis-ankara.org.tr

U.S. Consulate General in Istanbul
To access: http://www.usisist.org.tr

Foreign Embassies *(Continued)*

Turkmenistan
U.S. Embassy in Ashgabat
To access: http://www.usemb-
  ashgabat.usia.co.at

Ukraine
U.S. Embassy in Kiev
To access: http://www.usemb.kiev.ua

United Arab Emirates
U.S. Embassy in Abu Dhabi
To access: http://www.usembabu.gov.ae

United Kingdom
U.S. Embassy in London
To access: http://www.usembassy.org.uk

Uruguay
U.S. Embassy in Montevideo
To access: http://www.embeeuu.gub.uy

Uzbekistan
U.S. Embassy in Tashkent
To access: http://www.freenet.uz/usis/
  wwwhemb.htm

Vietnam
U.S. Embassy in Hanoi
To access: http://members.aol.com/
  nomhawj/embassy/home.htm

Zambia
U.S. Embassy in Lusaka
To access: http://www.zamnet.zm/
  zamnet/usemb/welcome.html

United States Information Agency

If you know the trick, this site lets you access news reports, transcripts, and analyses of events around the world prepared by the U.S. Information Agency.

Under federal law, the USIA can distribute its reports only outside the United States. The Internet poses a problem since it has no national boundaries. The USIA has sidestepped this issue by creating two home pages—one for U.S. consumption and one for use outside the country.

If you use the address http://www.usia.gov, you reach the basic home page, which doesn't offer a whole lot. But if you use http://www.usia.gov/usis.html, you reach the international home page—and most of the good stuff.

Besides the news reports, the site offers a daily digest of foreign media reactions to a major foreign policy issue or event. The reactions are culled from newspapers, magazines, and broadcast media around the world. The digest is available in English, Spanish, French, Russian, and Arabic.

Another highlight is a collection of lengthy publications about government-related topics. Some of the available titles are *Arms Control and Disarmament: The U.S. Commitment; Basic Readings in U.S. Democracy; The Civil Rights Movement and the Legacy of Martin Luther King Jr.; The Marshall Plan: Investment in Peace; A Media Guidebook for Women; Outline of the American Economy; Outline of American History; Outline of American Literature;* and *An Unfettered Press.*

In addition, the site has an extensive collection of reports about U.S. policy toward countries around the world, five electronic USIA journals, information about the Fulbright grant program, and collections of reports about such topics as foreign policy and security, economic issues, democracy and human rights, and the Year 2000 computer problem.

Vital Stats:

Access method:	WWW
To access:	http://www.usia.gov/usis.html

United States Institute of Peace

The United States Institute of Peace site has numerous reports about international conflict. The institute is an independent federal institution created and funded by Congress.

Some of the reports available are *Preventing Genocide in Burundi; Can Nigeria Make a Peaceful Transition to Democratic Governance?; Zaire's Crises of War and Governance; Future U.S. Engagement in Africa: Opportunities and Obstacles for Conflict Management; Muddling Toward Democracy: Political Change in Grassroots China; Beyond the Asian Financial Crisis; Kosovo: Escaping the Cul-de-Sac; Managing NATO Enlargement;* and *Between Impediment and Advantage: Saddam's Iraq.*

The site also offers the institute's bimonthly magazine, papers from a conference on virtual diplomacy, information about grants and fellowships, a catalog of books published by the institute, and links to dozens of other Internet sites devoted to international relations.

Vital Stats:

Access method: WWW
To access: http://www.usip.org
E-mail: usip_requests@usip.org

U.S. State Department

The U.S. State Department site offers an amazing collection of documents about U.S. foreign policy, foreign countries, and travel abroad. Without question, it's one of the most important and useful government sites on the Internet.

The site offers the State Department's annual human rights report, a list of countries of the world, the State Department magazine *Dispatch*, an annual report titled *Patterns of Global Terrorism*, lists of contacts at American embassies and consulates around the world, books based on declassified State Department documents, and a directory of foreign embassies in the United States.

It also has the *Guide to Doing Business with the Department of State*, numerous publications for travelers, guides to the commercial environment in countries around the world, the names of foreign diplomats (and their spouses) in the United States, a list of phone numbers for State Department country desk officers for every country in the world, transcripts of daily State Department briefings, a directory of State Department employees, information about international adoptions and international child abductions, and much more.

Vital Stats:

Access method: WWW
To access: http://www.state.gov
E-mail: doswork@uic.edu

GOVERNMENT

CONGRESS

Committee Hearings

This bare-bones site offers transcripts of selected hearings by House committees. Most committees offer hearings back to 1997, although a few committees have not yet posted any transcripts.

The hearings are separated by committee, and unfortunately there is no search engine. This means you have to browse manually through each committee's offerings to find what you want.

Vital Stats:

Access method:	WWW
To access:	http://commdocs.house.gov/committees

Congress Today

The highlight of this site is a searchable database of congressional votes from 1996 to the present. You can search it by member, subject, or month. The site is operated by C-SPAN.

Other highlights include schedules of House and Senate actions for the current day, a calendar of House and Senate committee hearings for the current month, a congressional directory, House and Senate committee rosters, and a "Find Your Representative" feature that lets you search by Zip Code, state, or member last name.

Vital Stats:

Access method:	WWW
To access:	http://congress.nw.dc.us/c-span
E-mail:	viewer@c-span.org

Congressional Budget Office

This site offers current federal budget and economic projections, historical budget data, and a monthly budget review from the Congressional Budget Office, a nonpartisan agency that provides Congress with economic and budget information.

The site also has a large collection of full-text reports about various topics. The reports cover such subjects as climate change and the federal budget, defense base closures, competition in ATM markets, Social Security and private saving, the proposed tobacco settlement, expanding health insurance coverage for children, the economic and budget outlook for the next decade, proposals to subsidize health insurance for the unemployed, innovative financing of highways, tax reform, and water use conflicts in the West, among many others.

Finally, the site has congressional testimony by CBO officials, cost estimates for all bills ordered reported by congressional committees, and information about job openings at the CBO.

You also can sign up at the site to receive e-mail notifications when new CBO reports on a variety of subjects are issued.

Vital Stats:

Access method:	WWW
To access:	http://www.cbo.gov
E-mail:	webmaster@cbo.gov

Congressional Quarterly VoteWatch

The Congressional Quarterly VoteWatch site lets you examine the voting record of any member of Congress. The site is a project of Time Warner's Pathfinder and Congressional Quarterly (the publisher of this book).

If you want to check votes by your own member of Congress, you can search by the representative's last name, your Zip Code, or your voting district. You also can search by popular bill name, keyword, or subject. Each vote listing links to an article that describes the bill.

The site also has stories about the latest key votes in the House and Senate, along with details about how each representative or senator voted.

Vital Stats:

Access method:	WWW
To access:	http://pathfinder.com/CQ
E-mail:	webmaster@cqalert.com

Congressional Quarterly's American Voter

The "On the Job" section of Congressional Quarterly's American Voter has extensive information about each member of Congress—much of it not available from Internet sites operated by Congress itself.

For each member, the site provides a biographical profile, a list of key staff contacts, phone numbers, e-mail addresses for those members who have them, results of primary and general elections, a record of recent key votes, the text of recent floor speeches, a list of bills and resolutions introduced during the current session, and records of committee votes. You can search the member information by name, Zip Code, or state.

Other sections of the site offer lists of postal addresses, e-mail addresses, and phone numbers for all members of Congress; lists of Democratic and Republican leaders in each chamber; a list of cabinet members; background information about members of the Supreme Court; annotated links to other political sites on the Internet; and information about each House and Senate committee, including a list of members, the names of staff members, the committee's address and phone number, and details about the panel's jurisdiction.

Vital Stats:

Access method:	WWW
To access:	http://voter.cq.com
E-mail:	jsteiger@cqalert.com

FEDNET

You can listen to live broadcasts of floor debates in the House and Senate, selected congressional hearings, and congressional news conferences at the FEDNET site. To listen to the broadcasts, which are provided by Federal Network Inc., you must have the free RealAudio software installed in your computer.

The site also has schedules of floor actions in the House and Senate, selected congressional hearings (along with witness lists), and congressional news conferences. A small archive offers recordings of recent congressional events.

Vital Stats:

Access method:	WWW
To access:	http://www.fednet.net
E-mail:	kcarney@fednet.net

GAO Daybook

GAO Daybook is a mailing list that distributes a daily listing of reports and testimony released by the General Accounting Office, which is the investigative arm of Congress. The GAO conducts audits, surveys, investigations, and evaluations of federal programs, usually at the request of members of Congress.

Vital Stats:

Access method:	E-mail
To access:	Send an e-mail message to majordomo@www.gao.gov
Subject line:	
Message:	**subscribe daybook**
E-mail (questions):	documents@gao.gov

HillSource

The HillSource site provides digests of activities in the U.S. House of Representatives, publications about Republican positions on various issues, press releases from House Republican leaders, and media advisories. It's operated by the House Republican Conference.

Vital Stats:

Access method:	WWW
To access:	http://hillsource.house.gov
E-mail:	hrcwebmaster@mail.house.gov

Independent Counsel's Report to the United States House of Representatives

This site has the full text of the report that Independent Counsel Kenneth Starr submitted to the House of Representatives about his investigation of President Bill Clinton in the fall of 1998. It's operated by the Government Printing Office.

Besides the initial report, the site has a House report calling for release of the Starr document, supplemental materials that Starr submitted following the initial report, and responses to the report from the White House.

Vital Stats:

Access method:	WWW
To access:	http://icreport.access.gpo.gov
Email:	gpoaccess@gpo.gov

The Office of the Clerk On-line Information Center

This site, which is operated by the Office of the Clerk of the U.S. House of Representatives, has records of all roll call votes taken in the House since 1990. The votes are recorded by bill, so it's a lengthy process to compile a particular representative's voting record.

The site also has lists of committee assignments, a telephone directory for members and committees, mailing label templates for members and committees, rules of the House, information about the types of documents that are available from the Legislative Resource Center, election statistics from 1920 to the present, biographies of Speakers of the House, biographies of women who have served since 1917 (when the first woman was elected to the House), and a virtual tour of the House Chamber.

Vital Stats:

Access method:	WWW
To access:	http://clerkweb.house.gov

Office of the Majority Whip

The Office of the Majority Whip site provides minute-by-minute accounts of activities on the floor of the U.S. House of Representatives, with links to bills that are being debated. The site is operated by House majority whip Tom DeLay.

The site also has a House Calendar, speeches by DeLay, and electronic versions of *The Whipping Post* and *The Whip Notice,* which report on upcoming House activities. *The Whipping Post* is published daily when Congress is voting, and *The Whip Notice* is published weekly when Congress is in session. Both publications are also available through electronic subscriptions (see The Whip Notice and The Whipping Post, p. 170).

Vital Stats:

Access method: WWW
To access: http://majoritywhip.house.gov
E-mail: Webmaster@mail.house.gov

Office of Technology Assessment Archive

The Office of Technology Assessment Archive has copies of every report issued by the congressional Office of Technology Assessment from 1986 to 1995. The reports are arranged by years, and you also can search the whole archive by keywords or concepts. The National Academy Press operates the site.

The site is similar to the OTA Legacy (next entry), which has every report that OTA issued during its existence from 1972 to 1995.

Vital Stats:

Access method: WWW
To access: http://www.ota.nap.edu
E-mail: dellmore@nas.edu

The OTA Legacy

The OTA Legacy offers every report issued by the congressional Office of Technology Assessment, which existed from 1972 until 1995. The site is operated by the Woodrow Wilson School of Public and International Affairs at Princeton University. It's similar to the Office of Technology Assessment Archive (previous entry), which has reports issued from 1986 to 1995.

The site has more than 100,000 pages of detailed reports about aging, agricultural technology, arms control, biological research, cancer, computer security, defense technology, economic development, education, environmental protection, health and health technology, information technology, space, transportation, and many other subjects. The reports are organized in alphabetical, chronological, and topical lists.

Besides the reports, the site has lots of background information about the OTA.

Vital Stats:

Access method: WWW
To access: http://www.wws.princeton.edu:80/~ota
E-mail: ota@edith.princeton.edu

Penny Hill Press

The Penny Hill Press site offers abstracts of hundreds of publications by the Congressional Research Service, a division of the Library of Congress that provides research for congressional members and committees. The abstracts are arranged in dozens of categories, including abortion, civil rights and liberties, criminal justice, defense, education, environmental protection, foreign countries and regions, government information, health policy, immigration, public lands, rural affairs, science policy, and women's issues, among many others.

Users can order the full text of CRS reports from Penny Hill Press for a fee or request free copies from their member of Congress.

Vital Stats:

Access method:	WWW
To access:	http://www.pennyhill.com
E-mail:	congress@pennyhill.com

Subcommittee on Rules and Organization of the House

This site has a huge collection of materials about the legislative process. It's operated by the Subcommittee on Rules and Organization of the House, which is part of the House Rules Committee.

The highlights of the site are dozens of reports by the Congressional Research Service. Some of the available titles are *Legislative Research in Congressional Offices: A Primer; How to Follow Current Federal Legislation and Regulations; Hearings in the House of Representatives: A Guide for Preparation and Conduct; Investigative Oversight: An Introduction to the Law, Practice, and Procedure of Congressional Inquiry; How Measures are Brought to the House Floor: A Brief Introduction; A Brief Introduction to the Federal Budget Process;* and *Presidential Vetoes, 1789–1996: A Summary Overview.*

The site also has the full text of the House rules manual, publications titled *How Our Laws Are Made* and *House Protocol: A Guide on Process and Procedure in the House of Representatives,* and transcripts of hearings on such topics as unfunded mandates and civility in the House of Representatives.

Vital Stats:

Access method:	WWW
To access:	http://www.house.gov/rules_org

THOMAS

Although THOMAS still lacks some features promised at its unveiling by Speaker Newt Gingrich in January 1995, it's an excellent resource for congressional information. The site is operated by the Library of Congress.

THOMAS's highlight is undoubtedly its collection of searchable databases. They offer the full text of all bills introduced in Congress, summaries of bills introduced in Congress, information about the status of all bills, and reports by House and Senate committees.

The site also offers special links to the full text of bills that are expected to receive floor action in the House or Senate during the current week, bills that the full House or Senate voted on in the previous week, and major bills and amendments introduced in Congress. You can browse the major bills links by topic, popular or short title, bill number or type, and whether the bills have been approved. In addition, THOMAS has the full text of the *Congressional Record* back to 1990 and publications titled *How Our Laws Are Made* and *Enactment of a Law.*

Some of the features promised but still lacking are records of how specific members of Congress vote on particular bills and records of all floor and committee actions.

Vital Stats:

Access method:	WWW
To access:	http://thomas.loc.gov
E-mail:	thomas@loc.gov

United States General Accounting Office

The U.S. General Accounting Office, which is the investigative arm of Congress, offers the full text of its reports on this site. The reports cover such topics as the federal budget, civil rights, education, environmental protection, health, international affairs, national defense, social services, and veterans affairs, among many others. You can learn about new reports added to the site by subscribing to the GAO Daybook mailing list (p. 164).

The site also has lists of recently released GAO reports; annual indexes of GAO reports from 1996 to the present; a special section of reports and other documents about the Year 2000 computing crisis; links to other sites that offer archives of GAO reports; internal GAO policy and guidance reports about assessing the reliability of computer data, designing evaluations, and using structured interviewing techniques; recent decisions of the GAO comptroller general; and information about how to report allegations of fraud, waste, abuse, or mismanagement of federal funds.

Vital Stats:

Access method:	WWW
To access:	http://www.gao.gov
E-mail:	webmaster@www.gao.gov

U.S. House of Representatives

The U.S. House of Representatives site provides a wealth of congressional information. It has up-to-the-minute reports about current actions on the House floor, schedules of upcoming floor and committee votes and hearings, and links to sites that offer the full text of bills introduced in Congress and the *Congressional Record.*

The site also has the full text of *How Our Laws Are Made,* the House ethics manual, links to WWW pages operated by House members and committees, the Declaration of Independence and the U.S. Constitution, amendments to the Constitution that have been proposed but not ratified, information about touring Capitol Hill, and maps of Washington, D.C., and of Washington's subway system.

U.S. Legislative Branch

This Library of Congress site provides a superb collection of links to other sites about Congress and the legislative process. The links are conveniently arranged by subject, making it easy to find what you want.

Some of the subjects include congressional megasites, committees of Congress, congressional organizations and commissions, e-mail addresses for Congress, calendars and schedules, floor proceedings, legislation, the U.S. Code, House and Senate rules, the *Congressional Record,* roll call votes, the legislative process, and congressional news and analysis.

The United States Senate

The United States Senate site has everything from a virtual tour of the Senate to explanations of the legislative process.

It offers records of how senators voted (arranged by bill), schedules of upcoming committee meetings and hearings, the Senate legislative calendar, a link to another site that offers a daily digest of Senate and House activity, the *Standing Rules of the Senate,* and a list of committee reports issued during the previous week.

It also has contact information for senators, links to the home pages of those senators and committees that are online, a glossary of Senate terms, a bibliography of publications about the Senate, and information about visiting the Senate, including services for visitors with disabilities.

Vote Smart Web

The Vote Smart Web has a great collection of information about Congress, campaigns, and elections. The site presents lots of original information of its own, and it also has links to dozens of the best Internet sites for political information. Simply put, Vote Smart Web is a political junkie's dream come true.

Vote Smart Web is run by Project Vote Smart, which is the major program of the Center for National Independence in Politics. The center is a nonpartisan, nonprofit organization that provides voters with information about issues and candidates.

For each member of Congress, Vote Smart Web provides contact and biographical information, annotated samples of the member's voting record on numerous issues, information about the member's committee assignments, detailed campaign finance information for the 1995–1996 election cycle for representatives and 1995–1998 for senators, evaluations of the member's voting record by various special interest groups, and the member's answers to an issues questionnaire prepared by Project Vote Smart.

The site also has information about the status of major bills pending before Congress.

Vital Stats:

Access method:	WWW
To access:	http://www.vote-smart.org
E-mail:	webmaster@vote-smart.org

The Whip Notice and *The Whipping Post*

The Whip Notice and *The Whipping Post* are electronic versions of newsletters that report on upcoming activities in the U.S. House of Representatives.

The Whip Notice is published weekly when Congress is in session, and *The Whipping Post* is published daily when Congress is voting. Both publications are produced by House majority whip Tom DeLay, and you can subscribe to them at his Web site.

Vital Stats:

Access method:	WWW
To access:	http://majoritywhip.house.gov/mail
E-mail (questions):	Webmaster@mail.house.gov

ELECTIONS

Campaign Finance Data on the Internet

The Campaign Finance Data on the Internet site provides extensive campaign finance information for federal candidates. The files combine tables provided by the Federal Election Commission and provide them in database format. The site is operated by the American University School of Communication.

Vital Stats:

Access method:	WWW
To access:	http://www.soc.american.edu/campfin
E-mail:	cochran@american.edu

Center for Responsive Politics

This site provides numerous databases containing detailed campaign finance data. It's operated by the Center for Responsive Politics, a public interest organization.

One of the most interesting databases provides information about contributors to federal political campaigns. You can search the database by contributor name, Zip Code, employer, or recipient.

Other databases offer information about contributions by political action committees to federal candidates, financial disclosure statements filed by all members of Congress, detailed campaign finance profiles of each member of Congress, information about travel expenses that House members received from private sources for attending meetings and other events, activities of registered federal lobbyists, and activities of foreign agents who are registered in the United States.

The site also has a list of all "soft money" donations to political parties of $100,000 or more in the current election cycle, data about "leadership" political action committees associated with individual politicians, and much more.

Vital Stats:

Access method:	WWW
To access:	http://www.crp.org
E-mail:	webmaster@crp.org

FECInfo

FECInfo provides an extraordinary collection of federal campaign finance data. The site uses data from the Federal Election Commission, but it is not operated by the FEC. Instead, its author is a former FEC employee named Tony Raymond—who deserves three cheers from anyone interested in campaign finance issues.

FECInfo has oodles of searchable databases that provide itemized information about receipts and expenditures by federal candidates and political action committees. The data are quite detailed. For example, for candidates you can search for contributions by Zip Code. The site also has data on soft money contributions, lists of the top political action committees in various categories, lists of the top contributors from each state, and lots, lots more.

Vital Stats:

Access method: WWW
To access: http://www.tray.com/fecinfo
E-mail: Info@tray.com

Federal Election Commission

This site is operated by the Federal Election Commission (FEC), which regulates federal political spending. The highlight is a database of campaign reports filed from May 1996 to the present by House and presidential candidates, political action committees, and political party committees. Senate reports are not included because they're filed with the secretary of the Senate.

The site also has summary financial data for House and Senate candidates in the current election cycle, abstracts of court decisions pertaining to federal election law from 1976 to 1997, a graph showing the number of political action committees in existence each year from 1974 to the present, and a directory of national and state agencies that are responsible for releasing information about campaign financing, candidates on the ballot, election results, lobbying, and other issues.

Another useful feature is a collection of brochures about federal election law, public funding of presidential elections, the ban on contributions by foreign nationals, independent expenditures supporting or opposing a candidate for federal office, contribution limits, filing a complaint, researching public records at the FEC, and other topics.

Finally, the site provides information about how to register to vote, the FEC's legislative recommendations, its annual report, a report about its first twenty years in existence, its monthly newsletter, election results for the most recent presidential and congressional elections, and campaign guides for corporations and labor organizations, congressional candidates and committees, political party committees, and nonconnected committees.

Vital Stats:

Access method: WWW
To access: http://www.fec.gov
E-mail: webmaster@fec.gov

Federal Voting Assistance Program (FVAP)

The Federal Voting Assistance Program (FVAP) site has a calendar of upcoming elections, information about how to apply for an absentee ballot, details about legislative initiatives affecting elections, links to state government sites that offer election results, and the *Voting Assistance Guide,* which has information about the procedures for registering and voting in each state. The site is operated by the Office of the Secretary of Defense.

Vital Stats:

Access method:	WWW
To access:	http://www.fvap.gov
E-mail:	vote@fvap.gov

POLICIES, REGULATIONS, AND OPERATIONS

FinanceNet

FinanceNet, which is primarily aimed at accountants, auditors, and financial managers, seeks to improve financial management at all levels of government. It's a project of the National Performance Review (now the National Partnership for Reinventing Government).

One of FinanceNet's most interesting features is an extensive listing of government assets, such as property and loans, that are for sale. FinanceNet also has extensive files relating to financial management, including documents about federal acquisition through computers, congressional testimony, calendars of events, meeting minutes, newsletters, legislation, articles, news about employment opportunities, requests for comments about draft publications, and press releases. It also provides links to lots of related Internet sites.

Vital Stats:

Access method:	WWW
To access:	http://www.financenet.gov
E-mail:	webmaster@financenet.gov

National Partnership for Reinventing Government

The National Partnership for Reinventing Government, formerly known as the National Performance Review, has hundreds of documents about reinventing government. It has information about initiatives to improve government, presidential directives about customer service, extensive information about the Government Performance and Results Act, case studies, a bibliography about government reinvention, speeches, press releases, links to other Internet sites about reforming government, links to related sites, and the full text of *The Blair House Papers,* a book by President Bill Clinton and Vice President Al Gore about reinventing government.

Vital Stats:

Access method:	WWW
To access:	http://www.npr.gov

Office of Governmentwide Policy

Through original documents and links to other sites, this site provides information about a wide range of federal government policies. It's operated by the General Services Administration.

The site has information about federal policies regarding accessibility, aircraft management, asset management, best practices, computers for education, electronic commerce, acquisitions, fleet management, mail management, personal property management, real property, transportation management, travel management, information technology, and many other topics.

Vital Stats:

Access method:	WWW
To access:	http://policyworks.gov
E-mail:	webmaster@policyworks.gov

Plain Language Action Network

This site's highlight is a document titled *Writing User-Friendly Documents*. It has tips about engaging your readers, writing clearly, identifying your audience, organizing your document, using active voice, using short sentences, addressing one person, using the present tense, using informative headings, dividing material into short sections, and other writing techniques.

The site is operated by the Plain Language Action Network (PLAN), a government-wide group that's attempting to improve communications from the federal government to the public. PLAN was established by the Office of Management and Budget and the National Partnership for Reinventing Government, which was then known as the National Performance Review.

The site also has examples of plain language regulations, letters, forms, and manuals, and links to other sites with documents about writing in plain language.

Vital Stats:

Access method:	WWW
To access:	http://www.plainlanguage.gov
E-mail:	info@plainlanguage.gov

Project on Government Secrecy

Numerous official documents about government secrecy are available from the Project on Government Secrecy site. It's operated by the Federation of American Scientists.

The site has executive orders on classification policy, administration speeches and memos on access to information, documents about declassification of documents from numerous federal agencies, documents from the Secrecy Policy Board, annual reports and other documents from the Information Security Oversight Office, the annual report from the Assassination Records Review Board, the 1997 *Report of the Commission on Protecting and Reducing Government Secrecy,* links to other Internet sites about government secrecy, and lots more.

Vital Stats:

Access method:	WWW
To access:	http://www.fas.org/sgp
E-mail:	saftergood@igc.org

REGINFO.GOV

This site is a one-stop source for federal regulatory information, primarily through links to other sites. It's operated by the Regulatory Information Service Center, which is part of the General Services Administration.

The only original publication at the site is the semiannual *Unified Agenda of Federal Regulatory and Deregulatory Actions,* which describes federal regulations that are under development. But it also has links to other sites that provide regulations and paperwork reviews that are pending or completed at the Office of Management and Budget, the *Federal Register,* the Code of Federal Regulations, federal statistical information, legislation, federal judiciary materials, the *United States Government Manual,* state and local government information, and more.

Vital Stats:

Access method:	WWW
To access:	http://reginfo.gov
E-mail:	RISC@gsa.gov

U.S. Consumer Product Safety Commission

The U.S. Consumer Product Safety Commission site provides a wide range of information about the CPSC's regulation of more than 15,000 consumer products used in the home, at school, or for recreation.

The site's highlight is a collection of dozens of CPSC publications about such topics as children's furniture, toy safety, recreational safety, fire and burn prevention, household products, art materials, indoor air quality, and poisoning prevention.

The site also offers publications for businesses, information about how to report unsafe products to the CPSC, a calendar of CPSC activities, press releases, and notices published in the *Federal Register.*

Vital Stats:

Access method:	WWW
To access:	http://www.cpsc.gov
E-mail:	mcohn@cpsc.gov

United States Immigration and Naturalization Service

This site includes immigration laws, forms, and notices published in the *Federal Register*. It's operated by the U.S. Immigration and Naturalization Service.

The site also has information about how to apply for U.S. citizenship, a report titled *Cracking Down on Alien Smuggling*, annual statistics about immigration to the United States, data regarding the number of illegal aliens, state population estimates of legal permanent residents and aliens eligible to apply for naturalization, information for employers, information about careers with the U.S. Border Patrol, and press releases.

Vital Stats:

Access method:	WWW
To access:	http://www.ins.usdoj.gov

U.S. Office of Government Ethics Home Page

The U.S. Office of Government Ethics Home Page has numerous publications about ethics rules and laws affecting the executive branch of the federal government. Some of the available titles are *Standards of Ethical Conduct, Conflicts of Interest and Government Employment, Gifts of Travel and Other Benefits,* and *Rules for the Road.*

The site also has the text of executive orders and laws governing ethics, a list of federal agencies that have ethics-related authority, a list of ethics officials at federal agencies, reports about new ethics legislation, background information about the office, and links to other Web sites related to government ethics.

Vital Stats:

Access method:	WWW
To access:	http://www.usoge.gov
E-mail:	webmaster@oge.gov

U.S. Office of Special Counsel

The U.S. Office of Special Counsel site offers information about laws covering the activities of federal employees. It has descriptions of prohibited personnel practices, details about rules under the Hatch Act regarding political activities by government employees, an explanation of the Office of Special Counsel's whistleblower hotline, a guide to federal employee rights and remedies, and much more.

Vital Stats:

Access method:	WWW
To access:	http://www.access.gpo.gov/osc/index.html
E-mail:	wwwadmin@www.access.gpo.gov

WHITE HOUSE

E-Mail to the White House

You can send e-mail to the president, the vice president, the first lady, and the vice president's wife through the Internet. But don't expect to develop a regular e-mail correspondence with the White House.

That's because there's no system for e-mail replies from the White House. You'll get an e-mail acknowledgment when you send a message, but you won't get a personalized response. If you want a personal response, you have to include your postal address in your message.

Here are the White House addresses:

President Bill Clinton: president@whitehouse.gov
Vice President Al Gore: vice.president@whitehouse.gov
First Lady Hillary Rodham Clinton: first.lady@whitehouse.gov
Vice President's Wife Tipper Gore: mrs.gore@whitehouse.gov

Vital Stats:

Access method:	E-mail
To access:	Send e-mail messages as described

The Independent Counsel and Impeachment

This site from the University of North Texas Libraries offers a large selection of documents related to Independent Counsel Kenneth Starr's investigation of President Bill Clinton.

Through documents loaded at the site and links to other sites, it provides Starr's initial report and supplemental materials, a transcript of Clinton's grand jury testimony, White House responses to Starr's report, a letter from Starr in which he did not rule out further impeachment referrals, remarks by Clinton at a religious leaders' breakfast, the statute providing for an independent counsel, Senate impeachment rules, House of Representatives resolutions and reports, various documents from the 1974 impeachment inquiry involving Richard M. Nixon, and other documents.

Vital Stats:

Access method:	WWW
To access:	http://www.library.unt.edu/info/willis/govdocs/impeach/impeachpage.html
E-mail:	griffith@library.unt.edu

Office of Management and Budget

This site has statements of administration policy regarding specific bills pending before Congress, Office of Management and Budget circulars about such topics as management of federal information resources and federal procurement, a list of regulations and paperwork currently under review by OMB, and the full text of the *Government-wide Performance Plan for FY 1999.*

The site also has copies of proposed and final rules submitted to the *Federal Register,* congressional testimony by OMB officials, press releases, lists of job openings at OMB, and reports about the costs and benefits of federal regulations, the Paperwork Reduction Act, federal statistical programs, and related subjects.

Vital Stats:

Access method:	WWW
To access:	http://www.whitehouse.gov/WH/EOP/OMB/html/ombhome.html

Office of National Drug Control Policy

Through original documents and links to other sites, this site provides a wide range of information about drug use, prevention and education, treatment, science and medicine, enforcement efforts, and international issues. It's operated by the White House Office of National Drug Control Policy (ONDCP).

Some of the site's highlights include a report titled *National Drug Control Strategy,* an ONDCP statement on using marijuana for medical purposes, a status report about state marijuana initiatives, and a special section of documents for parents.

The site also has information about how to contact the ONDCP Drug Policy Information Clearinghouse, a document titled *Response to Drug Use and Violence: A Directory and Resource Guide of Public- and Private-Sector Drug Control Grants,* a map of high-intensity drug trafficking areas throughout the country, a calendar of conferences, press releases, congressional testimony and speeches, and links to lots of related sites.

Vital Stats:

Access method:	WWW
To access:	http://www.whitehousedrugpolicy.gov
E-mail:	ondcp@ncjrs.org

Welcome to the White House

When it was first unveiled to much media hype in October 1994, Welcome to the White House was a major disappointment. Basically, it just provided links to other federal government sites on the Internet. The links were somewhat useful, but lots of other sites had better link collections.

The site has been updated and improved somewhat, although it's still primarily a glorified group of links. The links are arranged in two ways: by agency and by topic.

The site's best feature is its collection of White House documents, such as speeches by the president and transcripts of press briefings. These same documents are available at several other sites on the Internet, but Welcome to the White House arranges them quite nicely. You can search all the White House documents released since the beginning of the Clinton administration, the contents of this site, executive orders, recordings of the president's Saturday radio addresses, and White House photographs.

Welcome to the White House also has information about White House offices and agencies such as the Council of Economic Advisers and the Office of Management and Budget, a virtual historical tour of the White House, portraits and biographies of each president and first lady, information about touring the White House, and the White House for Kids, a section that offers basic information about the president, the vice president, and kids and pets who have lived in the White House.

Alas, a previous highlight was missing during a recent visit: a sound clip of Socks meowing.

Vital Stats:

Access method:	WWW
To access:	http://www.whitehouse.gov
E-mail:	feedback@www.whitehouse.gov

White House Publications

Through this Web page, you can sign up to receive automatically new White House publications by e-mail. The "Quick Subscription" option lets you subscribe to documents in more than twenty categories, and the "Custom Subscription" option lets you fine-tune your subscription to specific documents.

The following categories are available:

- Everything
- Computers and Communications
- Economy
- Education
- Environment
- Executive Acts
- Foreign Affairs
- Government Activities
- Healthcare
- International Security and Defense
- Justice and Crime
- Legislation
- Party Politics
- Personnel Announcements
- Science
- Science and Technology
- Social Issues
- Technology

- Daily Press Briefings
- Instructions (FAQs)
- Policy Briefings
- Remarks by President, Vice President, First Lady
- Speeches on Major Topics

Vital Stats:

Access method: WWW
To access: http://www.pub.whitehouse.gov/publications/
                      subscription-registration.html
E-mail: feedback@www.whitehouse.gov

HEALTH
AND MEDICINE

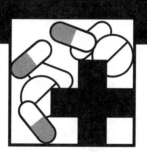

AIDS

AIDS Clinical Trials Information Service

The AIDS Clinical Trials Information Service has detailed information about clinical trials of drugs for the treatment of HIV/AIDS that are open for enrollment. The site is a joint project of the Centers for Disease Control and Prevention, National Institute of Allergy and Infectious Diseases, Food and Drug Administration, and National Library of Medicine.

The site also has a database of bibliographic references for journal articles about the interim or final results of HIV/AIDS-related clinical trials, a fact sheet about AIDS clinical trials, a list of FDA-approved drugs for HIV infection and AIDS-related conditions, press releases about clinical trials, and links to other Internet sites that have information about AIDS clinical trials.

Vital Stats:

Access method: WWW
To access: http://www.actis.org
E-mail: actis@actis.org

AIDS in the Workplace

The AIDS in the Workplace site has results from a national survey about how businesses are responding to AIDS, print ads that can be used in employee newsletters, a bibliography, links to related Web sites, and information about kits for managers and labor leaders that can be ordered from the Centers for Disease Control and Prevention, which operates the site.

Vital Stats:

Access method: WWW
To access: http://www.brta-lrta.org
E-mail: brta-lrta@cdcnpin.gov

AIDSNews

AIDSNews is a mailing list that distributes AIDS-related documents from the Centers for Disease Control and Prevention and other federal agencies.

Documents distributed through the list include the center's *Daily News Update*, selected articles from the *Morbidity and Mortality Weekly Report*, information about clinical trials, conference announcements, and news about funding opportunities.

Vital Stats:

Access method:	E-mail
To access:	Send a blank e-mail message to aidsnews-subscribe@cdcnpin.org
Subject line:	
Message:	
E-mail (questions):	info@cdcnpin.org

CDC National Prevention Information Network

The CDC National Prevention Information Network site, which is operated by the Centers for Disease Control and Prevention, is primarily devoted to information about HIV and AIDS. However, it also offers some materials about sexually transmitted diseases and tuberculosis.

The site offers a database that has descriptions of more than 19,000 HIV/AIDS service organizations, a database that provides information about private and government funding opportunities for community-based and HIV/AIDS service organizations, government reports about various aspects of HIV/AIDS, articles about AIDS from the CDC's *Morbidity and Mortality Weekly Report*, and the CDC's *Daily News Update*, which summarizes articles about AIDS, sexually transmitted diseases, and TB from newspapers, wire services, magazines, and journals.

It also has the full text and selected tables about AIDS prevalence from the *HIV/AIDS Surveillance Report*, a CDC publication titled *Glossary of HIV/AIDS-Related Terms*, numerous bibliographies of AIDS-related materials, the CDC *Guide to Selected HIV/AIDS Related Internet Resources*, and numerous fact sheets, brochures, and other publications.

Vital Stats:

Access method:	WWW
To access:	http://www.cdcnac.org
E-mail:	info@cdcnpin.org

HIV/AIDS Treatment Information Service

This site has numerous articles, brochures, and other publications about the treatment of HIV and AIDS. It's sponsored by seven U.S. Public Health Service agencies.

Some of the available titles are *HIV Protease Inhibitors and You, Caring for Someone with AIDS at Home, FDA Approved Drugs for HIV Infection and AIDS-Related Conditions,* and *Eating Defensively: Food Safety Advice for Persons with AIDS.* The site also has numerous links to other Internet sites that offer treatment information.

Vital Stats:

Access method:	WWW
To access:	http://www.hivatis.org
E-mail:	atis@hivatis.org

ALCOHOL AND DRUG ABUSE

National Institute on Alcohol Abuse and Alcoholism

The National Institute on Alcohol Abuse and Alcoholism site has a database containing abstracts and bibliographic references to journal articles, books, conference papers, reports, and other works about alcohol abuse and alcoholism. The database contains about 100,000 records back to the late 1960s.

The site also has pamphlets about alcoholism, aging and alcohol abuse, drinking and pregnancy, and how to reduce your drinking; a list of free research monographs and other publications that can be ordered online; the full text of *Alcohol Alerts,* a quarterly publication that has news about research findings; and much more. The institute is part of the National Institutes of Health.

Vital Stats:

Access method: WWW
To access: http://www.niaaa.nih.gov
E-mail: niaaaweb-r@exchange.nih.gov

National Institute on Drug Abuse

The National Institute on Drug Abuse site offers fact sheets about specific drugs, drug abuse and pregnancy, women and drug abuse, and other topics. It also has a guide for parents about drug use among young people, a report titled *Economic Costs of Alcohol and Drug Abuse in the United States,* articles about research, extensive grant information, a catalog of the institute's publications, therapy manuals for treating cocaine addiction, materials for teachers about addiction and various drugs, and press releases.

In addition, the site has speeches and congressional testimony by NIDA officials, links to other Internet sites about drug abuse, a publication for schools and community groups titled *Preventing Drug Use among Children and Adolescents: A Research-Based Guide,* and reports titled *Anabolic Steroids: A Threat to Mind and Body; Heroin: Abuse and Addiction; Inhalant Abuse: Its Dangers Are Nothing to Sniff At; Methamphetamine: Abuse and Addiction;* and *Nicotine Addiction.*

The institute is part of the National Institutes of Health.

Vital Stats:

Access method: WWW
To access: http://www.nida.nih.gov
E-mail: Information@lists.nida.nih.gov

PREVline (Prevention Online)

PREVline offers hundreds of files about alcohol, tobacco, and other drugs from the National Clearinghouse for Alcohol and Drug Information. The site has publications about prevention, resource guides, basic descriptions of street drugs, a publications catalog, a directory of drug abuse and alcoholism treatment and prevention programs, teaching kits, and links to recent news articles about alcohol, tobacco, and other drugs.

Vital Stats:

Access method:	WWW
To access:	http://www.health.org
E-mail:	webmaster@health.org

BIBLIOGRAPHIC INFORMATION

Combined Health Information Database

This site offers more than a dozen databases that provide bibliographic information about journal articles, directories, videotapes, books, bibliographies, newsletters, and reports about various diseases and conditions. The site is a joint effort of the National Institutes of Health and the Centers for Disease Control and Prevention.

The site has separate databases with references to materials about AIDS education, Alzheimer's disease, arthritis and musculoskeletal and skin diseases, cancer patient education, cancer prevention and control, comprehensive school health, deafness and communication disorders, diabetes, digestive diseases, disease prevention and health promotion, epilepsy education and prevention, health promotion and education, kidney and urologic diseases, maternal and child health, medical genetics and rare disorders, oral health, prenatal smoking cessation, and weight control.

You can search an individual database or all the databases together. Each database record provides a title, abstract, and availability information.

Vital Stats:

Access method:	WWW
To access:	http://chid.nih.gov
E-mail:	chid@aerie.com

Dr. Felix's Free MEDLINE Page

This site provides links to all of the Internet sites that offer free access to MEDLINE. MEDLINE is a database created by the National Library of Medicine that contains references to nearly nine million articles from medical journals.

Besides the links, Dr. Felix offers brief summaries of what's provided at each MEDLINE site. Where available, it includes the site name, a list of the available databases, dates of database coverage, frequency of updates, registration requirements, usage restrictions, and details about available document delivery services.

The site also has links to MEDLINE tutorials from various sources, links to other sites that list free MEDLINE sources, and links to papers about MEDLINE.

Vital Stats:

Access method:	WWW
To access:	http://www.docnet.org.uk/felix-frames.html
Mirror:	http://www.beaker.iupui.edu/drfelix
E-mail:	medline@grhlib.demon.co.uk

Internet Grateful Med

Internet Grateful Med provides access to fifteen databases prepared by the National Library of Medicine that are part of the MEDLARS system. Most of the databases provide bibliographical information for articles published in the medical literature. To help with your searches, the site provides a detailed user's manual.

The premier database is MEDLINE, which has bibliographic information for more than 8.5 million articles published from 1966 to the present. Almost three-quarters of the listings also have an abstract. The data cover more than 3,700 biomedical journals about medicine, nursing, dentistry, veterinary medicine, and the preclinical sciences. The database is updated daily.

Following are brief descriptions of the other databases:

- AIDSDRUGS has records about more than 240 chemical and biological agents currently being evaluated in AIDS clinical trials. Each entry includes standard chemical names, synonyms and trade names, CAS registry numbers, protocol ID numbers, pharmacological action, adverse reactions and contraindications, physical and chemical properties, and manufacturer's name. The database also contains a bibliography of relevant articles.

- AIDSLINE offers bibliographic citations for more than 124,000 journal articles, government reports, technical reports, books, audiovisual items, and other materials about AIDS published from 1980 to the present. The database is updated weekly.

- AIDSTRIALS has records about more than 700 open and closed clinical trials of substances being tested for use against AIDS, HIV infection, and AIDS-related opportunistic diseases. Each record has information about the title and purpose of the trial, diseases studied, patient eligibility criteria, contact persons, agents tested, and trial locations. The database is updated biweekly.

- BIOETHICSLINE provides more than 53,000 bibliographic citations to journal articles, monographs, newspaper articles, court decisions, bills, audiovisual materials, and other items published from 1973 to the present about policy issues in health care and biomedical research. Some of the topics covered are euthanasia and other end-of-life issues, organ donation and transplantation, allocation of health care resources, patients' rights, professional ethics, new reproductive technologies, genetic intervention, abortion, behavior control and other mental health issues, AIDS, human experimentation, and animal experimentation.

- ChemID is a chemical dictionary file for more than 340,000 compounds. For each chemical, the database provides the CAS registry number, molecular formula, generic names, trivial names, other synonyms, and related information.

- DIRLINE contains records about more than 17,000 health and biomedical information sources. The records cover organizations, government agencies, information centers, professional societies, voluntary associations, support groups, academic and research institutions, and research facilities. Each record has the resource name, address, and telephone number, along with descriptions of services, publications, and holdings.

- HealthSTAR provides bibliographic citations for more than 2.5 million journal articles, technical and government reports, meeting papers, and books published from 1975 to the present. The items cover both clinical and nonclinical aspects of medicine, including such topics as evaluation of patient outcomes, effectiveness of procedures and programs, health care administration, and health care planning. The database is updated monthly.

- HISTLINE offers about 155,000 bibliographic records for monographs, journal articles, books, and other materials about the history of health related professions. The database covers publications from 1964 to the present, and it's updated weekly.

- HSRPROJ provides about 3,000 records concerning research in progress that's funded by federal and private grants and contracts. The types of information available for each project vary, but they frequently include a project summary, the names of performing and sponsoring agencies, the name and address of the principal investigator, the beginning and ending years of the project, and the study design and methodology. The database is updated quarterly.

- OLDMEDLINE has bibliographic information for articles published in international biomedical journals from 1964 to 1965. The database contains more than 307,000 records.

- POPLINE offers bibliographic citations for more than 250,000 journal articles, monographs, reports, and other items published from 1970 to the present about family planning, population law and policy, and primary health care, including maternal and child health in developing countries.

- SDILINE has bibliographic information for all materials added to MEDLINE in the most recent complete month. The database is updated monthly and usually offers about 31,000 new citations each month.

- SPACELINE provides bibliographic citations for more than 140,000 journal articles, books, papers, and other items about space life sciences.

- TOXLINE has bibliographic information about more than 2.4 million articles, reports, and other items about toxicological, pharmacological, biochemical, and physiological effects of drugs and other chemicals.

Vital Stats:

Access method:	WWW
To access:	http://igm.nlm.nih.gov
E-mail:	access@nlm.nih.gov

National Library of Medicine

The National Library of Medicine site has dozens of bibliographies on such topics as medical treatment of heroin addiction, acupuncture, malaria, thalidomide, genetic testing for cystic fibrosis, interventions to prevent HIV risk behaviors, breast cancer screening in women ages forty to forty-nine, public health informatics, dietary supplements, cervical cancer, and confidentiality of electronic health data, among many others.

It also has links to National Library of Medicine sites that provide free access to the MEDLINE database of references to medical journal articles, Grateful Med software to use in accessing MEDLINE, descriptions of more than forty databases offered by the library, information for visitors and researchers, a sample of images and animations from the Visible

Human Project, information about telemedicine projects around the country, a staff directory, and much more.

Vital Stats:

Access method: WWW
To access: http://www.nlm.nih.gov

PubMed

PubMed provides free searching of all nine million citations in MEDLINE, a database that provides bibliographical information for the biomedical literature. It also contains citations that have not yet been entered in MEDLINE.

MEDLINE is a database created by the National Library of Medicine that covers the fields of medicine, nursing, dentistry, veterinary medicine, the health care system, and the preclinical sciences. The database has citations from more than 3,800 biomedical journals published in the United States and seventy foreign countries. Records are available back to 1966.

PubMed also provides links to Web sites operated by dozens of journals that are indexed in the database. PubMed is operated by the National Center for Biotechnology Information at the National Library of Medicine.

Vital Stats:

Access method: WWW
To access: http://www.ncbi.nlm.nih.gov/PubMed
E-mail: info@ncbi.nlm.nih.gov

CANCER

CancerNet

CancerNet, which is operated by the National Cancer Institute, offers hundreds of files about prevention, diagnosis, and treatment of cancer.

There are documents about risk factors and possible causes of cancer, unconventional treatment methods, side effects frequently experienced by cancer patients, coping with cancer, caring for cancer patients, clinical trials of new cancer drugs, and sources of cancer information. Many of the documents are available in Spanish versions.

The site also has abstracts of recent journal articles about cancer and links to more than two dozen other cancer sites on the Internet.

Vital Stats:

Access method:	WWW
To access:	http://wwwicic.nci.nih.gov
E-mail:	comments@icic.nci.nih.gov

Cancer Trials

This site offers background information about clinical trials of cancer therapies, including such topics as clinical trials and insurance coverage, how clinical trials affect cancer research, and deciding whether to participate in a trial. The site is operated by the National Cancer Institute (NCI).

It also has a step-by-step guide to searching an NCI database of current clinical trials (and a link to the database), news about clinical trials and cancer research, and a page where you can sign up to receive e-mail updates about new items on the site.

Vital Stats:

Access method:	WWW
To access:	http://cancertrials.nci.nih.gov

National Action Plan on Breast Cancer

This site has fact sheets about such topics as hereditary susceptibility and clinical trials, press releases, and calendars of events related to breast cancer. The National Action Plan on Breast Cancer is a public-private partnership coordinated by the U.S. Department of Health and Human Services.

The site also has information about grants, links to Internet sites about clinical trials, and links to dozens of Internet sites that have information about breast cancer.

Vital Stats:

Access method: WWW
To access: http://www.napbc.org
E-mail: info@napbc.org

National Cancer Institute

The National Cancer Institute site has details about how to contact the Cancer Information Service, which provides information about cancer to the public and health professionals. The site also has a calendar of upcoming cancer-related meetings, budget data for the institute, links to Internet sites operated by NCI branches, and information about research being conducted or supported by NCI.

In addition, it has a link to CancerNet (p. 192), an NCI Internet site that offers hundreds of documents for cancer patients and physicians.

Vital Stats:

Access method: WWW
To access: http://www.nci.nih.gov
E-mail: rstephen@exchange.nih.gov

DIRECTORIES AND SEARCH ENGINES

Department of Health and Human Services

This site primarily provides links to Internet sites operated by Department of Health and Human Services (HHS) agencies such as the Administration on Aging, Centers for Disease Control and Prevention, Food and Drug Administration, National Institutes of Health, and the Substance Abuse and Mental Health Services Administration.

It also has budget information, speeches and congressional testimony by department officials, reports about HHS-related bills pending before Congress, recent laws and executive orders related to HHS, press releases, and background information about the department.

Vital Stats:

Access method:	WWW
To access:	http://www.os.dhhs.gov
E-mail:	webmaster@os.dhhs.gov

healthfinder

The healthfinder site is an excellent place to start a search for health information on the Internet. It provides links to hundreds of federal publications about health topics and to hundreds of consumer health sites on the Internet. All of the sites have been evaluated for quality by the Department of Health and Human Services, which operates healthfinder.

Vital Stats:

Access method:	WWW
To access:	http://www.healthfinder.gov
E-mail:	healthfinder@health.org

National Health Information Center

The National Health Information Center offers a database containing contact information for more than 1,000 private organizations and government agencies that provide health information to the public. The database has links to Web sites operated by those groups that have them. The site also has a calendar of national health observances that includes contact information for each event.

Vital Stats:

Access method:	WWW
To access:	http://nhic-nt.health.org
E-mail:	nhicinfo@health.org

National Institutes of Health

The National Institutes of Health (NIH) site is a gateway to the dozens of Internet sites operated by NIH offices and institutes.

The site also has a searchable index of diseases currently being investigated at NIH or by NIH-supported scientists, links to the most requested NIH publications about various health topics, a list of toll-free phone numbers for NIH information hotlines, a searchable NIH telephone book, a map of the NIH campus, a calendar of events, press releases, and much more.

Vital Stats:

Access method:	WWW
To access:	http://www.nih.gov
E-mail:	nihinfo@od31tm1.od.nih.gov

NIH Web Search

This site is a search engine that looks for documents on more than 100 Web sites operated by various components of the National Institutes of Health. You can search by numerous variables, and both basic and complex queries are available.

Vital Stats:

Access method:	WWW
To access:	http://search.info.nih.gov
E-mail:	webmaster@www.nih.gov

DISABILITIES

ABLEDATA

ABLEDATA offers a database containing detailed information about more than 24,000 products designed for people with disabilities. The products range from white canes to voice output programs. The database contains descriptions of each product, along with price and company information. ABLEDATA is funded by the National Institute of Disability and Rehabilitation Research, which is part of the U.S. Department of Education.

The site also has links to hundreds of Web sites with disabilities-related information, fact sheets about assistive technology devices ranging from wheelchairs to winter sports equipment, and consumer guides about wheelchair selection, office equipment for people with visual disabilities, accessible housing, and assistive technology for people with spinal cord injuries.

Vital Stats:

Access method:	WWW
To access:	http://www.abledata.com
E-mail:	KABELKNAP@aol.com

The Access Board

The Access Board site provides information about creating an accessible world for people with disabilities. The site is operated by the U.S. Architectural and Transportation Barriers Compliance Board, which is an independent federal agency that enforces the Architectural Barriers Act.

The site has technical assistance bulletins, information about how to file a complaint under the Architectural Barriers Act, links to dozens of Internet sites that offer accessibility information, and accessibility guidelines for buildings and facilities, transportation vehicles, and telecommunications equipment.

Vital Stats:

Access method:	WWW
To access:	http://www.access-board.gov
E-mail:	info@access-board.gov

Disabilities and Managed Care

This site's highlight is an excellent collection of links to reports and other sites about managed care and people with disabilities. It's operated by the U.S. Department of Health and Human Services.

Other than the links, the site offers very little. It has abstracts of more than 100 current and recent studies about managed care and people with disabilities, basic information about how managed care affects people with a particular disability, and technical details about how the growth of managed care has affected Medicaid, Medicare, and private insurance programs that serve people with disabilities.

Vital Stats:

Access method:	WWW
To access:	http://managedcare.hhs.gov
E-mail:	aspe@lewin.com

National Council on Disability

This site has more than twenty reports published by the National Council on Disability, an independent federal agency that makes recommendations to the president and Congress about disability issues.

Some sample titles are *Access to the Information Superhighway and Emerging Information Technologies by People with Disabilities; ADA Watch: A Report to the President and the Congress on Progress in Implementing the Americans with Disabilities Act; Achieving Independence: The Challenge for the Twenty-first Century; Inclusionary Education for Students with Disabilities: Keeping the Promise; Meeting the Unique Needs of Minorities with Disabilities;* and *Wilderness Accessibility for People with Disabilities.*

Vital Stats:

Access method:	WWW
To access:	http://www.ncd.gov
E-mail:	mquigley@ncd.gov

National Rehabilitation Information Center

This site offers extensive information about disabilities and rehabilitation. One of its highlights is a database containing bibliographic information about more than 12,000 reports, books, articles, and other items about physical, mental, and psychiatric disabilities, independent living, vocational rehabilitation, special education, assistive technology, law, employment, and other issues as they relate to people with disabilities. A similar database contains records on more than 38,000 documents published from 1956 to 1992.

Other databases describe more than 1,300 resources for disability information and more than 300 disability research programs. The site also offers *The NARIC Guide to Resources for the Americans with Disabilities Act*, details about how to design accessible Web pages, a calendar of events, and lots more.

The National Rehabilitation Information Center is funded by the National Institute on Disability and Rehabilitation Research (NIDRR), which is part of the U.S. Department of Education.

Vital Stats:

Access method:	WWW
To access:	http://www.naric.com/naric
E-mail:	wendling@mindspring.com

Trace Research and Development Center

The Trace Research and Development Center site has extensive information about disabilities and creating an accessible world for people with disabilities. The center, which is located at the University of Wisconsin–Madison, is supported by the National Institute on Disability and Rehabilitation Research of the U.S. Department of Education.

The site has an especially strong collection of information about computer access for people with disabilities, including guidelines for designing accessible Web sites, information about major ongoing programs addressing Web access issues, information about accessibility software and hardware, a calendar of events, and much more.

The site also has databases containing descriptions of thousands of assistive technology products, toys and computers for kids with disabilities, assistive technology funding resources, articles and publications about disabilities and rehabilitation, and rehabilitation training materials. In addition, it offers numerous documents about creating access for people with disabilities, the American with Disabilities Act and other laws, financing assistive technology, and telecommunications access.

Vital Stats:

Access method:	WWW
To access:	http://trace.waisman.wisc.edu
E-mail:	web@trace.wisc.edu

ENVIRONMENTAL HEALTH

National Institute of Environmental Health Sciences

This site has a small collection of publications about environmental health. Some of the available titles are *Lead: The #1 Environmental Hazard to Many Children; Women's Health and the Environment; Breast Cancer: Susceptibility and the Environment; Questions and Answers about EMF; Medicine and the Layman: Environment and Disease; Lead and Your Health;* and *With Respect to Life: Protecting Human Health and the Environment through Laboratory Animal Research.* The National Institute of Environmental Health Sciences is part of the National Institutes of Health.

The site also has information about three major research projects currently under way at the institute. The projects are investigating how chemical- and disease-susceptibility genes vary from person to person, the levels of chemicals we carry in our bodies, and the effects of chemical mixtures on health.

Vital Stats:

Access method:	WWW
To access:	http://www.niehs.nih.gov
E-mail:	webcenter@niehs.nih.gov

National Pesticide Telecommunications Network

This site has more than a dozen articles about toxicology issues such as bioaccumulation, carcinogenesis, toxic effects on skin, movement of pesticides in the environment, and pesticide regulation. It's a joint project of Oregon State University and the U.S. Environmental Protection Agency.

The site also offers contact information and links to Web sites operated by pesticide companies, contact information for state and regional poison control centers around the country, links to pesticide databases at other Internet sites, links to EPA documents about pesticides, and links to Web sites operated by state pesticide regulatory agencies.

Vital Stats:

Access method:	WWW
To access:	http://ace.orst.edu/info/nptn
E-mail:	nptn@ace.orst.edu

National Toxicology Program

The highlight of this site is a report listing all chemicals that are suspected or known to be carcinogens. The site also has extensive technical information about chemicals tested by the National Toxicology Program, *Federal Register* notices, a calendar of events, press releases, and abstracts of long-term carcinogenesis studies, short-term toxicity studies, immunotoxicity studies, reproductive toxicity studies, and teratology studies.

Vital Stats:

Access method:	WWW
To access:	http://ntp-server.niehs.nih.gov
E-mail:	Rowley@niehs.nih.gov

FOOD AND NUTRITION

Center for Food Safety and Applied Nutrition

The Center for Food Safety and Applied Nutrition site has everything from background information about the fat substitute Olestra to a book titled *Foodborne Pathogenic Microorganisms and Natural Toxins*—otherwise known as the "Bad Bug Book." The center is part of the Food and Drug Administration.

The site has information about food labels, health fraud, safe food handling, mercury in fish, eating disorders, food allergies, osteoporosis and other bone diseases, biotechnology, food additives, and pesticides and chemical contaminants, among many other subjects.

It also has an explanation of which federal agencies regulate food safety, details about how to report problems to the FDA, press releases, and links to dozens of other Internet sites that provide food and nutrition information.

Vital Stats:

Access method:	WWW
To access:	http://vm.cfsan.fda.gov
E-mail:	lrd@cfsan.fda.gov

Food and Nutrition Information Center

This site's highlight is a searchable database that contains nutrient data for thousands of foods. It also has a link to another site that provides nutritional information for more than 1,000 fast-food items. The site is operated by the Food and Nutrition Information Center, which is part of the National Agricultural Library.

Some of the other resources available include the report titled *Dietary Guidelines for Americans,* information about the food guide pyramid, a report about how well American diets conform to recommended healthy eating patterns, the recommended dietary allowances from the National Academy of Sciences, and a report titled *Food and Nutrition Resource Guide for Homeless Shelters, Soup Kitchens, and Food Banks.*

It also has a large collection of links to food and nutrition information divided by subject and bibliographies of publications about eating disorders, food allergies, foodborne illness, herbal medicine, nutrition and cancer, nutrition and cardiovascular disease, nutrition and diabetes, nutrition during pregnancy and breastfeeding, sports nutrition, vegetarian nutrition, weight control, and other topics.

Vital Stats:

Access method:	WWW
To access:	http://www.nal.usda.gov/fnic
E-mail:	fnic@nal.usda.gov

The National Food Safety Database

This site offers hundreds of articles and publications about food safety from the Food and Drug Administration, the Agriculture Department, and other sources. The site is funded primarily by the Agriculture Department.

You can browse or search the database. Some of the available publications are *Foodborne Illness: What Consumers Need to Know; Safe Food at Parties and Picnics; Hamburger Safety Tips; Food Additives; Monosodium Glutamate; Salt Substitutes; Slow Cooker Safety; Bacteria on Cutting Boards; Preventing Foodborne Illnesses; Pesticides in the Food Supply; Microwaving Tips; USDA Complete Guide to Home Canning; How to Buy Pest Control Services; Non-Chemical Rodent Control; Avoiding Food and Drug Interactions;* and *Making Food Healthy and Safe for Children.*

The site also includes telephone numbers for food hotlines run by government agencies and food companies, contact information for Cooperative Extension Service agents and others around the country who can answer food safety questions, a calendar of meetings and conferences, and links to other food safety sites.

Vital Stats:

Access method:	WWW
To access:	http://foodsafety.org
E-mail:	mlt@gnv.ifas.ufl.edu

NutriBase

A database at this site lists nutrients for more than 19,300 food items. The data come from the U.S. Department of Agriculture, although the site is operated by CyberSoft, a company that produces nutrition books and software packages.

Vital Stats:

Access method:	WWW
To access:	http://www.nutribase.com
E-mail:	edp@nutribase.com

Office of Dietary Supplements

Limited information about dietary supplements is available at this site, which is operated by the Office of Dietary Supplements in the National Institutes of Health.

The site's highlights are two databases. Computer Access to Research on Dietary Supplements (CARDS) provides information about dietary supplement research currently funded by the federal government, and International Bibliographic Information on Dietary Supplements (IBIDS) contains bibliographic information for journal articles and other items about dietary supplements.

The site also has a report titled *Merging Quality Science with Supplement Research: A Strategic Plan for the Office of Dietary Supplements*, background information about the office, a calendar of conferences and meetings, press releases, links to related sites, and a page where you can sign up to receive news releases and information about upcoming conferences and meetings by e-mail.

Vital Stats:

Access method: WWW
To access: http://odp.od.nih.gov/ods
E-mail: ods@nih.gov

GENERAL

Administration on Aging

The Administration on Aging site offers numerous brochures, primarily on health topics. Some sample titles include *Home Modification and Repair, Decisions about Retirement Living, Looking Out for Depression, Taking Care of Your Teeth and Mouth, Hearing and Older People, Prostate Problems,* and *Volunteer Opportunities.*

Another highlight is the Eldercare Locator. It's a searchable database that provides information about assistance available for the elderly in cities around the country.

The site also has links to Web sites operated by state agencies on aging, directories of area agencies on aging and state long-term care ombudsmen, information about the Older Americans Act, the final report from the 1995 White House Conference on Aging, a directory of resource centers and technical assistance for practitioners in aging, and press releases.

In addition, it offers an article titled "Memory Loss: It's Not Inevitable"; extensive demographic information about older Americans, including projections of the older population to 2050; and links to numerous Internet sites that provide information for older Americans.

Vital Stats:

Access method:	WWW
To access:	http://www.aoa.dhhs.gov
E-mail:	esec@ban-gate.aoa.dhhs.gov

Agency for Health Care Policy and Research

The Agency for Health Care Policy and Research site has numerous consumer publications, including *Choosing and Using a Health Plan, Prescription Medicines and You, What You Should Know about Stroke Prevention,* and *Be Informed: Questions to Ask Your Doctor before You Have Surgery.*

In addition, the site has various health care statistics, news about upcoming conferences, speeches and congressional testimony by AHCPR officials, and announcements about grants and job vacancies.

Vital Stats:

Access method:	WWW
To access:	http://www.ahcpr.gov
E-mail:	info@ahcpr.gov

Centers for Disease Control and Prevention

This site offers an incredible collection of health-related databases, books, and documents. It's operated by the Centers for Disease Control and Prevention.

The site offers *Physical Activity and Health: A Report of the Surgeon General;* the full text of the *Morbidity and Mortality Weekly Report;* brochures from the National Center for Health Statistics about lead poisoning, preventing birth defects, and other topics; *Emerging Infectious Diseases,* a journal published by the National Center for Infectious Diseases; and brochures about chronic fatigue syndrome, Lyme disease, and malaria.

It also provides access to CDC WONDER, a huge database system that provides CDC reports, guidelines, and public health data; numerous publications from the National Center for Health Statistics; the *HIV/AIDS Surveillance Report,* a report published semiannually by the CDC that contains tabular and graphic information about U.S. AIDS and HIV case reports; a report about where to obtain birth, death, marriage, and divorce certificates; information about grant opportunities; contracting information; and lots, lots more.

Vital Stats:

Access method:	WWW
To access:	http://www.cdc.gov
E-mail:	netinfo@cdc.gov

CDC Diabetes and Public Health Resource

This site has publications about diabetes for patients, physicians, and public health researchers. It's operated by the Centers for Disease Control and Prevention.

Some of the highlights are a brochure titled *Diabetes at-a-Glance,* a lengthy patient guide titled *Take Charge of Your Diabetes,* a report for physicians titled *The Prevention and Treatment of Complications of Diabetes Mellitus: A Guide for Primary Care Practitioners,* diabetes prevalence and mortality data for each state, and information about diabetes control programs in each state.

Vital Stats:

Access method:	WWW
To access:	http://www.cdc.gov/nccdphp/ddt/ddthome.htm
E-mail:	cdcinfo@cdc.gov

CDC Travel Information

If you're planning a trip to a foreign country, the CDC Travel Information site is a must-see before you go. It has news about current disease outbreaks around the world, summaries from inspections of international cruise ships, and health recommendations for regions around the world. The site is operated by the Centers for Disease Control and Prevention.

One of the site's highlights is a book titled *Health Information for International Travel,* which has CDC recommendations for every country in the world, vaccination requirements for each country, and a large section of health hints for travelers.

The site also has schedules of recommended childhood immunization and booster shots, as well as articles about traveler's diarrhea, cholera, dengue fever, hepatitis A vaccine, precautions for HIV-infected travelers, malaria, rabies, and typhoid fever, among other topics.

Vital Stats:

Access method:	WWW
To access:	http://www.cdc.gov/travel
E-mail:	ncid@cdc.gov

CDC's Tobacco Information and Prevention Source (TIPS)

This site has articles about nicotine dependence, the prevalence of smoking, advertising, smoking cessation, economics, health consequences, international issues, legal and policy issues, secondhand smoke, smokeless tobacco, tobacco production, and youth, among other subjects. It's operated by the Centers for Disease Control and Prevention.

One of the highlights is a database containing bibliographic information and abstracts of journal articles, books, reports, government documents, legal documents, editorials, and other items about smoking and health. The database lists more than 56,000 items. A separate list has citations for tobacco-related articles published within the past four weeks.

The site also has guides to quitting smoking, a guide for employers on creating a smoke-free workplace, a timeline of significant developments related to smoking and health, descriptions of actions taken by the federal government to regulate tobacco, the executive summary of a 1994 report by the surgeon general titled *Preventing Tobacco Use among Young People,* and quizzes, posters, and facts for children and teens.

Vital Stats:

Access method:	WWW
To access:	http://www.cdc.gov/tobacco
E-mail:	ccdinfo@cdc.gov

CDC WONDER

CDC WONDER lets you analyze data maintained by the Centers for Disease Control (CDC) on such subjects as mortality, cancer incidence, hospital discharges, AIDS, behavioral risk factors, diabetes, and other topics. The system also provides access to reports and guidelines prepared by the CDC. Although CDC WONDER is aimed at public health professionals, anyone from journalists to academic researchers should find it enormously useful.

You must register online to access the data sets.

Vital Stats:

Access method:	WWW
Internet:	http://wonder.cdc.gov
E-mail:	cwus@cdc.gov

Committee on Commerce Tobacco Documents

This site has more than 40,000 tobacco company documents that the House Commerce Committee subpoenaed in late 1997 and early 1998. The documents arose from Minnesota's lawsuit against the tobacco companies.

Accessing the documents is a bit tricky. They are in PDF and TIFF formats, and in some cases you must view each page as a separate file. To complicate matters further, they're arranged by company.

To help you find what you're seeking, the committee offers a "privilege log" for each company's documents that provides basic descriptions of each document. You can search the logs for items of interest by using any word processing program. Once you identify a document, you must search for it by number in the site's database.

Vital Stats:

Access method:	WWW
To access:	http://www.house.gov/commerce/TobaccoDocs/documents.html
E-mail:	commerce@mail.house.gov

Consumer Health Information

This page is a one-stop source for more than 100 of the most popular consumer health publications produced by the National Institutes of Health.

It offers links to publications about aging, AIDS, alcohol abuse, Alzheimer's disease, anabolic steroids, anxiety disorders, arthritis, asthma, blood cholesterol, cancer, colds and flu, depression, diabetes, digestive diseases, eating disorders, environmental health, eye care, fibromyalgia, food allergies, heart disease, hearing, incontinence, inhalant abuse, kidney diseases, knee problems, learning disabilities, lupus, Lyme disease, marijuana, menopause, oral contraceptives, stroke, sudden infant death syndrome, urinary problems, vasectomy, and many other subjects.

You can browse the links by subject keywords or by the NIH institute that published the document.

Vital Stats:

Access method:	WWW
To access:	http://www.nih.gov/health/consumer/conicd.htm
E-mail:	nihinfo@od31tm1.od.nih.gov

Diabetes in America

This site provides the full text of *Diabetes in America,* a 733-page book published by the National Institute of Diabetes and Digestive and Kidney Diseases.

The book's thirty-six chapters cover such subjects as diagnostic criteria and screening for diabetes, the prevalence and incidence of various types of diabetes, physical and metabolic characteristics of persons with diabetes, risk factors, complications of diabetes, therapy for diabetes, health insurance and diabetes, pregnancy in preexisting diabetes, and diabetes in special populations.

Each chapter of the book is provided in a separate PDF (portable document format) file. You must have the Adobe Acrobat Reader software to view them, and this site links to an Adobe site where you can download the software for free.

Vital Stats:

Access method:	WWW
To access:	http://diabetes-in-america.s-3.com

Health Care Financing Administration

The Health Care Financing Administration (HCFA) site specializes in information about Medicare and Medicaid. It has numerous consumer publications, including *Medicare and You, What Everyone Should Know about Skilled Nursing Facilities under Medicare, Guide to Choosing a Nursing Home, Advance Directives, Medicare Hospice Benefits, Medicare Managed Care,* and *Medicare and Home Health Care.*

The site also has a directory of local contacts for Medicare information, a list of state and federal Medicaid contacts, a fact sheet about managed care in Medicare and Medicaid, tips for avoiding Medicare fraud, extensive statistics on Medicare and Medicaid, fact sheets about HCFA programs, speeches and congressional testimony by HCFA officials, an HCFA employee telephone directory, and information about contracting opportunities.

Vital Stats:

Access method:	WWW
To access:	http://www.hcfa.gov
E-mail:	WebMaster@hcfa.gov

The Initiative to Eliminate Racial and Ethnic Disparities in Health

This site has information about the goals announced by President Bill Clinton in February 1998 to eliminate racial and ethnic disparities in six health areas: infant mortality, cancer screening and management, cardiovascular disease, diabetes, HIV infection, and child and adult immunizations. It's operated by the Department of Health and Human Services.

The site has data about disparities in the six focus areas, answers to frequently asked questions, and links to lots of related Web sites.

Vital Stats:

Access method:	WWW
To access:	http://raceandhealth.hhs.gov
E-mail:	HealthDisparities@OSASPE.DHHS.Gov

Internet FDA

A wide range of information about the Food and Drug Administration's regulation of food, drugs, medical devices, and the blood supply is available on Internet FDA.

The site has information about the FDA's efforts to regulate tobacco; the weekly *FDA Enforcement Report*, which lists FDA-regulated products that are being recalled; *FDA Consumer*, a magazine designed for consumers; telephone numbers for many FDA offices and officials; brief summaries of laws that the FDA enforces; information about how to report problems with foods, drugs, and other products that the FDA regulates; lists of FDA publications; selected speeches and testimony by FDA officials; press releases; links to other FDA Internet sites; and much more.

Vital Stats:

Access method:	WWW
To access:	http://www.fda.gov

LTCARE-L

Subscribers to the LTCARE-L mailing list discuss research findings and public policy issues related to aging, physical and cognitive disability, and long-term care. The list is operated by the U.S. Department of Health and Human Services.

Vital Stats:

Access method:	E-mail
To access:	Send an e-mail message to listserv@list.nih.gov
Subject line:	
Message:	**subscribe LTCARE-L**
E-mail:	LTCARE-L-request@list.nih.gov

Medicare

This site has a wealth of information about Medicare, a federal program that provides health insurance to people age sixty-five and over, people who have permanent kidney failure, and certain people with disabilities. It's operated by the Health Care Financing Administration, which is part of the Department of Health and Human Services.

One of the site's highlights is a collection of consumer publications. Some of the available titles are *Medicare and You, What Everyone Should Know about Skilled Nursing Facilities under Medicare, Guide to Choosing a Nursing Home, Guide to Health Insurance for People with Medicare, Advance Directives, Medicare Hospice Benefits, Medicare and Home Health Care,* and *Medicare and Home Medical Equipment: How to Get Home Medical Equipment and Report Suspected Fraud.* Many of the publications are also available in Spanish.

The site also has documents about Medicare coverage of various diseases and medical procedures, details about how to report Medicare fraud and abuse, answers to common questions about Medicare and managed care, and a program that provides information about costs, premiums, and types of services provided by managed care plans in your area.

National Bioethics Advisory Commission

The highlight of the National Bioethics Advisory Commission site is a 125-page report the commission issued in June 1997 about human cloning. The NBAC, which was created by executive order in October 1995, makes recommendations to federal agencies on bioethical issues involving research with humans.

The site also has transcripts of meetings, press releases, a schedule of upcoming meetings, the NBAC charter, and a list of NBAC members.

Vital Stats:

Access method:	WWW
To access:	http://bioethics.gov
E-mail:	webmaster@psc.gov

National Eye Institute

The National Eye Institute site has brochures about age-related macular degeneration, cataracts, glaucoma, and diabetic eye disease, among other subjects. The institute is part of the National Institutes of Health.

The site also has information about clinical trials that are currently recruiting patients, research being conducted or supported by the National Eye Institute, grants and contracts, and visiting the institute.

In addition, it offers a directory of more than thirty national eye health-related organizations, a list of resources for people with visual impairments, information about financial assistance for eye care available through national organizations, tips for finding an eye care professional, an eye diagram, a glossary of eye-related terms, and lesson plans for grades 4–8.

Vital Stats:

Access method:	WWW
To access:	http://www.nei.nih.gov
E-mail:	2020@nei.nih.gov

National Heart, Lung, and Blood Institute

The National Heart, Lung, and Blood Institute (NHLBI) site offers publications about high blood pressure, obesity, asthma, smoking, coronary heart disease, sleep apnea, insomnia, sickle cell disease, heart and lung transplants, and hormone replacement therapy and heart disease, among other subjects. Some of the publications are designed for the public, while others are geared toward health professionals.

The site also has a catalog of NHLBI education materials, information about grants and contracts, a staff directory, details about studies that are seeking patients, press releases, and brief descriptions of NHLBI research laboratories.

Vital Stats:

Access method:	WWW
To access:	http://www.nhlbi.nih.gov/nhlbi/nhlbi.htm
E-mail:	pl29i@nih.gov

National Human Genome Research Institute

The National Human Genome Research Institute site has news about genetic discoveries, discussions of the ethical issues involved in human genetics research, background information about the Human Genome Project, grant information, fact sheets, press releases, and links to other Internet sites that offer genomic and genetic resources. The institute is part of the National Institutes of Health.

Vital Stats:

Access method:	WWW
To access:	http://www.nhgri.nih.gov
E-mail:	webmaster@nhgri.nih.gov

National Institute of Allergy and Infectious Disease (NIAID)

The National Institute of Allergy and Infectious Disease (NIAID) site specializes in information about AIDS. It has publications about AIDS research, pediatric AIDS, women and HIV infection, HIV vaccines, clinical trials for AIDS therapies, and related topics.

The site also offers information about allergies, asthma, chronic fatigue syndrome, emerging infectious diseases, food allergies, Lyme disease, malaria, sexually transmitted diseases, transplantation, tuberculosis, and other medical conditions and diseases. And it has grant and contract information, NIAID personnel information, details about clinical trials that are seeking volunteers, and news about technology transfer opportunities.

Vital Stats:

Access method:	WWW
To access:	http://www.niaid.nih.gov
E-mail:	ocpostoffice@flash.niaid.nih.gov

National Institute of Arthritis and Musculoskeletal and Skin Diseases

This site provides brochures about arthritis and exercise, arthritis pain, fibromyalgia, hip replacement, knee problems, lupus, Lyme disease, psoriasis, rheumatoid arthritis, shoulder problems, and other topics. It's operated by the National Institute of Arthritis and Musculoskeletal and Skin Diseases, which is part of the National Institutes of Health.

The site also has contact information for the National Arthritis and Musculoskeletal and Skin Diseases Information Clearinghouse, NIH consensus statements about optimal calcium intake and total hip replacement, information about research being conducted at the institute, results of clinical trials, workshop summaries, a calendar of events, and press releases.

Vital Stats:

Access method:	WWW
To access:	http://www.nih.gov/niams
E-mail:	NIAMSWEB-L@exchange.nih.gov

National Institute of Dental Research

The National Institute of Dental Research site has publications titled *Snack Smart for Healthy Teeth, A Healthy Mouth for Your Baby, Diabetes and Periodontal Disease,* and *Seal Out Dental Decay.* It also offers information about research being conducted at the institute, a calendar of events, press releases, and links to other dental-related Internet sites. The institute is part of the National Institutes of Health.

Vital Stats:

Access method:	WWW
To access:	http://www.nidr.nih.gov
E-mail:	nidrinfo@od31.nidr.nih.gov

National Institute of Diabetes and Digestive and Kidney Diseases

This site has extensive information about diabetes, digestive diseases, endocrine disorders, hematologic disorders, kidney disorders, nutrition, obesity, and urologic disorders. It's operated by the National Institute of Diabetes and Digestive and Kidney Diseases (NIDDK), which is part of the National Institutes of Health.

The site also has an NIDDK staff directory, press releases, and information about research funding available from the NIDDK, postdoctoral research training available from the NIDDK and the National Institutes of Health, NIDDK laboratories, and the National Digestive Diseases Information Clearinghouse.

Vital Stats:

Access method:	WWW
To access:	http://www.niddk.nih.gov

National Institute of Neurological Disorders and Stroke

The National Institute of Neurological Disorders and Stroke site offers dozens of pamphlets about disorders of the brain and nervous system. There are pamphlets about attention deficit disorder, autism, carpal tunnel syndrome, epilepsy, headaches, learning disabilities, multiple sclerosis, muscular dystrophy, Parkinson's disease, post-polio syndrome, restless legs, sleep apnea, spinal cord injury, and many other topics.

One of the site's highlights is its extensive collection of documents about stroke. They provide information about prevention, warning signs, risk factors, clinical trials, recovery, and research.

The site also has information about training programs, clinical studies, employment and grant announcements, and press releases.

Vital Stats:

Access method:	WWW
To access:	http://www.ninds.nih.gov
E-mail:	NINDSWebAdmin@nih.gov

National Sudden Infant Death Syndrome Resource Center

This site has background information about Sudden Infant Death Syndrome, details about state SIDS programs around the country, and a bibliography of materials about infant positioning and SIDS. It also has several major publications: *After Sudden Infant Death Syndrome: Facing Anniversaries, Holidays, and Special Events; The Death of a Child, The Grief of the Parents: A Lifetime Journey;* and *Sudden Infant Death Syndrome: Trying to Understand the Mystery.*

The center is operated by the Maternal and Child Health Bureau, which is part of the Department of Health and Human Services.

Vital Stats:

Access method:	WWW
To access:	http://www.circsol.com/SIDS
E-mail:	info@circsol.com

National Women's Health Information Center (NWHIC)

The National Women's Health Information Center site has answers to dozens of frequently asked questions about women's health, a database with contact information for women's health organizations, information about women's health-related legislation introduced in Congress, a calendar of women's health conferences and meetings, and links to many other health sites. The center is sponsored by the U.S. Public Health Service's Office on Women's Health.

Vital Stats:

Access method:	WWW
To access:	http://www.4woman.gov
E-mail:	4woman@soza.com

Office of Alternative Medicine

The highlight of this site is a database containing bibliographic citations for 90,000 articles, books, and other items about complementary and alternative medicine published from 1966 to 1997. It's operated by the Office of Alternative Medicine (OAM), which is part of the National Institutes of Health.

The site also has background information about various alternative medical treatments, answers to frequently asked questions about complementary and alternative medicine, a calendar of complementary and alternative medicine events worldwide, bibliographies about acupuncture and the treatment of chronic pain and insomnia, a list of specialty centers that are conducting research in the field, a list of OAM-funded research, a quarterly newsletter, and press releases.

Vital Stats:

Access method:	WWW
To access:	http://altmed.od.nih.gov
E-mail:	oam-info@altmed.od.nih.gov

Office of Animal Care and Use

This site is aimed at National Institutes of Health (NIH) employees, but it offers technical information that is helpful to anyone interested in the use of animals in biomedical research. Eighteen of the twenty-five NIH components use animals in their research.

Among the site's highlights are a lengthy publication from the National Research Council titled *Guide for the Care and Use of Laboratory Animals,* numerous NIH policy manuals on caring for animals and using them in research, and links to lots of related sites.

Vital Stats:

Access method:	WWW
To access:	http://oacu.od.nih.gov

Office of Disease Prevention

The Office of Disease Prevention site offers dozens of Consensus Development Statements on various medical topics. The statements, which result from National Institutes of Health conferences, evaluate scientific information related to biomedical technology.

There are statements about rehabilitation of persons with traumatic brain injury, diagnosis and treatment of attention deficit hyperactivity disorder, medical treatment of opiate addiction, acupuncture, genetic testing for cystic fibrosis, interventions to prevent HIV risk behaviors, breast cancer screening for women ages forty to forty-nine, and physical activity and cardiovascular health.

Other statements address optimal calcium intake, mortality and morbidity of dialysis, early identification of hearing impairment in infants and young children, impotence, diagnosis and treatment of early melanoma, diagnosis and treatment of depression in late life, and treatment of panic disorder, among other subjects.

Vital Stats:

Access method:	WWW
To access:	http://odp.od.nih.gov
E-mail:	webmaster@www.nih.gov

Office of Disease Prevention and Health Promotion

This site has the report *Nutrition and Your Health: Dietary Guidelines for Americans* and information about the Healthy People 2010 initiative. It's operated by the Office of Disease Prevention and Health Promotion.

Vital Stats:

Access method:	WWW
To access:	http://www.odphp.osophs.dhhs.gov
E-mail:	dbaker@osophs.dhhs.gov

Office of Minority Health Resource Center

The Office of Minority Health Resource Center offers the *Minority Health Resource Pocket Guide,* which lists federal and state minority health officials, federal health information centers and clearinghouses, national minority organizations, sources of health materials for minority populations, and minority-based colleges and universities.

The site also has information about services available from the center, legislative news, grant information, a calendar of events and conferences, a bimonthly newsletter titled *Closing the Gap,* searchable databases containing bibliographic information for publications about minority health, and the *Funding Guide,* which has information about grants and funding resources, state resources, the top twenty-five foundations, and writing proposals.

In addition, the site has a list of seventy health-related federal information centers and clearinghouses, listings of health professionals who volunteer to provide technical assistance to community-based organizations that are active in minority health issues, and a publication titled *Breast Cancer and Minorities: A Resource Guide.*

Vital Stats:

Access method:	WWW
To access:	http://www.omhrc.gov
E-mail:	lmosby@omhrc.gov

Office of Rare Diseases

The Office of Rare Diseases site has a list of about 2,000 rare diseases, a searchable database of current clinical trials involving rare diseases, news about research results, a calendar of events, and links to other Internet sites that provide information about rare diseases. The office is part of the National Institutes of Health.

Vital Stats:

Access method: WWW
To access: http://rarediseases.info.nih.gov/ord
E-mail: ordcomments@icic.nci.nih.gov

Organ Donation

This site seeks to promote organ and tissue donation. It's operated by the U.S. Department of Health and Human Services.

The site has an organ donor card that you can download and fill out, details about how to become an organ donor, answers to frequently asked questions, a discussion of common myths about organ and tissue donation, weekly U.S. transplantation statistics, a glossary of terms, extensive information about the National Organ and Tissue Donation Initiative, and links to related Web sites.

Vital Stats:

Access method: WWW
To access: http://www.organdonor.gov
E-mail: rlaeng@hrsa.dhhs.gov

Osteoporosis and Related Bone Diseases National Resource Center

This site provides information about osteoporosis, Paget's disease, osteogenesis imperfecta, hyperparathyroidism, fibrous dysplasia, and hypophosphatasia. It's operated by the Osteoporosis and Related Bone Diseases National Resource Center, which is supported by the National Institute of Arthritis and Musculoskeletal and Skin Diseases.

One of the site's highlights is a collection of two dozen fact sheets about alcohol and bone disorders, African American women and osteoporosis, biochemical markers of bone metabolism, depression and bone loss, fall prevention for older adults, peak bone mass in women, psychosocial consequences of osteoporosis, and women in clinical trials, among other subjects.

The site also provides more than two dozen bibliographies. They cover such topics as bone density and bone mass, calcium, eating disorders and bone density, estrogen and bone loss, exercise and postmenopausal women, female athletes and bone health, and men and osteoporosis.

Vital Stats:

Access method: WWW
To access: http://www.osteo.org
E-mail: orbdnrc@nof.org

GULF WAR ILLNESS

GulfLINK

GulfLINK offers a huge collection of information about illnesses that have struck veterans of the war in the Persian Gulf, which began with Iraq's invasion of Kuwait in August 1990 and ended in February 1991. The site is operated by the Office of the Special Assistant for Gulf War Illnesses in the Defense Department.

One of the site's highlights is an assortment of more than 40,000 recently declassified intelligence, medical, and operational documents from the gulf war. The documents include directives, plans, status reports, daily mission reports, logistics summaries, and personnel reports, among others.

GulfLINK also offers reports about gulf war illness from various government agencies, documents about medical research, case narratives of specific events during the gulf war, information about help available for veterans, testimony before congressional committees, narratives of various services' actions in the war, a map of the Persian Gulf theater, bibliographies about gulf war illness, and lots more.

The GulfLINK mailing list notifies subscribers when new documents are added to the site. You can sign up by going to the page at http://www.gulflink.osd.mil/mail_list.html.

Vital Stats:

Access method:	WWW
To access:	http://www.gulflink.osd.mil
E-mail:	brostker@gwillness.osd.mil

The Missing GulfLINK Files

This site has several hundred U.S. Department of Defense documents about the possible release of Iraqi chemical and biological weapons during the 1991 Persian Gulf war. It's operated by Insignia Publishing Company, a private firm.

The documents are part of a larger group that the Defense Department originally posted on its GulfLINK Internet site in July 1995. After the CIA complained that some of the documents were released too quickly and provided sensitive information, the Defense Department removed more than 300 of them. After another review, the department reposted nearly 100 of the documents in August 1996.

In November 1996 Insignia posted the full text of the more than 300 original documents on its Web site. You can read the documents individually or download the entire collection at once.

Vital Stats:

Access method:	WWW
To access:	http://www.insigniausa.com/resource/gulflink/gulflink.htm
E-mail:	InsigniaPC@aol.com

Presidential Advisory Committee on Gulf War Veterans' Illnesses

The Presidential Advisory Committee on Gulf War Veterans' Illnesses site has several reports by the committee, transcripts of committee hearings, and background information about the committee and its members.

Vital Stats:

Access method: WWW

To access: http://www.gwvi.gov

HUMAN RADIATION EXPERIMENTS

Human Radiation Experiments Information Management System (HREX)

This site provides searchable databases containing more than 250,000 pages of historical documents about human radiation experiments conducted during the cold war. The declassified documents originated with the Central Intelligence Agency and the departments of Defense, Energy, Health and Human Services, and Veterans Affairs. HREX is operated by the Energy Department.

Vital Stats:

Access method:	WWW
To access:	http://hrex.dis.anl.gov
E-mail:	hrex@dis.anl.gov

Office of Human Radiation Experiments

The Office of Human Radiation Experiments site offers extensive information about human radiation experiments conducted during the cold war. The office is part of the Energy Department.

The site provides the full text of recently declassified documents, oral histories with researchers involved in human radiation experiments, historical photographs, an Energy Department report that summarizes more than 400 human radiation experiments, descriptions of record sets about human radiation experiments located at various federal facilities, and links to other Internet sites that have information about the subject.

Vital Stats:

Access method:	WWW
To access:	http://tis.eh.doe.gov/ohre

MENTAL HEALTH

ALZHEIMER

The ALZHEIMER mailing list is designed for patients, caregivers, researchers, policy makers, students, and anyone else interested in Alzheimer's disease or related disorders. The list is operated by Washington University's Alzheimer Disease Research Center and supported by a grant from the National Institute on Aging.

Vital Stats:

Access method:	E-mail
To access:	Send an e-mail message to majordomo@wubios.wustl.edu
Subject line:	
Message:	**subscribe alzheimer**
E-mail (questions):	alzheimer-owner@wubios.wustl.edu

ALZHEIMER Page

The ALZHEIMER Page has an archive of messages posted to the ALZHEIMER mailing list (previous entry), links to dozens of other Internet sites about aging and dementia, and information about new Internet sites about the subjects. It's operated by Washington University's Alzheimer Disease Research Center and supported by a grant from the National Institute on Aging.

Vital Stats:

Access method:	WWW
To access:	http://www.biostat.wustl.edu/ALZHEIMER
E-mail:	alzheimer-owner@wubios.wustl.edu

Alzheimer's Disease Education and Referral Center

This National Institute on Aging site provides extensive information about Alzheimer's disease and related dementias.

The site has background information about Alzheimer's, reports about progress in unraveling the mysteries of Alzheimer's, information about Alzheimer's Disease Centers around the country that are conducting research, press releases about recent research results, a quarterly newsletter from the center, a list of publications that can be ordered from the center, a calendar of events, links to other federal Internet sites that provide information about Alzheimer's, and a link to another federal Internet site that has a database containing references to more than 4,000 books, articles, and other items about Alzheimer's.

National Institute of Mental Health

This site offers numerous publications about various types of mental illness. Some of the available titles are *Depression: Effective Treatments are Available; Plain Talk about Depression; Getting Treatment for Panic Disorder; Understanding Panic Disorder; Alzheimer's Disease; Attention Deficit Hyperactivity Disorder; Eating Disorders; Learning Disabilities; Medications— Mental Health/Mental Illness; Obsessive-Compulsive Disorder; Suicide Facts;* and *You Are Not Alone—Mental Health/Mental Illness.*

The site also has a report titled *Mental Illness in America: The NIMH Agenda;* background information about the NIMH, including a list of telephone contacts; information about NIMH studies that are seeking patients; and a huge calendar of mental health meetings.

National Mental Health Services Knowledge Exchange Network

This site provides information about prevention, treatment, and rehabilitation services for mental illness. It's operated by the National Center for Mental Health Services, which is part of the U.S. Department of Health and Human Services.

The site has fact sheets about alternative approaches to mental health care, anxiety disorders, choosing a therapist, eating disorders, mood disorders, paying for mental health services, schizophrenia, and related topics.

It also has a pamphlet about what to look for in managed mental health care, publications about mental health parity, papers about helping victims of natural disasters, a calendar of mental health conferences and events, statistics about mental health, and information about and links to research centers and clearinghouses on mental health issues.

In addition, it offers a database containing information about more than 2,000 organizations and government agencies that provide mental health services, a directory of organizations that provide psychiatric treatment, a database containing names and contact information for people interested in mental health issues, and a huge collection of links to other mental health resources on the Internet.

Substance Abuse and Mental Health Services Administration

The Substance Abuse and Mental Health Services Administration (SAMHSA) site has statistics about substance abuse and mental health, information about SAMHSA programs, and a calendar of managed care events. It also has grant information and a weekly report from SAMHSA about the status of legislation, upcoming conferences, grants, and new publications.

Vital Stats:

Access method: WWW
To access: http://www.samhsa.gov
E-mail: info@samhsa.gov

HISTORY

c.1492
c.1776
c.1861
c.1968
c.2000

Advisory Council on Historic Preservation

The Advisory Council on Historic Preservation site has background information about the national historic preservation program, the full text of the National Historic Preservation Act of 1966, an introduction to federal historic preservation laws, a list of state historic preservation officers, a calendar of historic preservation events, and a staff directory. The council is an independent federal agency.

Vital Stats:

Access method: WWW
To access: http://www.achp.gov
E-mail: achp@achp.gov

American Memory

Thousands of treasures from the Library of Congress collection are available through the American Memory site. It offers prints, photographs, documents, motion pictures, and sound recordings. The site is constantly being expanded, but here's a sample of what's available:

- More than 350 pamphlets written by African Americans between Reconstruction and the First World War.

- About 29,000 photographs of buildings, interiors, and gardens of renowned architects and interior designers taken from 1935 to 1955.

- More than 1,100 Civil War photographs taken by Mathew Brady and his assistants.

- Photographs, documents, and manuscripts documenting the conservation movement in the United States from 1850 to 1920.

- Printed broadsides from the Continental Congress and the Constitutional Convention.

- More than 600 daguerreotypes taken from 1842 to 1862 by the Mathew Brady studio.

- More than 25,000 photographs of turn-of-the-century America from the Detroit Publishing Company.

- Photographs of rural America during the 1930s and of the defense and war mobilization effort from 1939 to 1944.

- Transcripts of interviews from the Federal Writers' Project, 1936–1940.

- Motion pictures from 1897 to 1916 of New York City, San Francisco before and after the earthquake, the Westinghouse Works, and President William McKinley at the Buffalo World's Fair.

- Portraits taken by Carl Van Vechten from 1932 to 1964.

- Portraits of presidents and first ladies from 1789 to the present.

- Recordings of political speeches by American leaders during World War I and the 1920 election.

- Photographs, playbills, and motion pictures related to vaudeville and popular entertainment from 1870 to 1920.

- Books, pamphlets, and other artifacts from the campaign for woman suffrage, 1848–1921.
- Four notebooks from Walt Whitman.
- More than 14,000 photographs of Washington, D.C., from 1923 to 1959.
- Materials about Jackie Robinson and the history of baseball in general.
- Nearly 200 books containing first-person narratives about experiences in California during and after the Gold Rush.
- About 4,000 panoramic views of American main streets, landscapes, bathing beauties, disasters, and other events, taken between 1851 and 1991.
- Railroad maps of North America.
- Motion pictures made from 1898 to 1901 of the Spanish-American War and the Philippine Insurrection.
- George Washington's papers at the Library of Congress. The holdings include about 65,000 items created from 1741 to 1799.

Vital Stats:

Access method:	WWW
To access:	http://memory.loc.gov
E-mail:	ndlpcoll@loc.gov

The Architect of the Capitol Home Page

The Architect of the Capitol Home Page has a history of the Capitol building, pictures and documents about historic rooms in the Capitol, a description and history of the Capitol grounds, a map of the Capitol complex, details about visiting the Capitol, and information about the U.S. Botanic Garden.

Vital Stats:

Access method:	WWW
To access:	http://www.aoc.gov
E-mail:	feedback@aoc.gov

Franklin D. Roosevelt Library and Museum

The Franklin D. Roosevelt Library and Museum offers extensive background information about Franklin and Eleanor Roosevelt, more than 1,000 photos of them, information for researchers, and a list of library collections.

Vital Stats:

Access method:	WWW
To access:	http://www.academic.marist.edu/fdr
E-mail:	library@roosevelt.nara.gov

George Bush Presidential Library and Museum

The complete public papers of George Bush's presidency are available at this site. They consist primarily of speeches, White House statements, and press conference transcripts. You can browse the collection by month or use keywords to search all of it.

The site also has biographies of George and Barbara Bush, photographs from Bush's presidency, videos of a dozen of Bush's major speeches, information about conducting research at the library, and information about visiting the library, which is located in College Station, Texas.

Vital Stats:

Access method:	WWW
To access:	http://csdl.tamu.edu/bushlib/bushpage.html
E-mail:	library@bush.nara.gov

Images from the History of Medicine

This site provides nearly 60,000 historical medical images. The reproduced photographs, artworks, and printed texts are from the collection of the National Library of Medicine, which operates the site. The images include portraits, pictures of institutions, caricatures, genre scenes, and graphic art.

Vital Stats:

Access method:	WWW
To access:	http://wwwihm.nlm.nih.gov
E-mail:	hmdref@nlm.nih.gov

Jimmy Carter Library

This site has a guide to the holdings of the Jimmy Carter Library, the text of selected Carter speeches, a chronology of Carter's administration, oral history interviews with more than a dozen people, and a link to hundreds of photographs from Carter's presidency.

It also includes biographies of Jimmy and Rosalynn Carter, information about conducting research at the library, bibliographies of materials about the 1976 and 1980 presidential campaigns, and a bibliography of selected books about Carter's presidency.

Vital Stats:

Access method:	WWW
To access:	http://carterlibrary.galileo.peachnet.edu
E-mail:	library@carter.nara.gov

John F. Kennedy Library Home Page

The John F. Kennedy Library Home Page has a biography of Kennedy for young people, photographs, excerpts from recordings of speeches by Kennedy, an online exhibit about Jacqueline Bouvier Kennedy, and the text of speeches by John, Robert, and Edward Kennedy. The site also has catalogs of manuscripts, oral histories, audiovisual materials, the Ernest Hemingway Collection, and printed materials in the library's collection.

Vital Stats:

Access method:	WWW
To access:	http://www.cs.umb.edu/jfklibrary
E-mail:	library@kennedy.nara.gov

The Lyndon B. Johnson Library and Museum

When it's completed, this site will provide extensive information about the holdings of the Lyndon B. Johnson Library and Museum in Texas. The library's collection includes more than 44 million documents, a large holding of audiovisual material, and oral history interviews with more than 1,000 people.

A few items from the museum's collection are available online, and more will be added as the site is further developed. For now, there are a few transcripts of oral histories of people associated with Johnson, selected speeches by Johnson, and about a dozen photographs of Johnson and events in his presidency.

Vital Stats:

Access method:	WWW
To access:	http://www.lbjlib.utexas.edu
E-mail:	library@johnson.nara.gov

National Archives and Records Administration

The National Archives and Records Administration offers an amazing collection of research guides, online exhibits, databases, lesson plans, and other materials at this site.

Perhaps the most important feature is the NARA Archival Information Locator (NAIL), a searchable database with descriptions and copies of some of NARA's holdings. It's the working prototype of a future online catalog of all NARA holdings nationwide. The database currently has descriptions of nearly 374,000 documents, photographs, maps, and sound recordings, and digital copies of 83,000 items.

Another highlight is an excellent collection of brief publications for people doing genealogical research. The publications available include *Beginning Your Genealogical Research, Clues in Census Records 1850–1920, Immigration Records, Naturalization Records, Civil War Records,* and *Confederate Pension Records.* To provide further help with genealogical research, the site has catalogs of microfilm publications of census records, military service records, immigrant and passenger arrival records, and other items.

The site also has databases containing complete casualty lists for the Vietnam War and the Korean War, a database that contains descriptions of more than 170,000 documents related to the assassination of John F. Kennedy, and online exhibits that change regularly. When this book was being written, there were exhibits about World War II posters, the Declaration of Independence, the meeting of Richard M. Nixon and Elvis Presley, and other subjects.

Other features include the full text of the *Guide to Federal Records in the National Archives of the United States*, which has detailed information about records in the Archives' collection; schedules for lectures and book signings at the National Archives; information about presidential libraries and their holdings; information for archivists and records managers; and lots, lots more.

Vital Stats:

Access method:	WWW
To access:	http://www.nara.gov
E-mail:	webmaster@nara.gov (for questions about the site) or inquire@nara.gov (for research questions)

U.S. Colored Troops

A database at this site provides basic personal information about more than 230,000 soldiers who served in the U.S. Colored Troops during the Civil War. The site is operated by the National Park Service.

For each soldier, the database lists the first and last name, unit, company, rank when joined and left the military, and the number of the National Archives microfilm roll where further information is available.

The site also provides very limited information about 180 U.S. Colored Troops units and regiments, links to Web sites operated by National Park Service sites that are associated with African American history during the Civil War, links to Web sites of other Civil War battlefields, and information about how to obtain service records for Union and Confederate soldiers from the National Archives.

Eventually, the site will have basic personal information about every soldier who fought in the Civil War.

Vital Stats:

Access method:	WWW
To access:	http://www.itd.nps.gov/cwss/usct.html

JOBS AND EMPLOYMENT

JOBS

America's Career InfoNet

This site has a wide range of background information for job seekers. It's a service of America's Job Bank (next entry), which is a joint project of the U.S. Department of Labor and state Employment Services offices around the country.

It provides a brief description, an employment outlook, and average earnings for numerous occupations; basic demographic information for each state; and information about trends in the U.S. job market, including the fastest-growing occupations, occupations with the largest employment, occupations with declining employment, the highest paying occupations, and nontraditional occupations.

One of the site's highlights is the Career Resource Library, which provides annotated links to other sites about career paths, professional associations and labor unions, employment trends, businesses, relocating, education and training, salaries and wages, and related issues.

Vital Stats:

Access method:	WWW
To access:	http://www.acinet.org

America's Job Bank

America's Job Bank is a one-stop source for information about job openings nationwide. Job seekers also can enter electronic resumes for employers to search. The site is a joint project of the U.S. Department of Labor and state Employment Services offices around the country.

The site provides details about thousands of job openings. You can search the listings by using menus, keywords, or occupational codes. You can limit your search to jobs in particular states, or you can search the whole country.

The site also has publications about how to use the Internet for a job search and how to prepare your resume for the Internet, links to more than 1,000 Web sites operated by companies that are seeking employees, and links to Web sites operated by state Employment Services offices.

Vital Stats:

Access method:	WWW
To access:	http://www.ajb.dni.us

The Corporation for National Service

The Corporation for National Service site has background information about the federally sponsored domestic volunteer programs that the corporation oversees. They include AmeriCorps, Learn and Serve America, the National Senior Service Corps, and America Reads.

Vital Stats:

Access method:	WWW
To access:	http://www.cns.gov
E-mail:	eschmidt@cns.gov

Office of Personnel Management Home Page

The home page of the Office of Personnel Management (OPM) offers a huge collection of information about working for the federal government. It has federal salary tables, a list of more than 8,000 jobs filled by political appointments, a guide to buyouts of federal employees, regulations under the Family and Medical Leave Act, a guide that explains the special rights available to veterans in federal civil service employment, *Federal Register* notices, information about OPM workshops, and lots more.

Vital Stats:

Access method:	WWW
To access:	http://www.opm.gov
E-mail:	webmaster@opm.gov

Planning Your Future: A Federal Employee's Survival Guide

Although this site is aimed at federal employees who have been downsized, it offers useful information for anyone who is looking for a job. The site was created by employees of numerous federal agencies and is hosted by the U.S. Department of Labor.

Primarily through links to other sites, it has information about using the Internet in your job search, going back to school, preparing resumes and cover letters, researching the job market, and starting your own business. Other topics covered include federal retirement benefits, financial aspects of retirement, buyouts, and health and stress-related issues, among others.

A special section at the site has resources for career transition professionals.

Vital Stats:

Access method:	WWW
To access:	http://safetynet.doleta.gov
E-mail:	webmaster@doleta.gov

USA Jobs

USA Jobs, which is operated by the Office of Personnel Management, is the best Internet source for information about federal jobs.

USA Jobs has lists of federal job openings in the United States and overseas. The lists are updated daily. You can search the listings by type of job, location, and pay level. Once you locate a job of interest, you can apply online.

The site also has information about searching for a federal job, federal employment overseas, employment of people with disabilities, employment of veterans, student employment, federal salary and benefits, outplacement assistance, and other issues. It also has a downloadable version of the optional federal application, form OF-612.

Vital Stats:

Access method: WWW
To access: http://www.usajobs.opm.gov
E-mail: usajobs_webmaster@opm.gov

LABOR LAWS AND REGULATIONS

Job Accommodation Network (JAN)

Extensive information about the Americans with Disabilities Act (ADA) is available from the Job Accommodation Network (JAN). The site, which is a service of the President's Committee on Employment of People with Disabilities, has the text of the ADA, regulations, technical assistance manuals, information about how to file ADA complaints, publications about working with employees who have various disabilities, information about reasonable accommodation under the ADA, links to other Internet sites that offer disability and health information, and much more.

Vital Stats:

Access method:	WWW
To access:	http://janweb.icdi.wvu.edu
E-mail:	jan@jan.icdi.wvu.edu

National Labor Relations Board

The National Labor Relations Board site has decisions and orders of the board, background information about the NLRB, searchable versions of the board's Rules and Regulations, a list of field offices, the text of the National Labor Relations Act, and *Federal Register* notices.

The site also provides decisions of NLRB administrative law judges and the *Weekly Summary of NLRB Cases,* which summarizes all published NLRB decisions in unfair labor practice and representation election cases. The newsletter has links to the full text of the decisions.

Vital Stats:

Access method:	WWW
To access:	http://www.nlrb.gov
E-mail:	dbparker@nlrb.gov

Occupational Safety and Health Administration Home Page

The home page of the Occupational Safety and Health Administration (OSHA) has a wide range of information about protecting employees in the workplace. It offers dozens of safety-related fact sheets and numerous publications, including *Handbook for Small Business, Consultation Services for the Employer, Employee Workplace Rights, Employer Rights and Responsibilities, Federal Employer Rights and Responsibilities Following an OSHA Inspection, How to Prepare for Workplace Emergencies,* and *Guidelines for Workplace Violence Prevention Programs for Night Retail Establishments.* Another large collection of OSHA materials is available from the OSHA Technical Links site (p. 235).

The home page also has workplace injury and illness statistics, an OSHA report titled *The New OSHA—Reinventing Worker Safety and Health,* a searchable database of OSHA fact sheets, the full text of OSHA regulations, compliance guides and directives, a directory of OSHA offices around the country, press releases, speeches and congressional testimony by OSHA officials, and the full text of the Occupational Safety and Health Act of 1970.

In addition, it has lists of free publications available from OSHA, a list of states that conduct their own occupational safety and health inspections under plans approved by OSHA, a searchable database called "Frequently Cited OSHA Standards" that lets you determine the most frequently violated OSHA standards for a particular SIC code, links to other Internet sites that offer safety and health information, and lots more.

Vital Stats:

Access method:	WWW
To access:	http://www.osha.gov
E-mail:	suggest@osha-slc.gov

Pension Benefit Guaranty Corporation

The Pension Benefit Guaranty Corporation site has a pamphlet titled *Your Guaranteed Pension,* a searchable database of people who are owed pensions but cannot be found by employers, and proposed and final regulations. The PBGC insures the pensions of nearly 42 million people.

The site also includes the PBGC's annual report, congressional testimony and speeches by PBGC officials, background information about the agency, and a database of opinion letters from the Office of General Counsel.

Vital Stats:

Access method:	WWW
To access:	http://www.pbgc.gov
E-mail:	webmaster@pbgc.gov

President's Committee on Employment of People with Disabilities

This site offers dozens of fact sheets and other publications for businesses about the Americans with Disabilities Act and disability employment issues. It's operated by the President's Committee on Employment of People with Disabilities.

Some of the available publications include *Communicating With and About People with Disabilities, What to Do if You Have Been Discriminated Against, Essential Elements of an Effective Job Search, Myths and Facts about People with Disabilities, Guidelines for Conducting a Job Interview,* and *Cost and Benefits of Accommodations.*

The site also has background information about the committee and its projects, a list of state liaisons, speeches, press releases, and links to Web sites operated by companies that are interested in hiring people with disabilities.

Vital Stats:

Access method:	WWW
To access:	http://www.pcepd.gov
E-mail:	info@pcepd.gov

Technical Links

This site has information about hazards found in specific industries, how to recognize hazards, and how to evaluate and control them. The site, which is operated by the Occupational Health and Safety Administration, provides information through original documents and links to related Web sites. The site complements the Occupational Safety and Health Administration Home Page (p. 233).

Most of the information is divided into pages by technical subjects. Some of the topics covered are asbestos, carcinogens, ergonomics, fall prevention, fire safety, hand and power tools, hazardous waste, heat stress, indoor air quality, latex allergy, needlestick injuries, noise and hearing conservation, personal protective equipment, radiofrequency radiation, reproductive hazards, solvents, video display terminals, and workplace violence.

Other pages address hazards in specific industries. There are pages about agricultural operations, general construction, health care facilities, logging, meat packing, nursing homes, oil and well gas drilling, ship building and repair, and textiles, among other industries.

Vital Stats:

Access method:	WWW
To access:	http://www.osha-slc.gov/SLTC
E-mail:	webmaster@osha-slc.gov

United States Department of Labor

The United States Department of Labor site has hundreds of documents about the workplace, including information about the minimum wage law, extensive details about the Family and Medical Leave Act, tips for avoiding clothes made in sweatshops, several reports about the use of child labor around the world, and documents about corporate citizenship.

It also has the *Small Business Handbook,* publications about the rights of women in the workplace, grant and procurement information for nonprofit organizations, publications about substance abuse in the workplace, *Federal Register* notices, summaries of laws and regulations enforced by the Labor Department, the sections of the Code of Federal Regulations that apply to the Labor Department, compliance materials for employers, and reports titled *Genetic Information and the Workplace, A Look at Employers' Costs of Providing Health Benefits, Working Together for Public Service, Care around the Clock: Developing Child Care Resources Before Nine and After Five,* and *Making Work Pay: The Case for Raising the Minimum Wage.*

In addition, it offers speeches and congressional testimony by Labor Department officials, press releases, and links to Internet sites operated by Labor Department agencies such as the Bureau of Labor Statistics, the Mine Safety and Health Administration, and the Occupational Safety and Health Administration.

Vital Stats:

Access method: WWW
To access: http://www.dol.gov
E-mail: webmaster@dol.com

U.S. Equal Employment Opportunity Commission

This site features information about how to file a job-related complaint with the Equal Employment Opportunity Commission (EEOC) alleging discrimination based on race, color, sex, religion, national origin, age, or disability.

One of its most useful features is a collection of fact sheets that describe what constitutes sexual harassment, racial discrimination, age discrimination, national origin discrimination, pregnancy discrimination, religious discrimination, and discrimination against people with disabilities. A special page offers information about the Americans with Disabilities Act, including publications titled *Your Responsibilities as an Employer* and *Your Employment Rights as an Individual with a Disability.*

The site also has the texts of laws enforced by the EEOC, including Title VII of the Civil Rights Act of 1964, the Equal Pay Act of 1963, the Age Discrimination Employment Act of 1967, Sections 501 and 505 of the Rehabilitation Act of 1973, Titles I and V of the Americans with Disabilities Act of 1990, and the Civil Rights Act of 1991.

Other highlights include guidance for small businesses about how to comply with equal employment opportunity laws, new and proposed regulations, enforcement statistics, press releases about EEOC suits and settlements, contact information for EEOC field offices around the country, background information about the commission, links to related sites, and a report titled *"Best" Equal Employment Opportunity Policies, Programs, and Practices in the Private Sector.*

Vital Stats:

Access method: WWW
To access: http://www.eeoc.gov

WorkNet@IRL

WorkNet@IRL offers the full text of numerous federal reports about women in the workplace, child labor, and other labor issues. It's operated by the School of Industrial and Labor Relations at Cornell University.

The site offers reports by the Commission on the Future of Worker-Management Relations (Dunlop Commission), the Glass Ceiling Commission, the Commission on Family and Medical Leave, the Labor Department's International Child Labor Study Office, the National Commission on Retirement Policy, and the Task Force on Excellence in State and Local Government through Labor-Management Cooperation.

Vital Stats:

Access method: WWW
To access: http://www.ilr.cornell.edu/lib/bookshelf.html
E-mail: cf13@cornell.edu

LAW AND JUSTICE

COURTS

The Federal Judicial Center Home Page

The Federal Judicial Center Home Page offers a great collection of books and reports about judicial topics, extensive background information about the center, and links to other Internet sites that have federal court opinions, Supreme Court rules, the Federal Rules of Evidence, and publications from the Bureau of Justice Statistics. The Federal Judicial Center, which was created by Congress, is the federal courts' agency for research and continuing education.

The books and reports cover such topics as arbitration, attorneys' fees, civil litigation, sentencing guidelines, mandatory minimum prison terms, electronic media coverage of federal courts, diversity in the courts, scientific evidence, the history of federal courts, and the role of gender in the federal courts, among others.

Vital Stats:

Access method: WWW
To access: http://www.fjc.gov
E-mail: webmaster@fjc.gov

The Federal Judiciary Homepage

The Federal Judiciary Homepage, which is operated by the Administrative Office of the U.S. Courts, provides limited information about the federal court system.

It has a document titled *Understanding the Federal Courts,* a report about wiretaps, a directory of bulletin board systems and automated voice response systems operated by federal courts, a long-range plan by the Judicial Conference of the United States, selected articles from the monthly newsletter of the federal courts, press releases about such topics as court caseloads and bankruptcy filings, and answers to frequently asked questions about federal judges, filing a case, jury duty, and other topics.

Vital Stats:

Access method: WWW
To access: http://www.uscourts.gov

FindLaw

The FindLaw site provides a searchable database of U.S. Supreme Court opinions from 1893 to the present. It's operated by FindLaw, a private company.

You can browse the database by year and *United States Reports* volume number, and you can search it by citation, case title, and keywords. The cases are in HTML format and have hyperlinks to those previous decisions that have been loaded on the site.

The site also has a copy of the U.S. Constitution that has hyperlinks to Supreme Court decisions through June 29, 1992, and links to lots of other Internet sites that offer Supreme Court information.

Vital Stats:

Access method:	WWW
To access:	http://www.findlaw.com/casecode/supreme.html
E-mail:	write@findlaw.com

Georgetown University Legal Explorer

Opinions from the U.S. Court of Appeals for the District of Columbia Circuit and the U.S. Court of Appeals for the Federal Circuit are provided by the Georgetown University Legal Explorer. Opinions from the D.C. Circuit are available from March 1995 to the present, and opinions from the Federal Circuit are available from August 1995 to the present. The site is operated by the Edward Bennett Williams Law Library at Georgetown University.

Vital Stats:

Access method:	WWW
To access:	http://www.ll.georgetown.edu/lr/lg/justice.html
E-mail:	webweavr@law.georgetown.edu

Law Journal Extra!

The Law Journal Extra! site offers the full text of decisions from all the U.S. Circuit Courts of Appeals since November 1995. The cases are separated by circuit. The site is operated by the New York Law Publishing Company, a private legal publisher.

Vital Stats:

Access method:	WWW
To access:	http://www.ljextra.com/courthouse/feddec.html
E-mail:	feedback@ljextra.com

Legal Information Institute

The Legal Information Institute site provides U.S. Supreme Court decisions, the *Federal Rules of Evidence,* the *Federal Rules of Civil Procedure,* and much more. It's operated by the Cornell Law School.

Of particular interest is a page that has links to recent newsworthy decisions of state and federal courts around the country. To reach the page directly, use the address http://www.law.cornell.edu/focus/liieye.htm.

The site's highlight is undoubtedly its collection of U.S. Supreme Court decisions from May 1990 to the present. New decisions are posted the same day they're released by the

Court. The institute also operates a mailing list called liibulletin (next entry) that sends out syllabi of Supreme Court decisions as they're placed on the Internet.

In addition to recent Supreme Court decisions, the site offers nearly 600 historic pre-1990 Supreme Court decisions in cases involving such topics as school prayer, abortion, administrative law, copyright, and trademarks; the Court's current calendar; a schedule of oral arguments; Supreme Court rules; and pictures, biographies, and lists of decisions by current Court members.

The site also has the full text of the U.S. Constitution, the U.S. Code as of January 1996, and Articles 1–9 of the Uniform Commercial Code.

Vital Stats:

Access method:	WWW
To access:	http://www.law.cornell.edu
E-mail:	lii@law.mail.cornell.edu

---

liibulletin

The liibulletin is a mailing list that sends out syllabi of U.S. Supreme Court decisions as they're placed on the Internet, along with instructions about how to obtain the full text of the decisions. The list is operated by Cornell Law School's Legal Information Institute (previous entry).

Vital Stats:

Access method:	E-mail
To access:	Send an e-mail message to listserv@listserv.law.cornell.edu
Subject line:	
Message:	**subscribe liibulletin** *your name, address, phone*
E-mail (questions):	liibulletin-owner@listserv.law.cornell.edu

---

The Oyez Project

The Oyez Project offers recordings of oral arguments from more than 250 historic Supreme Court cases back to 1956. The site is operated by Northwestern University, with support from the National Endowment for the Humanities and the National Science Foundation.

The recordings are digitized from tapes in the National Archives. To listen to the cases, you must have RealAudio software installed on your computer. Oyez offers a link to another Internet site where you can download the RealAudio software for free.

Some of the cases available are *Planned Parenthood v. Casey, Hustler Magazine v. Falwell, Regents of the University of California v. Bakke, Roe v. Wade, Furman v. Georgia, Griswold v. Connecticut,* and *New York Times v. Sullivan.* The database can be searched by title, citation, subject, and date. For each case, the site provides recordings of oral arguments and text listing the facts of the case, the constitutional question involved, and the Court's conclusion.

Oyez also provides brief biographies of all current and former justices and a virtual tour of the Supreme Court building.

U.S. Bankruptcy and District Courts

Many federal bankruptcy and district courts operate Web sites. The information available varies from site to site, but often includes recent opinions, local court rules, court calendars, dockets, general court orders, job listings, and contact information for judges and clerks.

Vital Stats:

Access method:	WWW
To access:	See box starting on next page

United States Circuit Court of Appeals Decisions

This site lets you search all opinions of U.S. Circuit Courts of Appeals that are available on the Internet. The opinions are loaded on numerous computers, but the search engine lets you search all of them at once with a single query. The site is operated by Cornell University's Legal Information Institute.

Vital Stats:

Access method:	WWW
To access:	http://supct.law.cornell.edu/Harvest/brokers/ circuit-x/fancy.query.html

U.S. Court of Appeals for the Federal Circuit

This site has decisions from the U.S. Court of Appeals for the Federal Circuit from January 1997 to the present. It also has rules for the Federal Circuit, a court calendar, a list of new cases filed in the last ninety days, biographies of the judges, and links to other Internet sites that have older Federal Circuit opinions.

Unfortunately, nearly all the documents—including the opinions—have been compressed in a self-extracting format that makes them unusable on most Macintosh computers.

Vital Stats:

Access method:	WWW
To access:	http://www.fedcir.gov
E-mail:	mcdermottp@cafc.uscourts.gov

Bankruptcy Courts by State and District

Arizona Bankruptcy Court
To access: http://www.azb.uscourts.gov

Arkansas Eastern District Court
To access: http://www.are.uscourts.gov

California Central Bankruptcy Court
To access: http://www.cacb.uscourts.gov

California Central District Court
To access: http://www.cacd.uscourts.gov

California Eastern Bankruptcy Court
To access: http://www.caeb.uscourts.gov

California Eastern District Court
To access: http://www.caed.uscourts.gov

California Eastern Probation Office
To access: http://www.caep.uscourts.gov

California Northern Bankruptcy Court
To access: http://www.canb.uscourts.gov

California Northern District Court
To access: http://www.cand.uscourts.gov

California Southern Bankruptcy Court
To access: http://www.casb.uscourts.gov

Colorado Bankruptcy Court
To access: http://www.ck10.uscourts.gov/
cobk

District of Columbia District Court
To access: http://www.dcd.uscourts.gov

Florida Middle Bankruptcy Court
To access: http://www.flmb.uscourts.gov

Georgia Middle Bankruptcy Court
To access: http://www.gamb.uscourts.gov

Georgia Northern Bankruptcy Court
To access: http://ecf.ganb.uscourts.gov/
index.html

Georgia Northern District Court
To access: http://www.gand.uscourts.gov

Idaho Bankruptcy/District Court
To access: http://www.id.uscourts.gov

Illinois Central District Court
To access: http://www.ilcd.uscourts.gov

Illinois Northern Bankruptcy Court
To access: http://www.ilnb.uscourts.gov

Illinois Northern District Court
To access: http://www.ilnd.uscourts.gov

Illinois Southern Bankruptcy Court
To access: http://home.stlnet.com/
~usbcsdil

Indiana Northern Bankruptcy Court
To access: http://www.innb.uscourts.gov

Indiana Northern District Court
To access: http://www.innd.uscourts.gov

Indiana Southern Bankruptcy Court
To access: http://www.insb.uscourts.gov

Indiana Southern District Court
To access: http://www.insd.uscourts.gov

Iowa Northern Bankruptcy Court
To access: http://www.ianb.uscourts.gov

Iowa Southern District Court
To access: http://www.iasd.uscourts.gov

Kentucky Western District Court
To access: http://www.kywd.uscourts.gov

Louisiana Eastern Bankruptcy Court
To access: http://www.laeb.uscourts.gov

Louisiana Eastern Pretrial Services Office
To access: http://www.laept.uscourts.gov

Louisiana Eastern Probation Office
To access: http://www.laep.uscourts.gov

Louisiana Middle District Court
To access: http://www.lamd.uscourts.gov

Louisiana Western Bankruptcy Court
To access: http://www.lawb.uscourts.gov

Bankruptcy Courts by State and District *(Continued)*

Maine Bankruptcy Court
To access: http://www.meb.uscourts.gov

Maine District Court
To access: http://www.med.uscourts.gov

Maryland District Court
To access: http://www.mdd.uscourts.gov/
city.htm

Massachusetts Bankruptcy Court
To access: http://www.mab.uscourts.gov

Michigan Western Bankruptcy/District Court
To access: http://www.miw.uscourts.gov

Minnesota Bankruptcy Court
To access: http://www.mnb.uscourts.gov

Mississippi Northern District Court
To access: http://www.msnd.uscourts.gov

Mississippi Southern District Court
To access: http://www.mssd.uscourts.gov

Missouri Eastern Bankruptcy Court
To access: http://www.moeb.uscourts.gov

Missouri Eastern District Court
To access: http://www.moed.uscourts.gov

Nebraska District Court
To access: http://www.nfinity.com/
~usdcne

Nevada Bankruptcy Court
To access: http://www.nvb.uscourts.gov

New Mexico Bankruptcy Court
To access: http://www.nmcourt.fed.us/
bkdocs

New Mexico District Court
To access:
http://www.nmcourt.fed.us/dcdocs

New Mexico Pretrial Services
To access: http://www.nmcourt.fed.us/
ptdocs

New Mexico Probation Office
To access: http://www.nmcourt.fed.us/
pbdocs

New York Eastern District Court
To access: http://www.nyed.uscourts.gov

New York Northern Bankruptcy Court
To access: http://www.nynb.uscourts.gov

New York Northern District Court
To access: http://www.nynd.uscourts.gov

New York Southern Bankruptcy Court
To access: http://www.nysb.uscourts.gov

New York Southern District Court
To access: http://www.nysd.uscourts.gov

North Carolina Eastern Bankruptcy Court
To access: http://www.nceb.uscourts.gov

North Carolina Middle Bankruptcy Court
To access: http://www.ca5.uscourts.gov/
ncmb

North Carolina Middle District Court
To access: http://www.ncmd.uscourts.gov

North Carolina Western Bankruptcy Court
To access: http://www.ncbankruptcy.org

North Dakota Bankruptcy Court
To access: http://www.ndb.uscourts.gov

Ohio Northern Bankruptcy Court
To access: http://www.ohnb.uscourts.gov

Ohio Northern District Court
To access: http://www.ohnd.uscourts.gov

Oregon District Court
To access: http://oregon.court.fed.us

Pennsylvania Eastern Bankruptcy Court
To access: http://www.paeb.uscourts.gov

Bankruptcy Courts by State and District *(Continued)*

Pennsylvania Eastern District Court
To access: http://www.paed.uscourts.gov

Puerto Rico District Court
To access: http://www.prd.uscourts.gov

Rhode Island Bankruptcy Court
To access: http://www.rib.uscourts.gov

South Dakota Bankruptcy Court
To access: http://www.sdb.uscourts.gov

South Dakota District Court
To access: http://www.sdd.uscourts.gov

Tennessee Western Bankruptcy Court
To access: http://www.tnwb.uscourts.gov

Texas Eastern District Court
To access: http://www.txed.uscourts.gov

Texas Eastern Probation Office
To access: http://www.txep.uscourts.gov

Texas Northern Bankruptcy Court
To access: http://www.txnb.uscourts.gov

Texas Northern District Court
To access: http://www.txnd.uscourts.gov

**Texas Southern District/
Bankruptcy Courts**
To access: http://www.txs.uscourts.gov

Texas Western Bankruptcy Court
To access: http://www.txwb.uscourts.gov

Texas Western District Court
To access: http://www.txwd.uscourts.gov

Utah Bankruptcy Court
To access: http://www.utb.uscourts.gov

Utah District Court
To access: http://www.utd.uscourts.gov

Vermont Bankruptcy Court
To access: http://usbcvt.court.fed.us

Virginia Eastern Bankruptcy Court
To access: http://www.vaeb.uscourts.gov

Virginia Western Bankruptcy Court
To access: http://www.vawb.uscourts.gov

Washington Eastern Bankruptcy Court
To access: http://www.waeb.uscourts.gov

Washington Eastern District Court
To access: http://www.waed.uscourts.gov

**Washington Western Bankruptcy
Court**
To access: http://www.wawb.uscourts.gov

Washington Western District Court
To access: http://www.wawd.uscourts.gov

Wisconsin Western District Court
To access: http://www.wiw.uscourts.gov

Wyoming Bankruptcy Court
To access: http://www.wyb.uscourts.gov

Wyoming District Court
To access: http://www.ck10.uscourts.gov/
  wyoming/district

U.S. Court of Appeals for the Second Circuit

This site provides opinions from the U.S. Court of Appeals for the Second Circuit from September 1995 to the present. It also has links to Internet sites that provide opinions from all the other federal circuit courts. The project is a joint effort of Pace University School of Law and Touro Law Center.

The Second Circuit includes Connecticut, Vermont, and New York.

Vital Stats:

Access method:	WWW
To access:	http://www.law.pace.edu/lawlib/legal/us-legal/judiciary/second-circuit.html
E-mail:	dwilliam@lawlib.law.pace.edu

U.S. Court of Appeals for the Fifth Circuit

The U.S. Court of Appeals for the Fifth Circuit site has opinions released by the court since 1990, docket sheets, local rules, rules governing complaints of judicial misconduct or disability, sample jury instructions for civil and criminal cases, and samples of an appellant's brief, appellee's brief, reply brief, and petition for rehearing. One feature lets you sign up to receive new opinions by e-mail automatically as they're released on the Internet.

The Fifth Circuit includes Mississippi, Louisiana, and Texas.

Vital Stats:

Access methods:	WWW, FTP
To access:	http://www.ca5.uscourts.gov *or* ftp://ftp.ca5.uscourts.gov
Login (FTP only):	**anonymous**
Password (FTP only):	your e-mail address
E-mail:	webmaster@ca5.uscourts.gov

U.S. Court of Appeals for the Seventh Circuit

This site offers opinions from the U.S. Court of Appeals for the Seventh Circuit from January 1993 to the present. The Seventh Circuit includes Illinois, Indiana, and Wisconsin.

The site also has Court rules and links to Internet sites that offer opinions from all the other federal appeals courts. It's operated by the Chicago-Kent College of Law.

Vital Stats:

Access method:	WWW
To access:	http://www.kentlaw.edu/7circuit
E-mail:	clc@chicagokent.kentlaw.edu

U.S. Court of Appeals for the Eighth Circuit

The U.S. Court of Appeals for the Eighth Circuit site has opinions issued since October 1995, a court calendar, docket sheets, local rules, the *Practitioner's Handbook for Appeals to the U.S. Court of Appeals for the Eighth Circuit,* a few documents in the *Jones v. Clinton* lawsuit, a report by the Circuit's Gender Fairness Task Force, and model civil and criminal jury instructions. It's operated by the Washington University School of Law.

The Eighth Circuit includes Arkansas, Iowa, Minnesota, Missouri, Nebraska, North Dakota, and South Dakota.

Vital Stats:

Access method: WWW
To access: http://ls.wustl.edu/8th.cir/cindex.html
E-mail: 8thcir@ls.wustl.edu

United States Courts for the Ninth Circuit

The United States Courts for the Ninth Circuit site has the *Capital Punishment Handbook,* manuals of model jury instructions, links to other Internet sites operated by federal courts, and a booklet titled *History and Guide to the U.S. Courts* that has extensive background information about the Ninth Circuit in particular and U.S. courts in general. The Ninth Circuit includes all federal courts in California, Oregon, Washington, Arizona, Montana, Idaho, Nevada, Alaska, Hawaii, Guam, and the Northern Mariana Islands.

The site does not offer opinions from Ninth Circuit courts. Opinions from the Ninth Circuit Court of Appeals are available from the Center for Information Law and Policy.

Vital Stats:

Access method: WWW
To access: http://www.ce9.uscourts.gov

U.S. Court of Appeals for the Tenth Circuit

This site offers opinions from the U.S. Court of Appeals for the Tenth Circuit filed from October 1997 to the present. You can browse the decisions by case name, docket number, and filing date, and you can search them using keywords. The site is operated by the Washburn University School of Law Library.

The Tenth Circuit includes Colorado, Kansas, New Mexico, Oklahoma, Utah, and Wyoming.

Vital Stats:

Access method: WWW
To access: http://lawlib.wuacc.edu/ca10
E-mail: zzwisn@acc.wuacc.edu

U.S. Federal Courts Finder

The U.S. Federal Courts Finder offers opinions from five federal circuit courts of appeals, along with links to Internet sites with opinions from the other circuits and from the U.S. Supreme Court. The site is operated by the Emory University School of Law Library.

The Emory site hosts opinions from the Federal, First, Fourth, Sixth, and Eleventh Circuit Courts of Appeals. For each circuit, cases are listed by the month they were decided and alphabetically by first party and second party. You also can search each circuit's cases by keywords, including docket numbers.

Vital Stats:

Access method:	WWW
To access:	http://www.law.emory.edu/FEDCTS
E-mail:	www@www.law.emory.edu

JUSTICE

Bureau of Alcohol, Tobacco, and Firearms

The Bureau of Alcohol, Tobacco, and Firearms site has details about how to deal with bomb threats and how to detect letter and package bombs, a list of arson and bombing attacks against abortion clinics from 1982 to the present, and the interim report of the National Church Arson Task Force.

It also has information about the Brady handgun law, the *Federal Firearms Regulation Reference Guide,* a report titled *Gun Dealer Licensing and Illegal Gun Trafficking,* pictures and descriptions of criminals wanted by the ATF, details about how to submit a Freedom of Information Act request, press releases, and a list of toll-free telephone numbers for ATF hotlines for reports about arson, bombs, illegal firearms activity, firearms theft, and firearms tracing.

Vital Stats:

Access method:	WWW
To access:	http://www.atf.treas.gov
E-mail:	atfmail@atfhq.atf.treas.gov

Federal Bureau of Investigation Home Page

This site's highlight is a collection of thousands of pages of previously secret documents that have been released under the Freedom of Information Act. There are documents about Lucille Ball, Klaus Barbie, Bonnie and Clyde, John Wilkes Booth, John Dillinger, Amelia Earhart, the Hindenburg disaster, Adolf Hitler, John Lennon, Mickey Mantle, Thurgood Marshall, the Mississippi burning case, Marilyn Monroe, Baby Face Nelson, Pablo Picasso, Elvis Presley, Jackie Robinson, the St. Valentine's Day Massacre, Francis Cardinal Spellman, Leon Trotsky, unidentified flying objects, and John Wayne, among other subjects.

The site also has crime reports, details about current FBI investigations, a brochure titled *A Parent's Guide to Internet Safety,* Internet safety tips for kids, tips for avoiding child abductions, a report and congressional testimony about the effects of encryption on law enforcement, and a report titled *Terrorism in the United States.*

Other highlights include tips on detecting mail bombs, a report about hate crimes, information about the science behind DNA testing, details about the FBI's ten most wanted fugitives, the monthly *Law Enforcement Bulletin,* speeches and congressional testimony by top FBI officials, information about touring FBI headquarters in Washington, D.C., a list of FBI field offices that includes addresses and telephone numbers, and information about employment opportunities.

Vital Stats:

Access method:	WWW
To access:	http://www.fbi.gov

Federal Bureau of Prisons

The Federal Bureau of Prisons site has detailed information about every federal prison, including its address, telephone number, security level, capacity, average daily population, number of staff, and directions to the facility.

The site also has extensive statistics about federal prisons and prisoners, details about how to get information about individual federal inmates, a list of executions of federal prisoners since 1927, employment information, and telephone numbers for state corrections departments nationwide.

Vital Stats:

Access method:	WWW
To access:	http://www.bop.gov
E-mail:	pjones@bop.gov

Justice Information Center

The Justice Information Center offers hundreds of reports about criminal and juvenile justice, links to other Internet sites that have similar information, and a database that provides summaries of reports, articles, books, and other items about criminal justice. The center is a service of the National Criminal Justice Reference Service.

The site has publications about corrections, courts, crime prevention, criminal justice statistics, drugs and crime, international issues, juvenile justice, law enforcement, research and evaluation, and victims of crime prepared by the National Institute of Justice, Bureau of Justice Statistics, Office for Victims of Crime, and other organizations.

Some of the available titles are *Boot Camps for Juvenile Offenders, Assessing the Exposure of Urban Youth to Violence, Civil Jury Cases and Verdicts in Large Counties, Drug Enforcement and Treatment in Prisons, HIV in Prisons, Improving Literacy Skills of Juvenile Detainees, Prison Sentences and Time Served for Violence, Trial Court Performance Standards, Managing Adult Sex Offenders in the Community, Working as Partners with Community Groups, Crime and Policing in Rural and Small-Town America, Gangs, Partnerships to Prevent Youth Violence, Policing Drug Hot Spots,* and *Responding to Child Sexual Abuse.*

Vital Stats:

Access method:	WWW
To access:	http://www.ncjrs.org
E-mail:	askncjrs@ncjrs.org

Justice Information Distribution List (JUSTINFO) *and* Juvenile Justice Electronic Mailing List (JUVJUST)

These two mailing lists are designed for criminal justice professionals.

JUSTINFO is a biweekly electronic newsletter that provides information about international criminal justice issues, criminal justice resources on the Internet, federal legislation, funding for criminal justice programs, and new products, publications, and services from the National Criminal Justice Reference Service.

JUVJUST provides information about juvenile justice issues. It's operated by the Office of Juvenile Justice and Delinquency Prevention.

Vital Stats:

Access method:	E-mail
To access:	Send an e-mail message to listproc@ncjrs.org
Subject line:	
Message:	**subscribe** *listname firstname lastname*
E-mail (questions):	askncjrs@ncjrs.org

National Archive of Criminal Justice Data

The National Archive of Criminal Justice Data provides more than 500 technical data sets related to criminal justice issues. Data are available about community studies, corrections, court case processing, crime and delinquency, and victimization, among other subjects. The archive is operated by the Inter-University Consortium for Political and Social Research and funded by several Justice Department agencies.

Vital Stats:

Access method:	WWW
To access:	http://www.icpsr.umich.edu/NACJD
E-mail:	nacjd@icpsr.umich.edu

Office of Justice Programs

The Office of Justice Programs site offers hundreds of reports about criminal justice topics, along with numerous documents about grants available from various agencies within the Justice Department.

The site has dozens of reports from the Bureau of Justice Statistics about capital punishment, carjacking, the cost of crime to victims, drug-related crime, elderly crime victims, female victims of violent crime, guns and crime, local prosecution of organized crime, murder in families, presale firearms checks, recidivism, school crime, sentencing, violence and theft in the workplace, and women in prison, among many other subjects.

It also offers lots of information from the Office of Juvenile Justice and Delinquency Prevention, including reports on corrections, courts, delinquency prevention, gangs, missing and exploited children, and violence and victimization.

Vital Stats:

Access method:	WWW
To access:	http://www.ojp.usdoj.gov
E-mail:	askocpa@ojp.usdoj.gov

U.S. Customs Service Web Site

The U.S. Customs Service Web Site has customs information for travelers, files for importers and exporters, photographs and descriptions of fugitives wanted by the Customs Service, press releases, procurement information, a list of Customs Service offices, and details about Customs Service enforcement programs aimed at stopping fraud, child pornography, drug smuggling, money laundering, high-tech smuggling, and vehicle and cargo theft.

Vital Stats:

Access method:	WWW
To access:	http://www.customs.ustreas.gov

U.S. Department of Justice

The U.S. Department of Justice site offers a huge, eclectic assortment of information, including documents from the Microsoft antitrust case, reports by the Justice Department's inspector general about such subjects as the alleged role of the Central Intelligence Agency in bringing cocaine into the United States, and extensive information about the Americans with Disabilities Act, including details about consent agreements and settlements of ADA lawsuits.

Other highlights include details about how the public can buy forfeited assets from the U.S. Marshals Service, federal guidelines for searching and seizing computers, information about investigations of computer crime, contact information for organizations that help crime victims, reports and statistics from the Drug Enforcement Administration, and a report titled *When Your Child Is Missing: A Family Survival Guide.*

It also has information about the administration's anti-gang and youth violence plan, speeches and grant information from the Violence against Women Office, complaints and consent decrees from the Civil Rights Division, speeches by the attorney general, press releases, links to other Justice Department Internet sites, and a special section for kids and youths that has materials about famous cases, drugs, crime prevention, staying safe on the Internet, child abduction, DNA testing, fingerprint identification, polygraph testing, and related subjects.

Vital Stats:

Access method:	WWW
To access:	http://www.usdoj.gov
E-mail:	web@usdoj.gov

United States Commission on Civil Rights Home Page

The United States Commission on Civil Rights Home Page has telephone numbers to call to file discrimination complaints, a publication titled *Getting Uncle Sam to Enforce Your Civil Rights,* a directory of civil rights agencies and offices, background information about the commission, a publications catalog, a list of regional offices, a calendar of meetings of the commission and state advisory committees, and press releases.

Vital Stats:

Access method:	WWW
To access:	http://www.usccr.gov
E-mail:	wwwadmin@usccr.gov

United States Sentencing Commission

This site provides reports to Congress by the United States Sentencing Commission about cocaine and federal sentencing policy, mandatory minimum penalties, penalties for fraud crimes involving elderly victims, sentencing policy for money laundering offenses, penalties for intentionally exposing people to HIV, sex crimes against children, and penalties for computer fraud and vandalism offenses, among other subjects.

The site also has a manual containing the federal sentencing guidelines, amendments to the guidelines, federal sentencing statistics by state, transcripts of public hearings, *Federal Register* notices, information about state sentencing commissions, and publications about public perceptions of the federal sentencing guidelines, corporate crime, environmental sanctions, money laundering, and other topics.

Vital Stats:

Access method:	WWW
To access:	http://www.ussc.gov
E-mail:	webmaster@ussc.gov

SCIENCE AND TECHNOLOGY

EARTH SCIENCES

Cascades Volcano Observatory

The Cascades Volcano Observatory site, which is operated by the U.S. Geological Survey, has a huge collection of documents and images about volcanoes. The site is particularly strong in information about volcanoes in the United States, although it also has some information about volcanoes in other countries.

The site has descriptions of specific volcanoes, photographs of volcanoes, an "armchair tour" of Mount Rainier, links to live views of volcanoes around the world, glossaries of volcano and glacier terminology, news about research being conduced at the Cascades Volcano Observatory, and abstracts of technical papers.

It also offers information about volcano monitoring, links to other volcano-related sites, and numerous publications, including *How Scientists Study Volcanoes, Twentieth-Century Volcanic Eruptions and Their Impact,* and *Volcanoes in Historical and Popular Culture.*

Vital Stats:

Access method:	WWW
To access:	http://vulcan.wr.usgs.gov
E-mail:	webmaster@mailvan.wr.usgs.gov

Department of the Interior Home Page

The Department of the Interior Home Page is a gateway to the vast wealth of material available from the department and its various bureaus on the Internet.

The site's primary feature is a collection of links to Internet sites operated by bureaus of the Interior Department, such as the Bureau of Land Management, Bureau of Reclamation, Fish and Wildlife Service, Minerals Management Service, National Biological Service, National Park Service, Office of Surface Mining, and the U.S. Geological Survey.

The site also has detailed information about the Interior Department's budget, directories of employees, information about employment opportunities at the department, and press releases.

Vital Stats:

Access method:	WWW
To access:	http://www.doi.gov
E-mail:	webteam@ios.doi.gov

Earthquake Information

The Earthquake Information site provides just that—anything and everything you might want to know about earthquakes. It's operated by the U.S. Geological Survey.

The site has an interactive map showing recent earthquakes worldwide, data about the latest earthquakes, documents about how to prepare for earthquakes, maps that estimate seismic hazards throughout the United States, information about the potential for large earthquakes in northern California, and maps showing the predicted intensity of shaking for earthquakes on the San Andreas fault or the Hayward fault in California.

The site also has answers to frequently asked questions about earthquakes, fact sheets about the Geological Survey's efforts to reduce earthquake losses, examples of science fair projects about seismology, and links to lots of other Internet sites that provide earthquake information.

Vital Stats:

Access method:	WWW
To access:	http://quake.wr.usgs.gov
E-mail:	webmaster@quake.wr.usgs.gov

Global Change Data and Information System

The Global Change Data and Information System is a one-stop source for links to other Internet sites that have collections of global change data and information. The site, which was created as part of the Global Change Research Act of 1990, provides few files of its own.

The links are primarily to federal government Internet sites operated by such agencies as the National Oceanic and Atmospheric Administration, the Agriculture Department, the Energy Department, the Environmental Protection Agency, NASA, the Interior Department, and the U.S. Geological Survey.

Vital Stats:

Access method:	WWW
To access:	http://www.gcdis.usgcrp.gov
E-mail:	webmaster@www.gcdis.usgcrp.gov

National Ocean Service

This site has information about the National Marine Sanctuary program, a list of products and services available from the National Ocean Service, background information about the service, and press releases.

Vital Stats:

Access method:	WWW
To access:	http://www.nos.noaa.gov
E-mail:	webmaster@ocean.nos.noaa.gov

U.S. Geological Survey

The U.S. Geological Survey (USGS) site is a gateway into the amazing collection of earth science information offered on the Internet by the USGS. It offers everything from an online exhibit about volcanoes to links to dozens of USGS Internet sites that provide information about biology, earthquakes, the environment, geology, mapping, marine geology, volcanoes, water resources, and related subjects.

The site also has lesson plans for teachers, press releases, links to other Internet sites that have earth science information, and much, much more.

Vital Stats:

Access method:	WWW
To access:	http://www.usgs.gov
E-mail:	webmaster@usgs.gov

USGS Branch of Earthquake and Geomagnetic Information On-line Information System

Both current and historical information about earthquakes is available at this site, which is operated by the National Earthquake Information Center.

The site has brief descriptions of earthquakes that occurred anywhere in the world during the previous three weeks, files with earthquake facts and statistics, and a database that provides values of the elements and parameters of the Earth's magnetic field.

Vital Stats:

Access method:	Telnet
To access:	telnet://neis.cr.usgs.gov
Login:	**qed**

WINDandSEA

This site provides more than 800 links to Internet resources about atmospheric and oceanic sciences. It was developed by library staff at the National Oceanic and Atmospheric Administration (NOAA).

The links are arranged by subject. Some of the topics included are the Chesapeake Bay, climate, coastal studies, coral reefs, fish, history of oceanic and atmospheric sciences, mapping and charting, marine biology, oceanography, weather, and wetlands.

A special page provides links to more than 100 NOAA pages aimed at students and teachers and to other educational sites about the Earth, oceans, and the atmosphere.

Vital Stats:

Access method:	WWW
To access:	http://www.lib.noaa.gov/docs/windandsea.html
E-mail:	reference@nodc.noaa.gov

TECHNOLOGY

Ernest Orlando Lawrence Berkeley National Laboratory

This site has information about science and technology research conducted at Ernest Orlando Lawrence Berkeley National Laboratory, which is managed by the University of California for the U.S. Department of Energy.

One of the site's highlights is an extensive collection of scientific articles. They cover such topics as accelerator and fusion research, astrophysics, batteries and fuel cells, computing and the Internet, engineering, environmental cleanup and waste handling, the future of science, human genome and DNA research, medical and risk-related research, nuclear science, physics, and X-ray research, among others.

One of the most interesting features is a collection of lessons prepared by the lab's Ethical, Legal, and Social Issues in Science educational outreach project. The lessons, which are targeted at middle school and high school students, cover such topics as basic and applied research, genetic patents and intellectual property, access to medical screening, indoor air pollution, and personal privacy and medical databases. Each lesson provides links to other Internet sites that offer related information. To reach the lessons directly, use the address http://www.lbl.gov/Education/ELSI/ELSI.html.

Vital Stats:

Access method:	WWW
To access:	http://www.lbl.gov
E-mail:	JBKahn@lbl.gov

Hybrid Electric Vehicle Program

The Hybrid Electric Vehicle Program site has information about hybrid electric vehicle projects by major auto manufacturers, news briefs about developments around the world, details about the components of a hybrid electric vehicle, a bibliography, and links to lots of related Internet sites. It's operated by the National Renewable Energy Laboratory.

Vital Stats:

Access method:	WWW
To access:	http://www.hev.doe.gov

Intelligent Mechanisms Group

The Intelligent Mechanisms Group site has videos, images, descriptive documents, and scientific papers about the development of planetary and space-based robotic systems. One of the site's highlights is an extensive collection of images and documents about Dante II, a walking robot that explored an active volcano in Alaska. The site is operated by NASA's Ames Research Center.

Vital Stats:

Access method:	WWW
To access:	http://img.arc.nasa.gov
E-mail:	sims@artemis.arc.nasa.gov

JPL Robotics

The JPL Robotics site has fascinating images, videos, and text descriptions of robotics and automation technologies being developed for everything from exploring the solar system to assisting with microsurgery. The site is operated by NASA's Jet Propulsion Laboratory.

The site has information about surface rovers and robotic balloons that are being developed to explore planets such as Mars, robots that will assist with detailed surgery, and other products. It also has links to other Internet sites that offer robotics information.

Vital Stats:

Access method:	WWW
To access:	http://robotics.jpl.nasa.gov
E-mail:	volpe@jpl.nasa.gov

NASA Space Telerobotics Program

Whether you just think robots are cool or you're doing sophisticated robotics research, the NASA Space Telerobotics Program site is a must-see. It offers videos, images, and text files about various kinds of robots being developed by NASA to service spacecraft in orbit, explore volcanoes on Earth, assemble structures in space, and roam across planet surfaces.

The site also has software programs that can be used when designing robots, links to dozens of other robotics resources on the Internet, links to Internet sites with robots you can manipulate with your computer, a "Cool Robot of the Week" link, and much more.

Vital Stats:

Access method:	WWW
To access:	http://ranier.hq.nasa.gov/telerobotics.html
E-mail:	dave.lavery@hq.nasa.gov

National Institute of Standards and Technology

The National Institute of Standards and Technology (NIST) site has case studies of cooperative efforts between the institute and industry, fact sheets about selected NIST programs, the *Guide to NIST,* congressional testimony, budget information, a staff directory, a calendar of workshops and conferences, and links to other Internet sites that provide science, technology, and standards information.

Oak Ridge National Laboratory (ORNL)

This site provides information about the Oak Ridge National Laboratory (ORNL), which conducts basic and applied research in materials sciences and engineering; physical, chemical, and engineering sciences; biological and life sciences; computer science; and manufacturing sciences and technologies. ORNL is part of the U.S. Department of Energy.

The site offers descriptions of major projects at ORNL, information about technologies available at the laboratory, press releases, bibliographies of ORNL publications, a searchable database of ORNL employees, information about employment opportunities, and links to other Internet sites operated by the laboratory.

Vital Stats:

Access method: WWW
To access: http://www.ornl.gov

Partnership for a New Generation of Vehicles (PNGV)

The Partnership for a New Generation of Vehicles site has background information about efforts to build an environmentally friendly car that has up to triple the fuel efficiency of today's midsize cars. The project is a public-private partnership between seven federal agencies and the "Big Three" automakers. The site is operated by the U.S. Department of Commerce.

Vital Stats:

Access method: WWW
To access: http://www.ta.doc.gov/pngv

Rocky 7

No, Rocky 7 doesn't promote a new Sylvester Stallone movie. Instead, it provides documents, data, images, and videos about tests of Rocky 7, a prototype of the kind of unmanned rover that will be sent to Mars in coming years. The site is a joint project of the Jet Propulsion Laboratory and the Planetary Data System Geosciences Node at Washington University.

Vital Stats:

Access method: WWW
To access: http://wundow.wustl.edu/rocky7
E-mail: Samad.Hayati@jpl.nasa.gov

SCAN

SCAN provides more than 200 mailing lists that offer sections of *Selected Current Aerospace Notices,* a publication that has summaries and bibliographic information for recently issued reports and journal articles about aeronautics and aerospace research.

You can subscribe to mailing lists about commercial and general aviation, aircraft noise and sonic boom, jet propulsion, launch vehicles and space vehicles, space probes, space stations, chemical processes and engineering, corrosion, electromagnetic radiation, structural mechanics, solar space power, weather forecasting, oceanography, aerospace medicine, nuclear physics, space commercialization, and urban technology and transportation, among other subjects.

Vital Stats:

Access method:	E-mail
To access:	Send an e-mail message to listproc@sti.nasa.gov
Subject line:	
Message:	**lists** (to get a list of lists)
Message:	**subscribe** *listname firstname lastname* (to subscribe to a list)
E-mail (questions):	helpdesk@sti.nasa.gov

Time Service Department

The Time Service Department site offers the time at the U.S. Naval Observatory, which is the official source of time used in the United States. The site also has a map of world time zones, technical information about such issues as GPS satellite timing operations, answers to frequently asked questions about time, and information about the development of new clocks.

Vital Stats:

Access method:	WWW
To access:	http://tycho.usno.navy.mil
E-mail:	res@tuttle.usno.navy.mil

WEATHER

Interactive Weather Information Network (IWIN)

Whether you're about to leave on an overseas trip or just want to know if you should carry an umbrella to work tomorrow, the Interactive Weather Information Network (IWIN) is the place for you. The site bills itself as "the National Weather Service's Internet data source," which sums things up pretty well.

IWIN offers detailed forecasts for each state, extensive national weather information, all weather warnings issued by the National Weather Service for the United States, current weather conditions for hundreds of cities around the world, and links to other Internet sites that offer satellite images of weather conditions around the world, current weather maps, weather movies, forecasts, and other weather information.

Vital Stats:

Access method:	WWW
To access:	http://iwin.nws.noaa.gov
E-mail:	W-IWIN.Webmaster@noaa.gov

National Hurricane Center/Tropical Prediction Center

This site offers current watches, warnings, forecasts, and analyses of hurricanes and other hazardous weather conditions in the tropics. It's operated by the National Hurricane Center/Tropical Prediction Center.

Other highlights include reports from previous hurricane seasons, descriptions of infamous Atlantic hurricanes, data about the deadliest and costliest U.S. hurricanes of this century, statistics about the number of U.S. hurricane strikes by state, and files showing past hurricane tracks.

The site also has a description of the Saffir-Simpson Hurricane Scale, lists of names that will be assigned to Atlantic and Pacific storms in upcoming years, and links to hundreds of other Internet sites that provide meteorological information.

Vital Stats:

Access method:	WWW
To access:	http://www.nhc.noaa.gov
E-mail:	brian@nhc.noaa.gov

National Severe Storms Laboratory

The National Severe Storms Laboratory site has lesson plans for teachers, weather-related coloring books for young children, information about weather careers, technical papers, information about research being conducted at the lab, links to other weather-related Internet sites, and answers to common questions about tornadoes, hurricanes, lightning, and thunderstorms. The laboratory is part of the National Oceanic and Atmospheric Administration.

Vital Stats:

Access method:	WWW
To access:	http://www.nssl.noaa.gov
E-mail:	www@whirlwind.nssl.noaa.gov

National Weather Service

The National Weather Service site is a one-stop source of weather information on the Internet. It provides few files of its own, but it has links to dozens of other sites that offer weather forecasts and warnings, climate data, and other information.

The site also has background information about the NWS, details about NWS modernization and restructuring efforts, procurement notices, press releases and story ideas for reporters, and links to Internet sites operated by NWS offices around the country.

Vital Stats:

Access method:	WWW
To access:	http://www.nws.noaa.gov
E-mail:	w-nws.webmaster@noaa.gov

National Weather Service Alaska Region

The National Weather Service Alaska Region site has weather forecasts, aviation-related weather information, river forecasts and flood watches, marine weather images, satellite images, summaries of historical Alaska climate data, a list of all the weather stations in Alaska, and related information.

Vital Stats:

Access method:	WWW
To access:	http://www.alaska.net/~nwsar
E-mail:	W-ARH.Webmaster@noaa.gov

National Weather Service Offices

More than 100 local National Weather Service offices around the country have home pages on the Internet. What's available varies among the sites, but they frequently offer forecasts, warnings about severe weather, information about floods or wildfires, aviation forecasts, marine forecasts, climate data, satellite and radar images, and links to other weather sites on the Internet.

Vital Stats:

Access method:	WWW
To access:	See accompanying box

National Weather Service Offices

Alabama

Birmingham
To access: http://www.acesag.auburn.edu/
    department/nws/index.html

Mobile
To access: http://www.srh.noaa.gov/
    FTPROOT/MOB/HTML/default.HTML

Arizona

Flagstaff
To access: http://www.wrh.noaa.gov/
    Flagstaff

Phoenix
To access: http://www.phx.noaa.gov

Tucson
To access: http://nimbo.wrh.noaa.gov/
    Tucson/twc.html

Arkansas

Little Rock
To access: http://www.srh.noaa.gov/
    ftproot/lzk/default.html

California

Eureka
To access: http://www.wrh.noaa.gov/
    Eureka

Hanford (San Joaquin Valley)
To access: http://www.wrh.noaa.gov/
    Hanford

Los Angeles/Oxnard
To access: http://www.nwsla.noaa.gov

Sacramento
To access: http://www.wrh.noaa.gov/
    Sacramento

San Diego
To access: http://nimbo.wrh.noaa.gov/
    Sandiego/nws.html

San Francisco
To access: http://www.nws.mbay.net/
    home.html

Colorado

Denver
To access: http://www.crh.noaa.gov/den

Grand Junction
To access: http://www.crh.noaa.gov/gjt

Pueblo
To access: http://www.crh.noaa.gov/
    pub/home.htm

Florida

Jacksonville
To access: http://www.nwsjax.noaa.gov

Melbourne
To access: http://sunmlb.nws.fit.edu

Miami
To access: http://www-mfl.nhc.noaa.gov

Tallahassee
To access: http://www.nws.fsu.edu

Tampa Bay/Fort Myters
To access: http://www.marine.usf.edu/nws

Georgia

Atlanta/Peachtree City
To access: http://www.srh.noaa.gov/
    FTPROOT/FFC/default.HTML

Guam

Tiyan
To access: http://www.nws.noaa.gov/
    pr/guam

Hawaii

Honolulu
To access: http://www.nws.noaa.gov/
    pr/hnl/index.html

Idaho

Boise
To access: http://www.boi.noaa.gov

Pocatello
To access: http://nimbo.wrh.noaa.gov/
    Pocatello/Pocatello.htm

National Weather Service Offices *(Continued)*

Illinois
Chicago
To access: http://taiga.geog.niu.edu/nwslot

Lincoln
To access: http://www.crh.noaa.gov/ilx/ilxhome.htm

Indiana
Indianapolis
To access: http://www.crh.noaa.gov/ind/start.htm

Iowa
Des Moines
To access: http://www.crh.noaa.gov/dmx/index.html

Quad Cities
To access: http://www.crh.noaa.gov/dvn

Kansas
Dodge City
To access: http://info.abrfc.noaa.gov/ddcdocs/nwsoddc.html

Goodland
To access: http://www.crh.noaa.gov/gld/index.htm

Topeka
To access: http://www.crh.noaa.gov/top

Wichita
To access: http://www.crh.noaa.gov/ict/index.html

Kentucky
Jackson
To access: http://www.crh.noaa.gov/jkl/index.html

Louisville
To access: http://www.crh.noaa.gov/lmk/welcome.htm

Paducah
To access: http://www.crh.noaa.gov/pah/index.html

Louisiana
Lake Charles
To access: http://www.srh.noaa.gov/FTPROOT/LCH/default.htm

Shreveport
To access: http://www.srh.noaa.gov/FTPROOT/SHV/default.html

New Orleans/Baton Rouge
To access: http://www.srh.noaa.gov/FTPROOT/LIX/default.HTML

Maine
Portland
To access: http://www.nws.noaa.gov/er/gyx

Maryland
Baltimore/Washington
To access: http://tgsv5.nws.noaa.gov/er/lwx

Massachusetts
Boston
To access: http://www.nws.noaa.gov/er/box

Michigan
Detroit/Pontiac
To access: http://www.crh.noaa.gov/dtx/start.htm

Gaylord
To access: http://www.crh.noaa.gov/apx/homepage.htm

Grand Rapids
To access: http://www.crh.noaa.gov/grr/index.html

Marquette
To access: http://www.crh.noaa.gov/mqt/mqt.htm

National Weather Service Offices *(Continued)*

Minnesota

Duluth
To access: http://www.crh.noaa.gov/
dlh/duluth.htm

Twin Cities
To access: http://www.crh.noaa.gov/
mpx /mpx.html

Mississippi

Jackson
To access: http://www.jannws.state.ms.us

Missouri

Kansas City/Pleasant Hill
To access: http://www.crh.noaa.gov/
eax/eax.htm

St. Louis
To access: http://www.crh.noaa.gov/
lsx/lsx.htm

Springfield
To access: http://www.crh.noaa.gov/
sgf/sgf1.htm

Montana

Billings
To access: http://www.wrh.noaa.gov/
Billings

Glasgow
To access: http://www.wrh.noaa.gov/
Glasgow

Great Falls
To access: http://www.wrh.noaa.gov/
Greatfalls

Missoula
To access: http://www.wrh.noaa.gov/
Missoula

Nebraska

Hastings
To access: http://www.crh.noaa.gov/
gid/gidhome.htm

North Platte
To access: http://www.crh.noaa.gov/lbf/
lbf.home.html

Omaha
To access: http://www.crh.noaa.gov/
oax/front.html

Nevada

Elko
To access: http://www.wrh.noaa.gov/Elko

Las Vegas
To access: http://www.wrh.noaa.gov/
Lasvegas

Reno
To access: http://www.wrh.noaa.gov/
Reno

New Mexico

Albuquerque
To access: http://www.srh.noaa.gov/
FTPROOT/ABQ/default.html

New York

Albany
To access: http://nwsfo.nws.cestm.
albany.edu

Binghamton
To access: http://www.nws.noaa.gov/
er/bgm

Buffalo
To access: http://www.wbuf.noaa.gov

New York City/Brookhaven
To access: http://sun20.ccd.bnl.gov/~nws

North Carolina

Newport
To access: http://www.eastnc.coastalnet.
com/weather/nwsmhx/nwsweb.htm

Raleigh
To access: http://www.nws.noaa.gov/
er/rah/frame/frame.html

National Weather Service Offices *(Continued)*

Wilmington
To access: http://nwsilm.wilmington.net

North Dakota
Bismarck
To access: http://www.crh.noaa.gov/bis/index.html

Grand Forks
To access: http://www.crh.noaa.gov/fgf/index.html

Ohio
Cleveland
To access: http://www.csuohio.edu/nws

Wilmington
To access: http://www.nws.noaa.gov/er/iln/iln.htm

Oklahoma
Norman
To access:
http://www.nssl.noaa.gov/~nws

Tulsa
To access: http://www.nwstulsa.noaa.gov

Oregon
Medford
To access: http://nimbo.wrh.noaa.gov/Medford/index.html

Pendleton
To access: http://www.wrh.noaa.gov/Pendleton

Portland
To access: http://www.wrh.noaa.gov/Portland

Pennsylvania
Philadelphia
To access: http://tgsv5.nws.noaa.gov/er/phi

Pittsburgh
To access: http://tgsv5.nws.noaa.gov/er/pit

State College
To access: http://bookend.met.psu.edu

Puerto Rico
San Juan
To access: http://www.upr.clu.edu/nws

South Carolina
Charleston
To access: http://wchs.csc.noaa.gov

Columbia
To access: http://tgsv5.nws.noaa.gov/er/cae

Greenville/Spartanburg
To access: http://www.nws.noaa.gov/er/gsp

South Dakota
Aberdeen
To access: http://www.crh.noaa.gov/abr/nwsabr.htm

Rapid City
To access: http://www.crhnoaa.gov/unr/index.htm

Sioux Falls
To access: http://www.crh.noaa.gov/fsd/homepage.htm

Tennessee
Knoxville
To access: http://www.srh.noaa.gov/FTPROOT/MRX/HTML/MRX.HTM

Memphis
To access: http://www.srh.noaa.gov/ftproot/meg/html/default.html

Nashville
To access: http://www.srh.noaa.gov/ftproot/ohx/html/ohx.html

National Weather Service Offices *(Continued)*

Texas

Amarillo
To access: http://www.srh.noaa.gov/
ftproot/ama/default.html

Brownsville
To access: http://www.srh.noaa.gov/
FTPROOT/BRO/html/default.HTML

Corpus Christi
To access: http://www.srh.noaa.gov/
FTPROOT/CRP/default.HTML

El Paso
To access: http://nwselp.epcc.edu

Fort Worth
To access: http://www.srh.noaa.gov/
FTPROOT/FWD/default.HTML

Houston/Galveston
To access: http://www.srh.noaa.gov/hqx

Lubbock
To access: http://cra.nws.noaa.gov/
nwslbb/index.html

Midland
To access: http://www.srh.noaa.gov/
FTPROOT/MAF/default.HTML

San Angelo
To access: http://www.srh.noaa.gov/
FTPROOT/SJT/default.html

San Antonio/Austin
To access: http://www.srh.noaa.gov/
FTPROOT/EWX/default.HTML

Utah

Salt Lake City
To access: http://nimbo.wrh.noaa.gov/
Saltlake/slc.noaa.html

Vermont

Burlington
To access: http://www.nws.noaa.gov/
er/btv

Virginia

Roanoke/Blacksburg
To access: http://www.bev.net/weather

Wakefield
To access: http://www.nws.noaa.gov/
er/akq

Washington

Seattle
To access: http://www.seawfo.noaa.gov/
new/index.html

Spokane
To access: http://nimbo.wrh.noaa.gov/
Spokane/index.html

West Virginia

Charleston
To access: http://www.nws.noaa.gov/er/rlx

Wisconsin

Green Bay
To access: http://www.crh.noaa.gov/
grb/index.html

La Crosse
To access: http://www.crh.noaa.gov/
arx/index.html

Milwaukee
To access: http://www.crh.noaa.gov/
mkx/welcome.htm

Wyoming

Cheyenne
To access: http://www.crh.noaa.gov/
cys/cyshome.htm

Riverton
To access: http://riw.weather.wyoming.
com

River Forecast Centers

More than a dozen National Weather Service River Forecast Centers operate sites on the Internet. The sites vary in their offerings, but typically they provide forecasts of river flows and stages, predictions of precipitation and water supplies, information about historical floods and the potential for new floods, weather forecasts, satellite and radar images, pictures of rivers, and links to other weather- and water-related sites on the Internet

Vital Stats:

Access method: WWW
To access: See accompanying box

River Forecast Centers

Alaska River Forecast Center
Anchorage, Alaska
To access: http://www.alaska.net/~akrfc

Arkansas-Red Basin River Forecast Center
Tulsa, Oklahoma
To access: http://info.abrfc.noaa.gov

California-Nevada River Forecast Center
Sacramento, California
To access: http://nimbo.wrh.noaa.gov/cnrfc

Colorado Basin River Forecast Center
Salt Lake City, Utah
To access: http://www.cbrfc.gov/home.html

Lower Mississippi River Forecast Center
Slidell, Louisiana
To access: http://www.srh.noaa.gov/ftproot/orn/html

Middle Atlantic River Forecast Center
State College, Pennsylvania
To access: http://crab.met.psu.edu

Missouri Basin River Forecast Center
Pleasant Hill, Missouri
http://www.crh.noaa.gov/mbrfc/index.html

North Central River Forecast Center
Chanhassen, Minnesota
To access: http://www.crhnwscr.noaa.gov/ncrfc/welcome.html

Northeast River Forecast Center
Taunton, Massachusetts
To access: http://tgsv5.nws.noaa.gov/er/nerfc

Northwest River Forecast Center
Portland, Oregon
To access: http://www.nwrfc.noaa.gov

Ohio River Forecast Center
Wilmington, Ohio
To access: http://www.nws.noaa.gov/er/iln/ohrfc.html

Southeast River Forecast Center
Peachtree City, Georgia
To access: http://www.srh.noaa.gov/ftproot/atr/html/main_p.htm

West Gulf River Forecast Center
Fort Worth, Texas
To access: http://www.srh.noaa.gov/wgrfc

SPACE

ASTEROIDS AND COMETS

Asteroid and Comet Impact Hazards

What's the chance that a meteor or comet will hit Earth? The Asteroid and Comet Impact Hazards site, which is operated by the National Aeronautics and Space Administration (NASA), has some answers.

The site has a list of near-Earth asteroids, a list of predicted close approaches to the Earth by asteroids and comets through 2020, testimony by NASA officials at congressional hearings, images of asteroid impacts, and news about grants.

It also provides documents and reports about impact hazards, a bibliography of scientific papers on impact hazards, and links to other Internet sites that offer related information.

Vital Stats:

Access method:	WWW
To access:	http://impact.arc.nasa.gov
E-mail:	dmorrison@mail.arc.nasa.gov

Comet Observation Home Page

The Comet Observation Home Page has hundreds of comet images, information about comets that are currently visible, summaries of comet observations, a glossary of comet terms, and links to other sites that have information about comets. It's operated by the Jet Propulsion Laboratory.

Vital Stats:

Access method:	WWW
To access:	http://encke.jpl.nasa.gov
E-mail:	csm@encke.jpl.nasa.gov

Near-Earth Asteroid Tracking Home Page

This site is operated by the Near-Earth Asteroid Tracking (NEAT) project, a Jet Propulsion Laboratory effort that searches the sky for near-Earth asteroids and comets.

It has news about new asteroid discoveries, answers to frequently asked questions about near-Earth comets and asteroids, images, videos, press releases, data on the number of asteroids detected by NEAT, a link to another site that offers about 20,000 images produced by NEAT, and links to related sites.

Vital Stats:

Access method:	WWW
To access:	http://huey.jpl.nasa.gov/~spravdo/neat.html
E-mail:	spravdo@pop.jpl.nasa.gov

Near-Live Comet Watching System

The Near-Live Comet Watching System has fantastic images of comet Hale-Bopp taken by people around the world. The site, which is operated by NASA, also has links to other Internet sites that provide information about comets.

Vital Stats:

Access method:	WWW
To access:	http://comet.hq.nasa.gov
E-mail:	gvarros@mail.hq.nasa.gov

Stardust

This site has information about NASA's Stardust mission to Comet Wild 2. The spacecraft, which is scheduled to launch in 1999, will fly to the comet, take pictures, and capture materials spewed out from the comet before returning to earth in 2006.

The site has extensive background information about the mission and the Stardust spacecraft, instructions for making a model of a comet in the classroom, a bibliography of books and popular articles about comets, news about comets, links to other Internet sites that provide comet information, and a lengthy list of books, Web sites, and museums that have materials about dinosaurs, comets, and asteroids.

A related mailing list distributes news about the mission by e-mail (next entry).

Vital Stats:

Access method:	WWW
To access:	http://stardust.jpl.nasa.gov
E-mail:	stardust@jpl.nasa.gov

Stardust Mailing List

This mailing list distributes status reports and press releases about the Stardust mission to Comet Wild 2. The spacecraft is scheduled to launch in 1999, travel to the comet for observations, and return to Earth in 2006.

Vital Stats:

Access method:	E-mail
To access:	Send an e-mail message to majordomo@sender.jpl.nasa.gov
Subject line:	
Message:	**subscribe stardust**
E-mail (questions):	stardust@jpl.nasa.gov

GENERAL

Earth from Space

This site, which is operated by NASA's Johnson Space Center, offers dozens of photos of Earth taken from space. You can select photos by clicking on a map of the Earth or by category: cities, Earth landscapes, Earth-human interactions, distinctive features, hurricanes and weather, Earth's water habitats, geographic regions, and technical search. You can order prints of any photographs at the site for a fee.

Vital Stats:

Access method:	WWW
To access:	http://earth.jsc.nasa.gov
E-mail:	chris.m.d'aquin1@jsc.nasa.gov

EXPRESS

Subscribers to the EXPRESS mailing list receive e-mail announcements when new materials are added to the NASA Spacelink site (p. 277). Spacelink is aimed at educators and students, although its thousands of files provide a huge amount of information for anyone interested in space exploration.

Vital Stats:

Access method:	E-mail
To access:	Send an e-mail message to listproc@spacelink.nasa.gov
Subject line:	
Message:	**subscribe EXPRESS** *firstname lastname*
E-mail (questions):	comments@spacelink.msfc.nasa.gov

International Space Station

This NASA site provides a huge amount of information about the *International Space Station,* which will be built in space during forty-four missions between late 1998 and 2004.

It has images, video clips, a book that provides background information about the space station and experiments that it will conduct, fact sheets about everything from the history of U.S. space stations to how the station will be assembled in space, news about work on the space station, updates about crew training, answers to frequently asked questions, information about international partners working on the project, links to related sites, and much more.

NASA also offers a mailing list called issnews (next entry) that offers e-mail updates about space station developments.

Vital Stats:

Access method:	WWW
To access:	http://station.nasa.gov
E-mail:	spstweb@ems.jsc.nasa.gov

issnews

Subscribers to NASA's issnews mailing list receive e-mail updates about developments involving the *International Space Station,* which will be built in space during forty-four missions between late 1998 and 2004.

Additional information about the space station is available at the International Space Station Web site (previous entry).

Vital Stats:

Access method:	E-mail
To access:	Send an e-mail message to majordomo@listserver.jsc.nasa.gov
Subject line:	
Message:	**subscribe issnews**
E-mail (questions):	spstweb@ems.jsc.nasa.gov

Jet Propulsion Laboratory

The Jet Propulsion Laboratory site, which is operated for NASA by the California Institute of Technology, contains an incredible collection of images of unmanned spacecraft, images taken by unmanned spacecraft, images from the Galileo mission to Jupiter, publications for educators, and text files about spacecraft missions.

The system has thousands of files, including information about numerous past and current space missions; extensive information about the Galileo mission to Jupiter, including animations, press releases, pictures of the spacecraft, and images taken by Galileo of asteroids, the moon, Earth, Venus, and Jupiter; and images of the collision of fragments from Comet Shoemaker-Levy 9 with Jupiter in July 1994.

The site also has press releases, status reports, and fact sheets on spacecraft missions; teachers' materials on such topics as comets, life in the universe, the solar system, and robotic spacecraft; links to other Internet sites at the Jet Propulsion Laboratory; and much, much more.

Vital Stats:

Access method:	WWW
To access:	http://www.jpl.nasa.gov

Kennedy Space Center

The Kennedy Space Center site, which has everything from a huge historical archive about NASA space missions to daily updates of current space shuttle flights, is one of NASA's best.

The historical archive has extensive information about all of NASA's missions dating back to the early days of rocketry. Although what's available varies among missions, the files often include pictures of the mission patch, images, movies, audio clips, news releases, and other documents.

The site also has information about visiting the center and viewing launches; a virtual tour of the space shuttle; the *Shuttle Reference Manual,* a book of several hundred pages that discusses all phases of shuttle operations; images of the space shuttle, rockets, launches, and landings; detailed procurement information; details about facilities at the Kennedy Space Center; links to lots of other NASA Internet sites; and links to Internet sites in other countries that have space information.

Vital Stats:

Access method:	WWW
To access:	http://www.ksc.nasa.gov
E-mail:	webteam@news.ksc.nasa.gov

ksc-press-release *and* shuttle-status

These two mailing lists provide information from NASA's Kennedy Space Center.

The first list, ksc-press-release, offers information about activities at the Kennedy Space Center. A separate digest version, which combines multiple messages into a single message sent out less frequently, is available as ksc-press-release-digest.

The second list, shuttle-status, provides daily news about preparations for upcoming launches of the space shuttle. A separate digest version is available as shuttle-status-digest.

Vital Stats:

Access method:	E-mail
To access:	Send an e-mail message to domo@news.ksc.nasa.gov
Subject line:	
Message:	**subscribe** *listname*

Lunar Prospector

This site has extensive information about NASA's first moon mission in twenty-five years: Lunar Prospector, which it launched in January 1998 to hunt for water ice on the moon.

Some of the site's highlights include information about past missions to the moon, a book titled *Where No Man Has Gone Before: A History of Apollo Lunar Exploration Missions,* answers to dozens of frequently asked questions about the moon and Lunar Prospector, images and video clips from the mission, mission status reports, a lunar atlas, and lesson plans for teachers.

The site has one downside: Someone needs to tell the site's designer that white text on a black background is extremely difficult to read.

Vital Stats:

Access method:	WWW
To access:	http://lunar.arc.nasa.gov
E-mail:	kbollinger@mail.arc.nasa.gov

NASA Headquarters

The NASA Headquarters site has a huge assortment of information—everything from the full text of books about space history to news about legislative activity affecting NASA. The site has thousands of files. Fortunately, it also has a search engine to help you quickly find what you're seeking.

Among the site's highlights are books about space history. Some of the available titles are *The Problem of Space Travel: The Rocket Motor; On the Shoulders of Titans: A History of Project Gemini; Chariots for Apollo: A History of Manned Lunar Spacecraft; The Partnership: A History of the Apollo-Soyuz Test Project; On Mars: Exploration of the Red Planet 1958–1978;* and *Destination Moon: A History of the Lunar Orbiter Program.*

The site also has a timeline of air and space developments, mission patches, links to online resources for educators, a publication titled *NASA Pocket Statistics,* NASA's strategic plan, congressional testimony by NASA officials, a weekly legislative activities report that summarizes floor activity in the House and Senate and NASA-specific activity on the floor or in committee, links to other NASA Internet sites that have procurement information, biographies of past and current astronauts, links to dozens of other NASA Internet sites, and much more.

Vital Stats:

Access method:	WWW
To access:	http://www.hq.nasa.gov

NASA Homepage

The NASA Homepage is the main entry point into the enormous resources that NASA makes available on the Internet. Although the site offers few files of its own, it has links to dozens of other NASA sites—including special collections of links to NASA photos, videos, and audio recordings.

The site also has NASA's budget, international space station bilateral agreements, press releases, and answers to frequently asked questions about such topics as how to become an astronaut, how to get a job or internship at NASA, where to get NASA photos and videos, how to get launch passes, and how to get a schedule of upcoming launches.

Vital Stats:

Access method:	WWW
To access:	http://www.nasa.gov
E-mail:	comments@www.hq.nasa.gov

NASA Image eXchange (NIX)

NIX is an effort to link photograph databases at many NASA sites so that you can search them simultaneously.

Not all of NASA's photo databases have been linked into NIX yet. Currently, you can search databases containing more than 300,000 images.

When you conduct a search, NIX returns thumbnail-sized images, text descriptions, image numbers, links to higher resolution images, links to more information, and links to the NASA center that stores each image.

One handy feature is "Browse," which lets you quickly access many of NASA's best photos. The feature provides sets of preselected images that are considered the best for a particular topic.

NIX is another NASA site where the designer needs to learn the basic fact that trying to read white text on a black background is very hard on the eyes.

Vital Stats:

Access method:	WWW
To access:	http://nix.nasa.gov
E-mail:	sti+nix@larc.nasa.gov

NASA Johnson Space Center Digital Image Collection

The NASA Johnson Space Center Digital Image Collection offers an incredible group of space images dating from Project Mercury to current space missions.

There are actually two image collections. The first offers 10,000 images of everything from astronauts to rocket launches to space shuttle interiors. The second has nearly 30,000 images of Earth. All the images are compressed in the JPEG format.

Vital Stats:

Access method:	WWW
To access:	http://images.jsc.nasa.gov
E-mail:	chris.m.daquin1@jsc.nasa.gov

NasaNews

If you Finger NasaNews, several NASA press releases will automatically scroll down your screen. The press releases, which are changed daily, provide status reports about the space shuttle and other NASA news.

If you want to save the press releases, turn on the capture feature in your communications software before you Finger the site.

Vital Stats:

Access method:	Finger
To access:	finger nasanews@space.mit.edu
E-mail:	pds-requests@space.mit.edu

NASA Search

From this page, you can search all of NASA's Web sites at once. A search lets you access hundreds of thousands of documents and images spread across dozens of NASA sites.

To conduct a basic search, you simply type words or phrases into a box. An options page lets you target your search more carefully. Instead of searching all sites, you can just search a category: news, education, press release, commerce, astronomy, images, history, software, administrative, or people. And instead of searching all NASA sites, you can choose to search just those sites at a particular facility.

Vital Stats:

Access method:	WWW
To access:	http://www.nasa.gov/search
E-mail:	comments@www.hq.nasa.gov

The NASA Shuttle Web

As its name suggests, the NASA Shuttle Web provides virtually everything you could possibly want to know about past, current, and future flights of the space shuttle. The site has text files, audio, images, and videos—everything from daily prelaunch status reports to information about how to request launch passes to videos taken by shuttle crew members.

Vital Stats:

Access method:	WWW
To access:	http://shuttle.nasa.gov
E-mail:	robert.d.eddy1@jsc.nasa.gov

NASA Shuttle-Mir Web

The NASA Shuttle-Mir Web has information about activities of NASA astronauts and Russian cosmonauts on the Mir space station. It has photos, videos, mission status reports, and information about the U.S. and Russian crew members who served on Mir.

Vital Stats:

Access method:	WWW
To access:	http://shuttle-mir.nasa.gov
E-mail:	robert.d.eddy1@jsc.nasa.gov

NASA Spacelink

Although NASA Spacelink is designed for teachers and students, it provides tons of valuable information for anyone interested in the National Aeronautics and Space Administration (NASA) and space exploration. It offers thousands of files about everything from how to become an astronaut to upcoming space shuttle flights.

Through original files or links to other NASA sites, the fully searchable Spacelink has information about launch dates and payloads, status reports about current missions, press releases, extensive historical information about past NASA missions, details about newsletters and workshops for teachers, lesson plans, images of Earth, information about NASA research programs, images from selected space shuttle flights, images from NASA's planetary probes, information about technology transfer, hundreds of subject-related links to other NASA sites, and much more.

NASA also operates a mailing list called EXPRESS (p. 272) that sends out announcements about new materials on Spacelink.

Vital Stats:

Access method:	WWW
To access:	http://spacelink.msfc.nasa.gov
E-mail:	comments@spacelink.msfc.nasa.gov

National Space Science Data Center

If you have any interest in space, make sure you visit the National Space Science Data Center. It has an incredible collection of hundreds of images, documents, data sets, and lesson plans about the planets, the moon, asteroids, comets, the solar system, galaxies, stars, the sun, and spacecraft. The center, which is operated by NASA, also has extensive information about specific space missions.

Vital Stats:

Access method:	WWW
To access:	http://nssdc.gsfc.nasa.gov/nssdc/gen_public.html
E-mail:	james@nssdca.gsfc.nasa.gov

press-release

Subscribers to the press-release mailing list automatically receive NASA press releases and other selected documents. The documents are delivered to subscribers' e-mail mailboxes.

Vital Stats:

Access method:	E-mail
To access:	Send an e-mail message to majordomo@lists.hq.nasa.gov
Subject line:	
Message:	**subscribe press-release**
E-mail (questions):	domo-admin@hq.nasa.gov

Space Calendar

The Space Calendar page provides a calendar of space-related events for the coming year. The calendar has information about launches, anniversaries, and celestial events such as meteor showers. It also provides more than 1,100 links to related home pages.

The calendar is hosted by the New Products Development Group at the Jet Propulsion Laboratory.

Vital Stats:

Access method:	WWW
To access:	http://NewProducts.jpl.nasa.gov/calendar
E-mail:	baalke@kelvin.jpl.nasa.gov

Trading Post 3

This site provides a catalog of NASA apparel, collectibles, memorabilia, and toys that you can order. The catalog has everything from freeze-dried ice cream to patches from various NASA missions.

There's one irony: you can't place an order online.

Vital Stats:

Access method:	WWW
To access:	http://nasastore.jsc.nasa.gov
E-mail:	tracyd@forrestersmith.com

Views of the Solar System

Views of the Solar System offers hundreds of breathtaking images, animations, and movies of the sun, each planet, moons, asteroids, comets, and meteors, along with extensive text files. The site, which is beautifully organized, is operated by Calvin Hamilton, a former employee of the Los Alamos National Laboratory.

Vital Stats:

Access method:	WWW
To access:	http://bang.lanl.gov/solarsys
E-mail:	Hamil9410@aol.com

PLANETS

Center for Mars Exploration (CMEX)

Is there a face on Mars? Is there life on Mars? Discussions of these questions—along with everything else you could possibly want to know about Mars—are available at the Center for Mars Exploration (CMEX) site. It's operated by NASA.

The site has images, information about current conditions on Mars, and lesson plans for teachers. However, its most useful resource is a huge collection of links to other Internet sites that provide images, news about Mars missions, a map of Mars, documents about human exploration of Mars, scientific papers, newsletters, and information about past, present, and future Mars missions.

Vital Stats:

Access method:	WWW
To access:	http://cmex-www.arc.nasa.gov
E-mail:	jtsutsui@mail.arc.nasa.gov

Kepler Mission: A Search for Habitable Planets

This site has information about the Kepler mission, a proposed NASA mission to discover hundreds of Earth-size planets. The site offers background documents about the mission, files about Johannes Kepler and his laws of planetary motion, an interactive educational software package about planet detection for the Macintosh, links to technical papers, and links to other Internet sites about planet detection.

Vital Stats:

Access method:	WWW
To access:	http://www.kepler.arc.nasa.gov
E-mail:	dkoch@mail.arc.nasa.gov

Mars Missions

This site is a one-stop source for information about recent, current, and future NASA missions to Mars. Separate pages are available for the following missions: Mars Pathfinder, Mars Global Surveyor, Mars Surveyor 98, and Mars Surveyor 2001. The items available for each mission vary, but they typically include photos, status reports, project documents, press conference transcripts, and links to related sites.

The site also has general background information about the Mars exploration program and educational materials for teachers.

Vital Stats:

Access method:	WWW
To access:	http://marsweb.jpl.nasa.gov
E-mail:	kirk.goodall@jpl.nasa.gov

Mars Today

Mars Today offers a daily poster showing current conditions on Mars and its relationship to Earth. It also has information about water on Mars and animations showing the orbits of Earth and Mars, the view of Mars from Earth, and the predicted Mars meteorology over the next year. The site is operated by NASA's Ames Research Center.

Vital Stats:

Access method:	WWW
To access:	http://humbabe.arc.nasa.gov

MGS-Status

Subscribers to the MGS-Status mailing list receive weekly e-mail reports about the Mars Global Surveyor mission. The spacecraft, which was launched in November 1996, is scheduled to map the planet until January 2000.

Vital Stats:

Access method:	E-mail
To access:	Send an e-mail message to majordomo@mgsw3.jpl.nasa.gov
Subject line:	
Message:	**subscribe mgs-status**
E-mail (questions):	owner-majordomo@mgsw3.jpl.nasa.gov

PDS Mars Explorer for the Armchair Astronaut

PDS Mars Explorer for the Armchair Astronaut lets you explore Mars from your computer. Starting with an image of Mars, you click on the area you want and the underlying software creates an image map of the Mars surface. Arrow buttons let you pan and zoom on any image. The site is operated by NASA's Planetary Data System Imaging Node.

Vital Stats:

Access method:	WWW
To access:	http://www-pdsimage.wr.usgs.gov/PDS/public/mapmaker
E-mail:	dlarsen@flagmail.wr.usgs.gov

Planetary Photojournal

The Planetary Photojournal is a searchable database that contains more than 1,300 images from various NASA missions to the planets and the solar system. You can click on a planet to view its images, or you can search all the images by spacecraft, feature name, date, and set. Each planet's page also has links to other sites with images of the planet.

The Planetary Photojournal is operated by NASA's Jet Propulsion Laboratory.

Vital Stats:

Access method: WWW
To access: http://photojournal.jpl.nasa.gov
E-mail: pds_imaging@www-pdsimage.jpl.nasa.gov

Planetary Rings Node

The Planetary Rings Node has animations, images, and documents about the ring systems of Jupiter, Saturn, Uranus, and Neptune. It's operated by NASA.

The site also has a glossary of terms related to planetary rings; images, data, and documents from the Voyager mission; forms to help planetary scientists plan, acquire, and interpret observations of the ringed planets; and links to related Internet sites.

Vital Stats:

Access method: WWW
To access: http://ringside.arc.nasa.gov
E-mail: showalter@ringside.arc.nasa.gov

Welcome to the Planets

Welcome to the Planets is a collection of about 200 of the best images from NASA's planetary exploration program. Besides images of each planet, it offers background data about each planet, images of asteroids and comets, and images and text about spacecraft that explored the planets. The site was created by the Jet Propulsion Laboratory.

Vital Stats:

Access method: WWW
To access: http://pds.jpl.nasa.gov/planets
E-mail: PDS_OPERATOR@jplpds.jpl.nasa.gov

TRANSPORTATION

Amtrak

Amtrak's Web site offers extensive information about traveling by train in the United States. The site gives details about schedules, routes, facilities available on trains, vacation packages, and special offers available through Amtrak. It also has congressional testimony by Amtrak officials, news releases, updates about Amtrak's Northeast Corridor high-speed rail project, links to other Amtrak sites, and links to sites operated by foreign railroads.

Vital Stats:

Access method:	WWW
To access:	http://www.amtrak.com
E-mail:	amtrak_p@ix.netcom.com

Bureau of Transportation Statistics

The Bureau of Transportation Statistics site offers an enormous collection of data and information about every facet of transportation in the United States. The bureau is part of the U.S. Department of Transportation.

The site's highlight is the National Transportation Library, which offers hundreds of publications from a variety of government and private organizations. They cover such subjects as aviation, bicycles and pedestrians, economics and finance, intelligent transportation systems, laws and regulations, parking, public transportation, rail transportation, and safety, among many others.

The site also has the *Transportation Statistics Annual Report, The Journal of Transportation and Statistics*, lists of other sources of transportation data, and links to hundreds of other transportation-related Internet sites.

Vital Stats:

Access method:	WWW
To access:	http://www.bts.gov
E-mail:	webmaster@bts.gov

FAA Y2K Program Office

This site describes what the Federal Aviation Administration is doing to contend with the Year 2000 computer problem. It has the FAA's plan for repairing computers to deal with the Y2K problem, a timeline of milestones and completion dates, speeches, and links to related sites.

For a series of reports highly critical of the FAA's Year 2000 efforts, see the United States General Accounting Office site (p. 168).

Vital Stats:

Access method:	WWW
To access:	http://www.faay2k.com

Federal Aviation Administration

The Federal Aviation Administration site has safety information, regulatory documents, and links to more than 100 aviation-related Internet sites.

The site has preliminary reports about aircraft accidents and incidents that occurred within the past ten days, press releases about safety- and security-related enforcement actions that seek penalties of $50,000 or more, quarterly lists of all enforcement actions, and a link to another FAA site that offers detailed accident and incident data.

It also has FAA newsletters and magazines, acquisitions information for contractors, speeches by FAA officials, biographies of FAA officials, instructions about how to make a Freedom of Information Act request, a publication titled *Journalist's Guide to the FAA,* and lots more.

Vital Stats:

Access method:	WWW
To access:	http://www.faa.gov
E-mail:	webmasterFAA@faa.dot.gov

Federal Transit Administration

The highlight of the Federal Transit Administration site is the National Transit Library, a collection of dozens of publications about mass transit from various government and private sources. Some of the subjects covered are access to transit, budget and funding, intelligent transportation systems, management of transit systems, planning, safety and security, and transit technology.

The site also includes congressional testimony and speeches by FTA officials, a calendar of events, and links to dozens of other transportation-related Internet sites.

Vital Stats:

Access method:	WWW
To access:	http://www.fta.dot.gov

National Highway Traffic Safety Administration

The highlight of this site may be its crash test data for cars, trucks, vans, and sport utility vehicles. It's operated by the National Highway Traffic Safety Administration.

The site also has numerous databases. Some of the more interesting ones provide information about active defects investigations, complaints that have been filed with the Office of Defects Investigation, and auto and truck recalls.

Other sections of the site provide information about air bags, child safety seats, school buses, accidents, and other topics.

Vital Stats:

Access method: WWW
To access: http://www.nhtsa.dot.gov
E-mail: webmaster@nhtsa.dot.gov

The National Transportation Safety Board

The National Transportation Safety Board (NTSB) site offers descriptions of more than 41,000 aviation accidents from 1983 to the present. The short reports describe the accidents, their probable cause, and contributing factors.

The site also has the board's final reports from 1996 to the present about transportation accidents of various types. There are reports about aviation, highway, marine, pipeline, hazardous materials, and railroad accidents.

Other highlights are statistics on aviation accidents, descriptions of cockpit voice recorders and flight data recorders, details about the NTSB's investigative process, speeches and testimony about safety issues by NTSB officials, a list of transportation safety improvements recommended by the agency, and press releases.

Vital Stats:

Access method: WWW
To access: http://www.ntsb.gov

Office of System Safety Home Page

The Office of System Safety Home Page has an amazing collection of databases that offer information about aviation accidents, incidents, and safety recommendations. It's operated by the Federal Aviation Administration.

The largest database has summary reports about aircraft accidents and incidents from the National Transportation Safety Board. Other databases offer reports about near midair collisions, incident reports from the FAA, NTSB safety recommendations and FAA responses, and safety recommendations from aviation authorities in the United States, Canada, and the United Kingdom.

The site also has data about aviation system indicators, a report about public interest in aviation safety data, a form that allows online ordering of selected FAA documents and videos, and the *Aviation Safety Statistical Handbook,* which contains detailed data about aircraft accidents and incidents.

Vital Stats:

Access method: WWW
To access: http://nasdac.faa.gov
E-mail: webmaster@asymail.faa.gov

U.S. Department of Transportation Homepage

The U.S. Department of Transportation (DOT) Homepage has extensive information about transportation—everything from tips for consumers about filing transportation-related complaints to dozens of files about managing fatigue in transportation.

The site also has DOT newsletters, press releases, speeches by the secretary of transportation, DOT budget information, the full text of U.S. policy about air transportation, extensive information for firms seeking DOT contracts, DOT acquisition manuals and regulations, links to Web sites operated by state transportation departments, and links to Web sites operated by DOT agencies such as the Bureau of Transportation Statistics, Federal Aviation Administration, Federal Highway Administration, Federal Railroad Administration, and National Highway Traffic Safety Administration, among others.

Vital Stats:

Access method:	WWW
To access:	http://www.dot.gov
E-mail:	dot.comments@ost.dot.gov

White House Commission on Aviation Safety and Security

The White House Commission on Aviation Safety and Security site has the full text of the commission's final report, which it released in February 1997. The site also has transcripts of public hearings conducted by the commission, statements by the president and vice president about aviation safety, and links to lots of other Internet sites devoted to aviation safety and security.

Vital Stats:

Access method:	WWW
To access:	http://www.aviationcommission.dot.gov
E-mail:	webmaster@www.aviationcommission.dot.gov

GLOSSARY

ASCII   A plain text format that includes no coding.

Baud   A rate that indicates how fast a modem can transfer information. The higher the number, the faster the transfer.

BBS   *See* Bulletin board system.

Bulletin board system (BBS)   A computer system that you can access by calling with a modem attached to a computer. BBSs typically have text files or computer programs that you can download. Most also have e-mail systems that allow you to exchange messages with other users.

Capture feature   A feature in most communications software programs that allows you to "capture" in a text file the information that is scrolling on your screen from an Internet site. After logging off the site, you can review the file by using your word processing program.

Communications software   A software program that allows your computer to "talk" with other computers.

Compressed file   A file that has been made smaller than its original size. Files are compressed to make them download more quickly and take up less space than regular files. To use them, you must decompress them back to their original size after downloading them. Usually, this requires using a decompression program. However, some files are "self-executing," meaning that you don't need a special program to decompress them. Their filenames have an EXE extension. For example, a self-executing file might be called **BBSGUIDE.EXE.** Self-executing files cannot be used on most Macintosh computers.

Decompressed file   *See* Compressed file.

Directory   An Internet site that has a comprehensive set of links to other Internet sites about one or more topics.

Download   To copy a file to your computer from a remote computer.

E-mail   Electronic messages written using a computer and sent to another person's computer. E-mail is basically private, although it can be intercepted as it travels across the Internet.

Extension   A three-letter code at the end of a filename that usually indicates what program was used to create the file. The extension is separated from the rest of the filename by a period. For example, on a file called **BBSGUIDE.W51**, the extension W51 indicates that the file was created with WordPerfect 5.1. Sometimes, the extension indicates which program was used to compress the file. For example, a file called **BBSGUIDE.ZIP** was compressed with the PKZIP compression program.

FAQ A list of frequently asked questions, along with answers.

File   A document, graphic image, sound, or computer program. You can download copies of files from Internet sites to your own computer.

File transfer protocol (FTP)   An Internet protocol used to transfer copies of files from one computer to another. Most publicly accessible FTP sites allow you to access them by using "anonymous FTP." To use anonymous FTP, type **anonymous** when asked for a login and type your e-mail address when asked for a password. This procedure allows you to access and download selected files on the computer without being a registered user of the machine.

Finger   A utility program you can use to receive basic information from a few federal Internet sites. For example, if you Finger NasaNews, a stream of NASA press releases will scroll onto your computer screen.

Freeware   A software program that you can use free of charge. Some federal Internet sites have freeware that you can download.

FTP   *See* File transfer protocol.

Garbage   Nonsensical characters that appear on your computer screen when you connect to an Internet site. They're commonly caused by noise on the telephone line or incorrect settings in your communications software.

Gateway   A connection that allows you to move from one computer system to another. Many federal Internet sites have gateways to other Internet sites.

GIF   *See* Graphics interchange format.

Graphics interchange format (GIF)   A popular format for compressing and storing graphic files such as photographs. You need a viewer program to decompress and open the files.

Home page   A site on the World Wide Web, which is part of the Internet.

Internet   A vast international network of computer networks.

Listserv   *See* Mailing list.

Login   A word or words that you must type to access some Internet sites after connecting to them.

Mail server   A computer that responds to e-mail requests for files. If you send a properly formatted e-mail message to a mail server, it will send back the file you requested.

Mailing list   Regular postings of topical e-mail messages to which you can subscribe. Some mailing lists allow discussion, and any message sent to the list goes to every subscriber. Some federal government mailing lists are one way only, and they are used to distribute press releases or other documents from government agencies.

Meta directory   A "directory of directories" that has links to many Internet directories about particular topics.

Mirror site   A duplicate version of a World Wide Web site located on a second computer. Mirrors are created for popular sites to lessen the load on them.

Modem   A piece of hardware that transforms data into electronic signals that computers can exchange over ordinary telephone lines.

Newsgroup   *See* Usenet newsgroups.

Password   A code used to access some Internet sites. At most publicly accessible FTP sites, **anonymous** is the password.

PDF file   A file in portable document format. These files can be read only by using Adobe Acrobat Reader software, which is available free at http://www.adobe.com/acrobat.

Prompt   A message from the Internet site asking what you want to do next. Some prompts present a list of options from which you can choose.

Server   A computer on the Internet that has files that are available to other computers. Any time you access an Internet site, you're connecting to a server.

Shareware   A computer program you can try for free. If you decide to keep it, you must send the shareware fee to the program's author. Some federal Internet sites have shareware programs that you can download.

Telnet   An Internet protocol that allows you to connect to another computer and use it as if it were sitting on your desk. For example, you can use Telnet to access electronic card catalogs at many federal libraries.

Uniform resource locator   An Internet address for a site or file.

Upload   To copy a file from your computer to another computer.

URL   *See* Uniform resource locator.

Usenet newsgroups   Thousands of discussion groups where users can exchange messages about specific topics.

User   A person who uses the Internet.

Wildcard   A capability that allows you to search for a file using only a partial filename. You can type part of the filename and a "wildcard" symbol such as *, and the computer will search for all files containing the partial name.

World Wide Web (WWW)   A hypertext-based interface to the Internet. Hypertext files have links to other, related files embedded within them. To access the related file, you click on the link.

WWW   *See* World Wide Web.

Zipped   *See* Compressed file.

INDEX

ABLEDATA, 196
Abortion, 167, 189, 240
Abortion clinic attacks, 248
Academic freedom, 102
Access Board, 196
Access EPA, 29, 135
Accessibility, for disabled, 196, 197, 198
Access methods, 4
Access to information. *See* Information access
Acid rain, 135
Acquired immunodeficiency syndrome. *See* AIDS and
   HIV
Acquisition Reform Network (ARNet), 56
Acquisitions. *See* Procurement
ACQWeb, 80
Acupuncture, 190, 214
ADA (Americans with Disabilities Act), 18, 197, 198,
   233, 234, 236, 251
Addresses, of Internet sites, 5
Administration for Children and Families, 68
Administration on Aging, 194, 204
Administrative education, 112
Administrative law, 23, 240
Administrative management, 15
Adobe Acrobat Reader, 65, 207
Adolescents, 23, 70, 71, 103, 107
Adoption
   international, 144, 159
   of wild horses and burros, 139
Adult education, 100, 108
Advance directives, 208, 209
Advisory Council on Historic Preservation, 224
Aeronautics. *See* Space
Aerospace medicine, 260
Aerospace research. *See* Space
AFDC (Aid to Families with Dependent Children), 68
Affirmative action, 15
Africa, 47, 99, 106, 158
African Americans
   black colleges and universities, 113
   black soldiers in Civil War, 106
   black students, 107
   culture and history, 27
   U.S. Colored Troops, 228
   writing of, 224
African languages, 102
Age Discrimination Employment Act of 1967, 236
Agencies, 10, 15, 16, 22. *See also specific agency names*
Agency for Health Care Policy and Research, 204
Agency for Toxic Substances and Disease Registry, 128

Aging, 166, 186, 204, 207, 209, 216, 220
   Administration on Aging, 194, 204
   demographic data, 204
   Eldercare Locator, 204
   elderly crime victims, 250, 252
   National Senior Service Corps, 231
   Older Americans Act, 204
   travel and, 144
   White House Conference on Aging, 204
Agriculture, 32-37, 33, 35, 48, 129, 202, 255
   AGRICOLA database, 34
   agricultural engineering, 34
   Agricultural Research magazine, 32
   Agricultural Research Service, 29, 32
   agricultural sciences, 22
   Agriculture Fact Book, 23, 36
   alternative farming, 32, 34
   animal science, 34
   aquaculture, 32
   biodynamic farming, 32
   biological production management systems, 33
   biomass crops, 120
   census data on, 21
   child labor in, 104
   conservation tillage, 32
   cooperative extension services, 34-35
   crops, 32, 33, 36, 37, 120
   dairy production, 36, 37
   Economic Research Service, 33-34, 36
   economics, 33, 34, 36
   Farm Bill, 35, 36
   farm income, 33
   farmland preservation, 32
   farm production expenses, 36
   fertilizer, 36
   foreign trade and market development, 33
   income and finances, 33, 36
   industrial uses of agricultural materials, 36, 37
   livestock inventories, 36, 37
   low-input farming, 32
   marketing, 33, 34
   migrant farm workers, 104
   National Agricultural Library, 32, 34, 35, 37, 201
   National Agricultural Statistics Service, 36
   North Carolina Cooperative Extension Service, 34-
      35
   occupational hazards, 235
   organic farming, 32
   pesticides, 23, 129, 131, 135, 199, 201, 202
   products and product development, 33, 34

publications, 22
regenerative, 32
research, 32, 33
Rural Development, 35
Rural Information Center, 34, 35
safety and health, 35
small-scale farming, 32
soil conservation and management, 33, 34
specialty crops, 36, 37
state fact sheets, 33
statistics on, 94
structure of, in U.S., 36
supply and demand, international, 36, 37
sustainable farming, 32
trade, 34, 36, 37
vegetable crops, 32, 36, 37
weather and, 36
World Agricultural Outlook Board, 36
See also Agriculture Department; Food and
    nutrition; Rural areas
Agriculture Department
    USDA Agricultural Baseline Projections to 2007, 33
    USDA Cooperative State Research, Education, and
        Extension Service, 35
    USDA Economics and Statistics System, 36
    USDA Forest Service Home Page, 142
    USDA Home Page, 36
    USDA Reports Electronic Mailing List, 36-37
AIDS and HIV, 184-185, 189, 206, 207, 208
    adolescents and, 104
    AIDS Clinical Trials Information Service, 184
    AIDSDRUGS database, 189
    AIDS in the Workplace, 184
    AIDSLINE database, 189
    AIDSNews, 184-185
    AIDS Patent Database, 52
    AIDSTRIALS database, 189
    bibliographies, 185, 189
    CDC National Prevention Information Network, 185
    clinical trials, 184, 189, 211
    drugs for, 184, 185
    education, 188
    food safety and, 185
    funding opportunities, 184, 185
    HIV/AIDS Surveillance Report, 185, 205
    HIV/AIDS Treatment Information Service, 185
    HIV vaccines, 211
    intentional exposure crimes, 252
    Internet resources, 185
    knowledge and attitudes, 93
    patient care, 185
    pediatric AIDS, 211
    prevalence of, 185
    research, 211
    risk behaviors, 190, 214
    service organizations, 185

Social Security benefits and, 66
    travel and, 206
    treatment, 185
    women and HIV infection, 211
Aid to Families with Dependent Children (AFDC), 68
Air bags, 285
Aircraft. See Aviation
Air Force Link, 80
Air Force News Service, 81
Air pollution, 130
Air quality, 29, 129, 135, 140
Alaska, 27, 104, 262
Alaska Public Lands Information Centers, 139
Albright, Madeleine K., 149
Alcohol and alcohol abuse, 186-187, 207
    aging and, 186
    Alcohol Alerts, 186
    Bureau of Alcohol, Tobacco, and Firearms, 248
    college prevention programs, 102
    economic costs, 186
    National Clearinghouse for Alcohol and Drug
        Information, 187
    National Institute on Alcohol Abuse and Alcoholism,
        186
    pregnancy and, 186
    prevention programs, 104, 187
    PREVline (Prevention Online), 187
    treatment programs, 187
    See also Drugs and drug abuse; Substance abuse
Aliens, 177
Allergies, 184, 201, 207, 211, 235
Alternative Farming Systems Information Center, 32
Alternative fuels, 120, 121, 124
Alternative Fuels Data Center, 120
Alternative medicine, 214
Alzheimer's disease, 188, 207, 220, 221
    ALZHEIMER mailing list, 220
    ALZHEIMER Page, 220
    Alzheimer's Disease Education and Referral Center,
        220-221
American Association of Colleges for Teacher
    Education, 104
American Federation of Teachers, 96
American Forces Press Service, 82, 83
American Indians, 17, 42, 61, 104
American Library Association, 12
American Memory, 224-225
American Revolution, 42
Americans with Disabilities Act (ADA), 18, 197, 198,
    233, 234, 236, 351
American University, 171
America Reads, 231
America's Career InfoNet, 230
America's Children: Key National Indicators of Child
    Well-Being, 68
America's Job Bank, 230

America's National Parks Electronic Bookstore, 139
AmeriCorps, 231
Ames Research Center, 258, 281
Amphibian malformations, 133
Amphibians, 128
Amtrak, 284
Anabolic steroids, 186, 207
Animals, 32, 128, 140
animal science, 34
    animal welfare, 32-33, 34
    Animal Welfare Information Center, 32-33
    laboratory animals, 214
    marine mammals, 132, 133
    Office of Animal Care and Use, 214
    veterinary medicine, 189, 191
Annual Energy Outlook, 24
Anonymous FTP, 289
Antarctica, 133
Anthrax, 78, 79, 82
Anthropology, 42
Anti-Ballistic Missile Protocol, 86
Antidumping investigations, 51
Antitrust issues, 20
Anxiety disorders, 207, 221
Apollo missions, 274, 275
Appalachia Educational Laboratory, 104
Applications and forms, 13
Aquaculture, 32
Arabic language, 106
Arbitration, 238
Architect of the Capitol Home Page, 225
Architectural and Transportation Barriers Compliance
  Board, 196
Architectural Barriers Act, 196
Architecture, 224
Archives, 27, 85, 151, 166, 227-228, 250
Argonne National Laboratory, 124
Arms control, 86, 158, 166
    Arms Control and Disarmament Agency, 86
    Arms Control and Disarmament Agreements, 24
Army, 2
    Army area handbooks, 27
    Army Center of Military History, 86
    Army Chemical and Biological Defense Command,
      78
    Army Homepage, 86-87
    Army Medical Department, 78
    Army Medical Research Institute of Chemical
      Defense, 79
    Army Medical Research Institute of Infectious
      Diseases, 79
    Army Recruiting Web Site, 87
Army Corps of Engineers, 142
ARNet (Acquisition Reform Network), 56
Arson, 116, 248
Arthritis, 188, 207, 211-212, 216

Arts and museums, 40-43
    art history, 98
    art materials, 176
    Arts.community, 40
    ARTSEDGE, 96
    arts education, 96, 106, 107, 111
    decorative arts, 41
    First 150 Years, The: The Traveling Exhibition, 40
    Franklin D. Roosevelt Library and Museum, 225
    John F. Kennedy Center for the Performing Arts, 40,
      96
    landscape painting, 110
    Lyndon B. Johnson Library and Museum, 227
    National Air and Space Museum, 40
    National Endowment for the Arts, 40-41, 96
    National Gallery of Art, 41
    National Museum of American Art, 41
    National Museum of Natural History, 42
    National Portrait Gallery, 42
    in rural areas, 35
    Smithsonian Institution, 42-43
    Smithsonian Institution Research Information
      System (SIRIS), 43
Asbestos, 235
ASCII format, 288
Asian American families, 70
Asian financial crisis, 158
AskERIC, 96
Asparagus, 34
Assassination Records Review Board, 175
Assassinations, 84, 175, 228
Assistive technology, 62, 75, 100, 196, 197, 198
Asteroids and comets, 270-271, 273, 278, 279, 282
    Asteroid and Comet Impact Hazards, 270
    Comet Observation Home Page, 270
    Hale-Bopp comet, 271
    Near-Earth Asteroid Tracking Home Page, 270
    Near-Live Comet Watching System, 271
    Shoemaker-Levy 9 comet, 273
    Stardust, 271
    Stardust Mailing List, 271
    Wild 2 comet, 271
Asthma, 207, 210, 211
Astronauts, 275, 277
Astrophysics, 257
Athletics and academics, 102
Atmospheric science, 256
Attention deficit disorders, 100, 212-213, 214, 221
Attorneys' fees, 238
Auctions, 16, 50, 57. *See also* Sales
Autism, 100, 213
Automation technologies, 258
Automobiles. *See* Vehicles
Aviation, 22, 260, 284, 285
    accidents and incidents, 80, 285, 286
    aircraft, 40, 84, 87, 175

air transportation policy, 287
Aviation Safety Statistical Handbook, 286
forecasts, 262
National Air and Space Museum, 40
noise, 260
safety and security, 286, 287
SR71 Blackbird spy plane, 40

"Bad Bug Book," 201
Balkans, 146
Ball, Lucille, 248
Ballistic missile defense systems, 80
Bankruptcy courts, 11, 238, 241, 242-244
Banks and banking, 54
bank failures, 62
    bank holding companies, 63
    bank ratings, 62
    Federal Reserve banks, 54-55
    foreign branches of U.S. banks, 63
    on the Internet, 62
    laws, 62
    mergers and acquisitions, 63
    statistics on, 62, 63
    U.S. branches of foreign banks, 63
Barbie, Klaus, 248
Baseball, 225
Base closure and realignment, 47, 82, 162
Batteries, 257
Battlefields, 141
Baud rate, 288
Bay of Pigs invasion, 146
BBS (bulletin board system), 11, 18-19, 288
Bears, 136
Behavioral sciences, 22
Behavior control, 189
Bibliographies, 16, 26
Bicycles, 284
Bilingual education, 103
Bill of Rights, 18
Biodiversity, 129
Biodynamic farming, 32
Bioenergy Information Network, 120
Bioethics, 189, 210
BIOETHICSLINE database, 189
Biofuels, 120
    Biofuels Information Center, 120
    Biofuels UPDATE, 120
Biological diversity, 140
Biological research, 166
Biological Resources Division, 128
Biological weapons. *See* Chemical and biological
    weapons
Biology, 121, 128, 256, 259
    biotechnology, 47, 51, 191, 201
    marine biology, 256
    paleobiology, 42

Biomass crops, 120
Biomedicine, 29, 189, 214
Biopower, 120
Biotechnology, 47, 51, 191, 201
Birds, 128, 140, 142
Birth certificates, 205
Birth defects, 205
Black colleges and universities, 113
Blacks. *See* African Americans; Minorities
Blair House Papers, The (Clinton and Gore), 174
Blindness, 27, 28, 196, 210
Blizzards, 133
Blood pressure, 210
Blood supply, 209
Board of Governors of the Federal Reserve System, 54
Boards, commissions, and committees, 15
Boating, 86
Bombs and bomb threats, 116, 248
Bonds, 54
Bone diseases, 201, 216
Bonnie and Clyde, 248
Books, 17, 22
    book fairs, 27
    bookstores, 26, 85, 139
    See also Publications; Reading
Boot camps, 249
Booth, John Wilkes, 248
Border Patrol, 177
BosniaLINK, 81
Bosnia Report, 144, 149
Boston Harbor pollution flow, 132
Botanical prints, 34
Botanic Garden, 225
Botany, 42
Brady, Mathew, 224
Brady handgun law, 248
Brain disorders, 212, 214
Breast cancer, 190, 192-193, 199, 214, 215
Breastfeeding, 201
Broadcasting, 147, 148, 149
Broadcasting Board of Governors, 148, 149
Budget, 16, 18, 24, 50, 162, 167, 168
Buffalo World's Fair, 224
Bulgaria, 124
Bulletin board system (BBS), 11, 18-19, 288
Bureau of Alcohol, Tobacco, and Firearms, 248
Bureau of Consular Affairs Home Page, 144, 150
Bureau of Diplomatic Security, 144-145
Bureau of Economic Analysis, 20, 93
Bureau of Export Administration, 46
Bureau of Justice Statistics, 238, 250
Bureau of Labor Statistics, 92, 93, 235
Bureau of Land Management, 139-140, 141, 142,
    254
Bureau of Reclamation, 142, 254
Bureau of the Census. *See* Census Bureau

Bureau of the Public Debt, 50, 54
Bureau of Transportation Statistics, 284, 287
Burma, 148
Burn prevention, 176
Burros, 139
Burundi, 158
Bush, George and Barbara, 226
Business and industry, 12, 13, 15, 46-53, 62-64
    Bureau of Export Administration, 46
    business development, 47-48, 53
    business financing, 47, 49
    case studies, 47
    Commerce Department, 49-50
    Federal Communications Commission, 62
    Federal Deposit Insurance Corporation, 62
    Federal Electronic Commerce Program Office, 46
    Federal Financial Institutions Examination Council,
        63
    HomePath, 63
    IBM Patent Server, 46-47
    industry trend data, 47
    International Trade Commission, 50-51
    and the Internet, 48
    marketing, 53
    National Credit Union Administration, 63-64
    National Gambling Impact Study Commission, 64
    Office of Economic Conversion Information, 47
    Office of the U.S. Trade Representative's Homepage,
        47
    Online Women's Business Center, 47-48
    Patent and Trademark Office, 46, 49, 51, 52
    Postal Service, 52
    Securities and Exchange Commission, 2, 52-53
    selling to the government, 49
    starting a business, 47-48, 231
    Tourism mailing list, 48-49
    Treasury Department, 50
    U.S. Business Advisor, 49
    U.S. Government Electronic Commerce Policy, 50
    USPTO Patent Databases, 52
    WhoWhere? Edgar, 53
    See also Small business

Cabinet members, 163
Calcium, 212, 214, 216
California, 225, 255
California Institute of Technology, 273
Cambodia, 148
Campaign finance, 134, 170, 171, 172
Campaign Finance Data on the Internet, 171
Cancer, 166, 192-193, 207
    breast cancer, 190, 192-193, 199, 214, 215
    Cancer Information Service, 193
    CancerNet, 192, 193
    Cancer Trials, 192
    carcinogens, 134, 199, 200, 235

cervical cancer, 190
    clinical trials, 192
    incidence of, 206
    melanoma, 214
    National Action Plan on Breast Cancer, 192-193
    National Cancer Institute, 192, 193
    nutrition and, 201
    patient care and education, 188, 192
    prevention and control, 188, 192
    research, 192, 193
    risk factors, 192
    screening, 208
    treatment, 192
Canyon WebWorks, 140
Capital punishment, 246, 250
Capitol and Capitol Hill, 27, 168, 225
Capture feature, 288
Carcinogens, 134, 199, 200, 235
Cardiovascular health, 201, 207, 208, 210, 214
Careers
    career and vocational schools, 19
    career counseling and education, 100
    Career Resource Library, 230
    information on, 14, 92
    See also Jobs
Cargo theft, 251
Carjacking, 250
CARL (Colorado Alliance of Research Libraries), 17
Carnegie Mellon Software Engineering Institute, 75
Carpal tunnel syndrome, 213
Cars. See Vehicles
Carter, Jimmy and Rosalynn, 226
Cascades Volcano Observatory, 254
Catalog of Federal Domestic Assistance, 17, 18, 61, 70
Catalog of U.S. Government Publications, 23
Cataracts, 210
Catholic University of America, 100
Caucasus Report, 145, 149
CBDNet, 56
CDC (Centers for Disease Control and Prevention),
    184, 188, 194, 205, 206
    CDC Diabetes and Public Health Resource, 205
    CDC National Prevention Information Network, 185
    CDC's Tobacco Information and Prevention Source
        (TIPS), 206
    CDC Travel Information, 205-206
    CDC WONDER, 205, 206
    Daily News Update, 184, 185
Cemeteries, 83
Census Bureau, 20, 49, 92, 93, 94
    Census and You, 92
    censusandyou mailing list, 92
    mailing lists, 92
    press releases, 29
    See also Demographic data
Census of Agriculture, 21

Census of Manufacturers, 23
Census of Population and Housing, 20
Center for Applied Linguistics, 103, 108
Center for Civic Education, 96
Center for Food Safety and Applied Nutrition, 201
Center for Information Law and Policy, 10
Center for Intelligent Information Retrieval, 13
Center for Mars Exploration (CMEX), 280
Center for National Independence in Politics, 170
Center for Responsive Politics, 171
Center for the Book, 27
Center for the Study of Intelligence, 145
Centers for Disease Control and Prevention. *See* CDC
Central Intelligence Agency. *See* CIA
Cervical cancer, 190
CFS (chronic fatigue syndrome), 205, 211
Charter of Paris for a New Europe, 86
Charter schools, 101, 112
Chemical and biological weapons, 78-79, 82, 86, 217
    Army Chemical and Biological Defense Command,
      78
    Army Medical Research Institute of Chemical
      Defense, 79
    Army Medical Research Institute of Infectious
      Diseases, 79
    Biological Weapons Convention, 86
    Chemical Weapons Convention, 86
    Nuclear, Biological, and Chemical Medical Defense
      Information Server, 78
Chemicals, 189, 199, 200
    chemical engineering, 259, 260
    chemical processes, 260
    Chemical Scorecard, 129
    chemical spills, 135
    ChemID database, 189
    chemistry, 121
    contaminants in food, 201
Chernobyl nuclear power plant, 124
Chesapeake Bay, 256
Children and families, 68-71
    Administration for Children and Families, 68
    adolescents, 23, 70, 71, 103, 107
    arts and humanities programs, 68
    at-risk children, 23
    books for children and parents, 69, 70
    child abuse and neglect, 69
    child care, 68, 69, 70, 104, 235
    Child Care Bulletin, 69
    child development, 70, 98
    child labor, 235, 236
    child pornography, 251
    ChildStats.gov, 68
    child support, 68, 70
    Child Support Enforcement, 68
    Coming Up Taller: Arts and Humanities Programs
      for Children and Youth at Risk, 68

consumer information, 14, 17
Council for Exceptional Children, 100
delinquency prevention, 250
demographic information, 68
disabilities and, 198
Family and Medical Leave Act, 231, 235
family leave, 70, 231, 235, 236
family planning, 190
family reunification programs, 70
fatherhood, 68
furniture for children, 176
illnesses of children, 69
kidnapping, 159, 248, 251
maternal and child health, 188, 190
missing children, 250, 251
National Child Care Information Center (NCCIC),
  69
National Clearinghouse on Child Abuse and Neglect
  Information, 69
National Parent Information Network (NPIN), 69-
  70
Office of the Assistant Secretary for Planning and
  Evaluation, 70
PARENTING-L mailing list, 70-71
publications, 17, 69, 70
reading and, 98
Safe Places to Play, 71
safety, 69
safety seats, 285
self-esteem of children, 98
single parents, 69
statistics, 68
television and, 69
video games and, 69
Web Pages for Kids around the Federal Government,
  71
Web sites for kids, 71
working parents, 69
writing and children, 69
YouthInfo, 71
China, 33, 148, 158
Chinese language, 106
Cholesterol, 207
Chronic fatigue syndrome (CFS), 205, 211
Churches, 94, 248
CIA (Central Intelligence Agency), 22, 145-146, 219,
  251
    Center for the Study of Intelligence, 145
    creation of, 151
    Electronic Document Release Center, 146
    Intelligence Reform Program, 84
    publications and maps, 146
CIAC-Bulletin mailing list, 74
Citizenship, U.S., 144, 177
Civic education, 96
Civic participation, 16

Civil litigation, 238
Civil rights, 15, 158, 167, 168, 236, 251, 252
   Civil Rights Act, 236
   Civil Rights Commission, 252
Civil service, 16, 231
Civil War, 17, 106, 139, 224, 227, 228
Civnet, 96-97
Classification policy, 146, 175
Clean Cities, 121
Clean Water Act, 134
Climate, 15, 33, 129, 133, 162, 256, 262
Clinical trials, 210, 211, 212, 213, 215, 216
Clinton, Bill, 2, 69, 81, 165, 174, 178, 208, 246
Clinton, Hillary Rodham, 178
Clocks, 260
Cloning, 210
Closing the Gap, 215
Clouds, 133
CMEX (Center for Mars Exploration), 280
Coal production, 122
Coastal areas, 135, 256
Coast Guard, 87
Cocaine, 186, 251, 252
Code of Federal Regulations, 14, 18, 24, 235
Coins, 50, 61
Colds, 207
Cold War, 145, 219
Colleges and universities, 102, 109
   academic freedom, 102
   academics and athletics, 102
   admission tests, 109
   affirmative action, 102
   alcohol and drug abuse prevention, 102
   black, 113
   budgeting for, at state level, 102
   collective bargaining in higher education, 102
   community colleges, 99
   community service learning, 102
   cost of higher education, 107
   crime on campus, 102
   distance learning, 102
   diversity in, 102
   faculty evaluation, 102
   faculty tenure, 102
   financial aid, 58, 105, 109, 111, 112
   funding, 102, 111
   high-risk students, 102
   minorities in, 107, 113
   multiculturalism in, 102
   preparing for college, 111
   sexual harassment in, 102
   stress reduction for students, 102
   technology and, 102
Colorado Alliance of Research Libraries (CARL)
   Databases, 17
Columbia University Libraries, 23

Combined Health Information Database, 188
Comet Hale-Bopp, 271
Comet Observation Home Page, 270
Comets. *See* Asteroids and comets
Comet Shoemaker-Levy 9, 273
Comet Wild 2, 271
Coming Up Taller: Arts and Humanities Programs for
   Children and Youth at Risk, 68
Commerce
   Commerce Business Daily, 18, 23, 49, 56, 58, 59
   Commerce Department, 47, 49-50, 56, 259
   See also Trade
Commission on Family and Medical Leave, 236
Commission on the Future of Worker-Management
   Relations, 236
Commission on the Roles and Capabilities of the U.S.
   Intelligence Community, 84
Commissions, 15
Committee for the National Institute for the
   Environment, 129
Committee Hearings, 162
Committee on Commerce Tobacco Documents,
   207
Committees, 15
Communication disorders, 188
Communications, 103, 110, 175
Communications software, 288
Communism, 145
Community case studies, 47
Community colleges, 99
Community development, 33, 35, 36, 47
Community facilities programs, 35
Community organizing, 18
Community projects, 18
Community Reinvestment Act, 54, 63
Community Right-To-Know program, 131
Community Services Block Grants, 68
Compendium of Federal Justice Statistics, 23
Competition issues, 20, 162
Complementary medicine, 214
Composting, 32, 120
Comprehensive Nuclear Test Ban Treaty, 86
Compressed files, 288
Comptroller of the Currency, 50
Computers, 74-76, 257
   CIAC-Bulletin mailing list, 74
   computer-assisted language learning, 102
   computer crime, 251, 252
   Computer Incident Advisory Capability, 74,
   75
   computer science, 22, 121, 259
   Computer Security Resource Clearinghouse, 74
   Computers for Learning, 97
   donating to schools, 97
   FedCIRC (Federal Computer Incident Response
   Capability), 75

Federal Y2K Commercial Off-the-Shelf (COTS)
   Product Database, 75
fraud, 252
hoaxes, 74
IT Policy On-Ramp, 75
President's Council on Year 2000 Conversion, 76
searching and seizing, 251
security, 74, 75, 84, 166
software, 53, 102
viruses, 74, 75
Year 2000, 13, 15, 63, 75, 76, 158, 168, 284
Conflict deterrence, 23, 158
Conflicts of interest, 177
Congress, 2-3, 10, 12, 162-170
   addresses, 16, 169
   bills, 11, 14, 18, 22, 24, 25, 28, 163, 167, 168, 170
   bills, administrative policy on, 179
   bills, cost estimates of, 162
   calendars and schedules, 24, 168
   campaign finance information, 134, 170, 171
   committee hearings, 162
   committees, 25, 162, 168, 170
   committee votes, 163
   Congress Today, 162
   directories, 16, 24-25, 162
   districts, 94
   documents, 25
   elections, 172
   e-mail addresses, 169
   FEDNET, 164
   financial disclosure statements, 171
   "Find Your Representative," 162
   floor proceedings, 169
   GAO Daybook, 164, 168
   General Accounting Office, 168
   hearings, 164
   intelligence and, 145
   legislation, 169
   legislative research, 167
   live broadcasts of floor debates, 164
   members, 16, 25, 163, 170
   news conferences, 164
   Office of Technology Assessment, 166
   organizations and commissions, 169
   OTA Legacy, 166
   Penny Hill Press, 166-167
   reports, 25
   resolutions, 24, 25, 28, 163
   technology and, 166
   THOMAS, 167
   U.S. Legislative Branch, 169
   Vote Smart Web, 170
   voting records, 162, 163, 169, 170
   See also House of Representatives; Senate
Congressional Budget Office, 162-163
Congressional Directory, 24-25

Congressional Quarterly's American Voter, 163
Congressional Quarterly VoteWatch, 163
Congressional Record, 14, 18, 22, 24, 25, 168, 169
Congressional Research Service, 3, 166, 167
Congressional Research Service Reports, 129
Conscientious objection, 86
Conservation movement, 224
Conservation tillage, 32
Consolidated Federal Funds Report, 21
Constitution, U.S., 16, 18, 25, 106, 168, 239, 240
Constitutional Convention, 224
Construction industry, 235
Consulates and embassies, 16, 144, 150, 151-157, 159
Consumer issues
   consumer disputes, 19
   Consumer Gateway, 14
   Consumer Health Information, 207
   Consumer Information Center, 17
   Consumer Product Safety Commission, 71, 176
   consumer protection rules, 20
   Consumer's Resource Handbook, 17
   information on, 10, 12, 13, 15, 17
Consumer price index, 54, 55, 92
Continental Congress, 224
Contracts, 16, 49, 53, 56-61
   CBDNet, 56
   General Services Administration, 60-61
   Ginnie Mae: Government National Mortgage
      Association, 57
   HUD, 18
   List of Defaulted Borrowers, 58
   Loren Data Corp., 58
   NAIS Email Notification Service, 59
   NASA Acquisition Internet Service (NAIS) Home
      Page, 59-60
   SBA PRO-Net, 48
   Small Business Administration, 53
   small-business contractors, 48
Cooperative extension services, 34-35
Copyright, 12, 16, 27, 28, 102, 240
Copyright Office, 27
Coral reefs, 133, 135, 256
Core Documents of U.S. Democracy, 18
Cornell Law School, 239, 240, 241
Cornell University, 36, 236
Coronary disease, 201, 207, 208, 210, 214
Corporal punishment, 101
Corporate citizenship, 235
Corporate crime, 252
Corporation for National Service, 231
Correctional education, 108
Corrections. See Prisons and prisoners
Corrosion, 260
Council for Exceptional Children, 100
Council of Economic Advisers, 25, 180
Council of the Great City Schools, 98

Council on Environmental Quality, 130
County and City Data Book, 23, 93
County Business Patterns, 93, 94
Courts, 238-247, 249
  appeals, 14
  bankruptcy, 11, 238, 241, 242-244
  circuit, 10, 11
  district, 10, 11
  federal court decisions, 239
  Federal Court Locator, 10
  Federal Judicial Center Home Page, 238
  Federal Judiciary Homepage, 238
  FindLaw, 238-239
  Georgetown University Legal Explorer, 239
  history of, 238, 246
  Law Journal Extra!, 239
  Legal Information Institute, 239-240
  liibulletin mailing list, 240
  media coverage, 238
  Oyez Project, 240-241
  State Court Locator, 10
  state courts, 10, 239
  U.S. Federal Courts Finder, 247
  See also Supreme Court; *specific courts*
Credit, 33
  credit cards, 17, 19, 54
  credit repair scams, 19
  credit reports, 20
Credit unions, 63-64
Crime, 12
  corporate crime, 252
  crime information for cities and countries, 148
  drug-related, 250
  elderly victims, 250, 252
  hate crimes, 23, 248
  international crime and criminal justice, 85, 250
  organized crime, 250
  prevention, 249, 251
  reports on, 15, 248
  in rural areas, 35, 249
  in schools, 250
  sentencing guidelines, 238, 250, 252
  sex crimes, 249, 252
  statistics on, 15
  Uniform Crime Report, 24, 93
  victims, 249, 250, 251
  See also Justice; Prisons and prisoners
Criminal justice, 12, 167, 249, 250
CRIS (Current Research Information System), 33
*Critical Foundations: Protecting America's
  Infrastructures,* 85
Critical Infrastructure Assurance Office, 81
Crops, 32, 33, 36, 37, 120
Crude oil production and prices, 122
Crustaceans, 140
Cryptology, 84-85, 248

C-SPAN, 162
Cuba, 147
Cuban missile crisis, 84
Currency, 14, 17, 50, 55, 61
Current Population Survey, 93, 94
Current Research Information System (CRIS), 33
Customs Service Web Site, 251
Cyanide, 78, 79
CyberSoft, 202
Cystic fibrosis, 190, 214

Daguerreotypes, 224
Daily-sales mailing list, 56-57
Dairy production, 33
Dance, 96
Dante II, 257
DEA (Drug Enforcement Administration), 251
Dead Sea Scrolls, 27
Deafness, 61, 100, 188, 204, 207, 214
Death certificates, 205
Death penalty, 246, 250
Declaration of Independence, 18, 27, 96, 168, 228
Declassification of documents, 146, 175
Decorative arts, 41
Deer, 141
Defense, 78-89, 167, 168
  ACQWeb, 80
  Air Force Link, 80
  Air Force News Service, 81
  Arms Control and Disarmament Agency, 86
  Army Homepage, 86-87
  Army Recruiting Web Site, 87
  BosniaLINK, 81
  Coast Guard, 87
  Critical Infrastructure Assurance Office, 81
  defense conversion, 47
  Defense Department, 2, 47, 80, 81, 82, 83, 84, 217,
    219
  Defense Department Inspector General, 83
  Defense Intelligence Agency, 81-82
  Defense Language Institute, 106
  DefenseLINK, 82
  DefenseLINK News by Email, 83
  Defense Nuclear Facilities Safety Board Server, 88
  Defense Technical Information Center (DTIC)
    Home Page, 82
  Intelligence Reform Program, 84
  MarineLINK, 84
  National Defense Panel, 82
  National Security Agency, 84-85
  National Security Council, 85
  Navy, 87
  Pentagon Book Store Online, 85
  President's Commission on Critical Infrastructure
    Protection, 85
  Selective Service System, 86

technology and, 166
Veterans Affairs Department, 83
See also Chemical and biological weapons; Military;
   Nuclear weapons
DeLay, Tom, 165, 170
Delinquency prevention, 250
Dementia, 220
Democracy, 18, 158
Demographic data, 12, 15, 20-21, 22, 92-94, 227
   Bureau of Labor Statistics, 92, 93, 235
   censusandyou mailing list, 92
   Census of Agriculture, 21
   Census of Manufacturers, 23
   Census of Population and Housing, 20
   children and families, 68
   churches, 94
   counties, 23, 93, 94
   Current Population Survey, 93, 94
   Earnings by Occupation and Education, 21
   elderly, 204
   FERRET, 93
   for genealogical research, 227
   Geospatial and Statistical Data Center, 93-94
   Historical Census Data Browser, 94
   housing, 20, 94
   i-net bulletin mailing list, 92
   North Carolina counties, 34
   population, 20, 35, 54, 93, 94, 135, 177, 190
   press-release mailing list, 92
   product-announce mailing list, 92
   on slave ownership, 94
   State and Metropolitan Area Databook, 11, 23
   Statistical Abstract of the United States, 11, 18, 23, 26,
     94
   Survey of Income and Program Participation, 93
   See also Census Bureau
Dental health, 188, 204, 212
Dentistry, 189, 191
Depression, 204, 207, 214, 216, 221
Design arts, 96
Detroit Publishing Company, 224
Diabetes, 188, 201, 206, 207, 208, 212
   CDC Diabetes and Public Health Resource, 205
   Diabetes in America, 207-208
   diabetic eye disease, 210
Dial-in access, 5
Dialysis, 214
Diesel fuel, 123
Dietary guidelines, 23, 33, 201, 215
Dietary supplements, 190, 202-203
Diet programs, 19, 188, 201
Digestive diseases, 188, 207, 212
Digest of Education Statistics, 24, 107
Digital Daily, The, 65
Digital Dispatch, 65
Digital television, 62

Dillinger, John, 248
Dinosaurs, 106, 271
Diplomatic security, 144-145
Directories, 288
DIRLINE database, 189
Disabilities, 13, 101, 196-198, 209
   ABLEDATA, 196
   Access Board, 196
   accessibility issues, 196, 197, 198
   accessible housing, 196
   Americans with Disabilities Act, 18, 197, 198, 233,
     234, 236, 351
   assistive technology, 62, 75, 100, 196, 197, 198
   children with, 98, 198
   Disabilities and Managed Care, 196-197
   disability benefits, 66
   discrimination and, 236
   education and, 100-101, 102, 110
   employment and, 197, 232, 233, 234
   inclusionary education, 197
   law, 197
   minorities with, 197
   National Council on Disability, 197
   National Institute on Disability and Rehabilitation
     Research, 196, 197, 198
   National Rehabilitation Information Center, 197-198
   products, 196
   research, 197, 198
   rights and responsibilities of parents, 98
   Trace Research and Development Center, 198
Disaster assistance, 53, 116
Disasters, 15, 116, 221, 225
Discrimination, 236, 252
Diseases
   disease clusters, 128
   infectious diseases, 79, 184, 205, 211
   outbreaks, 205
   prevention, 188, 214-215
   rare diseases, 188, 215-216
   See also specific diseases
Dispatch, 147, 159
Distance education, 100, 103, 107
Divorce certificates, 205
DNA testing and research, 248, 251, 257
Doctors, student loan defaults, 58
Documents, 12, 16, 18, 23-24
DOE. *See* Energy Department
DOE Information Bridge, 121
DOE Reports Bibliographic Database, 125
Dolphins, 133
Domestic assistance programs, 17
Domestic violence, 70, 251
Downloading, 288
Downtown revitalization, 35
Draft lotteries, 86
Dr. Felix's Free MEDLINE Page, 188

Drinking. *See* Alcohol and alcohol abuse
Drinking water, 129
DR-NRR mailing list, 121-122
Dropouts, 107, 113
Dr. Seuss, 103
Drugs and drug abuse, 186-187
   anabolic steroids, 186, 207
   cocaine, 186, 251, 252
   college prevention programs, 102
   crime and, 249
   Drug Enforcement Administration (DEA), 251
   Drug Policy Information Clearinghouse, 179
   drug-related crime, 250
   economic costs, 186
   enforcement efforts, 179
   heroin, 186, 190
   inhalant abuse, 186, 207
   marijuana, 179, 207
   National Clearinghouse for Alcohol and Drug Information, 187
   National Institute on Drug Abuse, 186
   Office of National Drug Control Policy, 179
   opiate addiction, 214
   pregnancy and, 186
   prevention programs, 102, 179, 186, 187
   PREVline (Prevention Online), 186
   research, 186
   smuggling, 251
   treatment programs, 179, 187
   violence and, 179
   women and, 186
   See also Medications; Substance abuse
Drunk driving. *See* Alcohol and alcohol abuse
DTIC (Defense Technical Information Center) Home Page, 82
Dunlop Commission, 236

Earhart, Amelia, 151, 248
Early childhood education, 68, 69, 97, 101, 111
Earnings by Occupation and Education, 21
Earth from Space, 272
Earthquake Information, 255
Earthquakes, 23, 116, 224, 255, 256
Earth sciences, 254-256
   Cascades Volcano Observatory, 254
   Earthquake Information, 255
   earthquakes, 23, 116, 224, 255, 256
   Geological Survey, 71, 128, 254, 255, 256
   geology, 140, 256
   Global Change Data and Information System, 255
   Interior Department Home Page, 254
   magnetic field of earth, 256
   National Ocean Service, 255
   NOAA Web Sites, 133
   oceanography, 110, 256, 260

   USGS Branch of Earthquake and Geomagnetic Information On-line Information System, 256
   volcanoes, 133, 254, 256, 258
   WINDandSEA, 256
Eastern Europe, 149
Easy Access for Students and Institutions (Project EASI), 109
Eating disorders, 201, 207, 216, 221
Ebonics, 103
ECENET-L mailing list, 97
Economics, 12, 15, 20-21, 54-55, 158, 162
   agricultural, 34
   Board of Governors of the Federal Reserve System, 54
   Bureau of Economic Analysis, 20, 93
   Bureau of Labor Statistics, 92
   Bureau of the Public Debt on the Net, 54
   Council of Economic Advisers, 25, 180
   Economic Census, 21
   economic conversion, 47
   economic development, 35, 36, 46, 166
   economic indicators, 25, 54
   Economic Report of the President, 18, 25
   Economic Research Service, 33-34, 36
   Economic Research Service Situation and Outlook Reports, 36
   Federal Reserve Banks, 54-55
   Historical Census Data Browser, 94
   Regional Economic Information System, 21
Ecosystems, 139, 142
ECPOLICY-L mailing list, 97-98
Education, 12, 15, 20-21, 69, 70, 96-113, 166, 167, 168
   administrative education, 112
   adult education, 100, 108
   after-school programs, 112, 113
   anti-bias education, 113
   ARTSEDGE, 96
   arts education, 96
   AskERIC, 96
   assessment, 100
   at-risk students, 103, 111
   bilingual education, 103
   block scheduling, 101
   career education, 19, 100
   civic education, 96
   Civnet, 96-97
   class size, 103, 112, 113
   computer accessibility technology, 111
   computers and, 97, 111, 175
   Computers for Learning, 97
   consumer information, 14
   corporal punishment, 101
   correctional education, 108
   crime in schools, 250
   disabled children, 100-101, 102, 110

discipline, 101
distance education, 100, 103
dress codes, 101
dropouts, 107, 113
early childhood education, 68, 69, 97, 101, 111
ECENET-L mailing list, 97
ECPOLICY-L mailing list, 97-98
EDInfo, 98
EDSITEment, 98
edtech mailing list, 105
educational management, 101
educational programming on television, 62
Educational Resources Information Center (ERIC), 98-99, 104-105, 112
Education Department, 96, 98, 105, 106, 109, 111-112
Education Department Search Page, 112
elementary education, 69, 70, 97, 101, 107, 110
English as a second language, 108, 109
ERIC Clearinghouse for Community Colleges, 99
ERIC Clearinghouse for Social Studies/Social Science Education, 99
ERIC Clearinghouse on Adult, Career, and Vocational Education, 100
ERIC Clearinghouse on Assessment and Evaluation, 100
ERIC Clearinghouse on Disabilities and Gifted Education, 100-101
ERIC Clearinghouse on Educational Management, 101
ERIC Clearinghouse on Elementary and Early Childhood Education, 69, 70, 97, 101, 107, 110
ERIC Clearinghouse on Higher Education, 102
ERIC Clearinghouse on Information and Technology, 102
ERIC Clearinghouse on Languages and Linguistics, 102-103
ERIC Clearinghouse on Reading, English, and Communication, 103
ERIC Clearinghouse on Rural Education and Small Schools, 104
ERIC Clearinghouse on Teaching and Teacher Education, 104
ERICNews, 104-105
evaluation, 100
extended school years, 103
FAFSA on the Web, 105
FCCsend mailing list, 105
FCCshare mailing list, 105
Federal Resources for Educational Excellence (FREE), 106
gifted children, 69, 98, 100-101, 103
goals for, 108
grammar, 102
health education, 104, 106
Hispanic-American students, 101

home schooling, 98, 101, 103
homework, 111
humanities, 98
of immigrants, 113
information and, 102
Internet and, 102, 103, 109, 111
languages and linguistics, 98, 102-103
legislation on, 98
library and information science, 102, 111
LingNet, 106
literacy, 108, 109, 111
local area networks for schools, 102
mainstreaming, 100
mentoring programs, 113
MIDDLE-L mailing list, 107
middle schools, 23, 107
multi-age classrooms, 101
multicultural programs, 70, 103, 104, 112
National Center for Education Statistics, 20, 107
National Clearinghouse for ESL Literacy Education (NCLE), 108
National Education Goals, 108
National Institute for Literacy Home Page, 108
National Literacy Advocacy, 109
National Public School Locator Search, 107
organizations, 112
outdoor education, 104
parental involvement, 113
perfectionist students, 101
physical education, 106
policy, 97
poverty and learning, 101
private schools, 104
Project EASI, 109
publications, 22, 98, 107, 111-112
Quest, 109
readiness for school, 107, 110, 111
reading, 17, 23, 98, 100, 103, 110, 111, 112
READPRO mailing list, 110
ReadyWeb, 110
reform, 107, 111, 112
Reggio Emilia approach, 101
research, 98, 100
resources, 23
rural education, 35, 104
school size and enrollment, 93, 101
science, 23, 106, 111
shy students, 101
single-sex, 113
small schools, 104
Smithsonian Education, 110-111
socialization skills of students, 101
social sciences, 22, 99
social studies, 99, 106
special education, 112, 197
spelling, 103

statistics on, 24, 98, 107

substance abuse programs, 101, 111, 112

technology and, 102, 105, 106, 112

tech-prep education, 103, 112

testing practices, 100, 111

This is MEGA Mathematics! 111

tutoring, 102

urban education, 69, 112

Urban Education Web, 112-113

violence in schools, 101, 103, 107, 111, 112, 113

vocational education, 19, 100, 106

writing, 103

year-round, 113

YouthInfo, 71

See also Colleges and universities; Schools; Teachers and teaching

EIA Email Lists, 122-123

Eldercare Locator, 204

Elderly. *See* Aging

Elections, 12, 170, 171-173

absentee ballots, 173

campaign finance, 134, 170, 171, 172

Campaign Finance Data on the Internet, 171

campaigns, 170, 172

Center for Responsive Politics, 171

congressional, 172

election law, 172

FECInfo, 172

Federal Election Commission, 171, 172

Federal Voting Assistance Program (FVAP), 173

presidential, 110, 172

results, 172, 173

speeches during 1920 election, 224

statistics, 165

See also Voting

Electric power, 122, 123, 131

Electric vehicles, 257

Electromagnetic fields, 199

Electromagnetic radiation, 260

Electronic benefits transfer, 46

Electronic catalogs, 46

Electronic commerce, 46, 49, 50, 59, 175

Electronic funds transfer, 46

Electronic grants, 46

Elementary education, 69, 70, 97, 101, 107, 110

El Niño weather system, 133

El Salvador, 151

E-mail, 288

E-mail addresses, 5

E-Mail to the White House, 178

Embargoes, 50

Embassies and consulates, 16, 144, 150, 151-157, 159

Emergency response and management, 15, 116-117, 126

Emerging Infectious Diseases, 205

Emory University School of Law Library, 247

Employment, 13, 16, 25, 54

Age Discrimination Employment Act of 1967, 236

benefits, 13

buyouts, 13, 231

civil service, 16, 231

cost trends, 92

demographic information by state, 230

of disabled persons, 234, 236

displaced workers, 93

downsizing, 13, 231

earnings by occupation, 21, 230

employee rights, 233

employer rights and responsibilities, 233

Employment Services offices, 230

Equal Employment Opportunity Commission, 21, 236

Equal Pay Act, 236

federal application form, 232

of foreign nationals, 46

health benefits, 23, 235

hiring, 48

immigrants and, 177

job hunting, 92

minimum wage, 235

Occupational Outlook Handbook, 92

publications, 17

resumes, 230, 231

rural youth and, 35

salaries and wages, 230, 231, 232

statistics, 93

students and, 232

trends, 230

unemployment, 25, 92, 93, 162

See also Federal employment; Job openings; Jobs; Labor

Emus, 32

Enactment of a Law, 168

Endangered Ecosystems of the United States, 128

Endangered plants, 140

Endangered species, 128, 131, 132, 133, 136, 140, 142

Endangered Species Act of 1973, 136

Endocrine disorders, 212

Energy, 15, 120-126

alternative fuels, 120, 121, 124

Alternative Fuels Data Center, 120

Bioenergy Information Network, 120

biofuels, 120

Biofuels Information Network, 120

Clean Cities, 121

DOE Information Bridge, 121

DR-NRR mailing list, 121-122

efficiency, 124, 125

EIA Email Lists, 122-123

Energy Efficiency and Renewable Energy Network (EREN), 122-123

Energy Information Administration, 122-123

GC-NRR mailing list, 121-122
International Nuclear Safety Center, 124
National Renewable Energy Laboratory, 120, 124-125, 257
Nuclear Regulatory Commission, 121, 125, 126
Office of Scientific and Technical Information, 125
PR-OPA mailing list, 121-122
publications, 121, 123
renewable, 120, 121, 122-125, 257
statistics, 123
supply and demand, 123
Tennessee Valley Authority, 125
See also Energy Department (DOE)
Energy Department (DOE), 97, 219, 255, 257
Bioenergy Information Network, 120
Clean Cities program, 121
Computer Incident Advisory Capability, 74, 75
DOE Information Bridge, 121
DOE Reports Bibliographic Database, 125
Home Page, 125-126
Nevada Operations Office, 88
nuclear facilities, 88-89, 124
Office of Civilian Radioactive Waste Management, 137
Engineering, 60, 121, 257, 259
English, 103, 110
English as a second language (ESL), 108, 109
Enterprise space shuttle, 40
Entomology, 34, 42
Environment, 15, 128-136, 256
Agency for Toxic Substances and Disease Registry, 128
Biological Resources Division, 128
Chemical Scorecard, 129
Committee for the National Institute for the Environment, 129
compliance issues, 134-135
Congressional Research Service Reports, 129
Council on Environmental Quality, 130
Envirofacts Warehouse, 129-130
environb-l mailing list, 130
Enviro-Newsbrief, 130
Environment, Safety, and Health Technical Information Services, 88-89
Environmental Defense Fund, 129
environmental impact statements, 131
environmental protection, 166, 167, 168, 257
environmental sciences, 121
Fish and Wildlife Service, 132, 136, 142, 254
fws-news mailing list, 132
global change, 106
global warming, 42, 120
industry reports, 131-132
internetnb-l mailing list, 130
legislation on, 130

National Institute for the Environment, 129
National Marine Fisheries Service, 132
National Wetlands Inventory, 132-133
NOAA Web Sites, 133
North American Reporting Center for Amphibian Malformations, 133
oppt-newsbreak mailing list, 130
publications, 17, 22, 135
research, 128
RTK NET, 134
sanctions, 252
Sector Facility Indexing Project, 134-135
State of the Coast, 135
wetlands, 129, 132-133, 135, 136, 140, 256
See also Environmental Protection Agency (EPA); Nuclear waste; Parks and public lands
Environmental health, 199-200, 207
National Institute of Environmental Health Sciences, 71, 199
National Pesticide Telecommunications Network, 199
National Toxicology Program, 200
Environmental Protection Agency (EPA), 19, 71, 129, 135-136, 199, 255
Access EPA, 29, 135
EPA Federal Register Mailing Lists, 131
epa-press mailing list, 130
EPA Sector Notebooks, 131-132
mailing lists, 130
Office of Enforcement and Compliance Assurance, 134-135
Online Library System (OLS), 29
press releases, 130
Epilepsy, 213
Equal Employment Opportunity Commission, 236
Equal Employment Opportunity File, 21
Equal Pay Act of 1963, 236
EREN (Energy Efficiency and Renewable Energy Network), 122-123
Ergonomics, 75, 235
ERIC (Educational Resources Information Center), 98-99
ERIC Database, 100
ERIC Digest, 100
ERICNews, 104-105
ERIC Clearinghouses
Adult, Career, and Vocational Education, 100
Assessment and Evaluation, 100
Community Colleges, 99
Disabilities and Gifted Education, 100-101
Educational Management, 101
Elementary and Early Childhood Education, 69, 70, 97, 101, 107, 110
Higher Education, 102
Information and Technology, 28, 96, 102
Languages and Linguistics, 102-103

Reading, English, and Communication, 103, 110
Rural Education and Small Schools, 104
Social Studies/Social Science Education, 99
Teaching and Teacher Education, 104
Urban Education, 69, 112
Ernest Orlando Lawrence Berkeley National
Laboratory, 257
ESL (English as a second language), 108, 109
Ethanol, 120
Ethical, Legal, and Social Issues in Science, 257
Ethics, 177, 189, 210, 211, 257
Euthanasia, 189
Evolution, 23
Executive branch, 12, 15, 16, 177
Executive orders, 11, 16, 85, 146, 175, 177, 180
Exercise, 205, 211, 214, 216
Exotic species, 141
Explorer, 89
Exports, 46, 49, 86, 151, 251
EXPRESS mailing list, 272, 278
Extensions, 288
Extension services, 34-35
Eye care, 207, 210

FAA (Federal Aviation Administration), 12, 285, 286,
287
FAA Y2K Program Office, 284
FAFSA on the Web, 105
Fair housing laws, 18
Fair use, 51
Fallout, 125
Families. *See* Children and families
Family and Medical Leave Act, 231, 235
Family leave, 70, 231, 235, 236
Family planning, 190
Family reunification programs, 70
Fannie Mae, 63
FAQs, 288
Farm Bill of 1996, 35, 36
Farmland preservation, 32
Farms and farming. *See* Agriculture
Farsi language, 106
Fast food, 201
Fat substitutes, 201
FBI (Federal Bureau of Investigation), 71, 93, 248
FCC (Federal Communications Commission), 62, 105
 FCC Daily Digest, 62
 FCCsend mailing list, 105
 FCCshare mailing list, 105
FDA (Food and Drug Administration), 19, 184, 194,
201, 202, 209
 FDA Consumer, 209
 FDA Enforcement Report, 209
FEC (Federal Election Commission), 171, 172
FECInfo, 172

FedCIRC (Federal Computer Incident Response
Capability), 75
Federal Acquisition Jumpstation, 59
Federal Acquisition Regulations, 56, 57, 59
Federal Aviation Administration (FAA), 12, 284, 285,
286, 287
Federal budget, 16, 18, 24, 50, 162, 167, 168
Federal Bulletin Board, 18-19
Federal Bureau of Investigation (FBI), 71, 93, 248
Federal Bureau of Prisons, 249
Federal Communications Commission. *See* FCC
Federal Computer Incident Response Capability
(FedCIRC), 75
Federal Court Locator, 10
Federal Credit Union Handbook, 63
Federal debt, 50, 54
Federal Deposit Insurance Corporation, 62
Federal depository libraries, 18, 24, 26
Federal Documents Task Force, 12
Federal Duck Stamp program, 136
Federal Election Commission (FEC), 171, 172
Federal Electronic Commerce Program Office, 46
Federal Emergency Management Agency (FEMA), 71,
116
Federal employment, 10, 12, 13, 16, 22, 177, 231, 232.
 See also Employment; Job openings
 America's Job Bank, 230
 Corporation for National Service, 231
 Federal Job Opportunity Board (FJOB), 12
 Office of Personnel Management, 231, 232
 USA Jobs, 232
Federal Financial Institutions Examination Council,
63
Federal Firearms Regulation Reference Guide, 248
Federal government information, finding on the Web,
22
Federal Highway Administration, 287
Federal Information Center, 10-11
Federal Interagency Council on Statistical Policy, 11
Federal Interagency Forum on Child and Family
Statistics, 68
Federalist Papers, 18
Federal Job Opportunity Board (FJOB), 12
Federal Judicial Center Home Page, 238
Federal Judiciary Homepage, 238
Federal Labor Relations Authority, 18
Federal Network Inc., 164
Federal Open Market Committee, 54
Federal Railroad Administration, 287
Federal Register, 18, 22, 24, 25, 176, 179
Federal Register Mailing Lists, 19
Federal Reserve Banks, 54-55
Federal Reserve Bulletin, 54
Federal Reserve System, 54
Federal Resources for Educational Excellence (FREE),
106

Federal Rules of Civil Procedure, 239
Federal Rules of Evidence, 238, 239
Federal Trade Commission (FTC), 14, 19-20
Federal Transit Administration, 285
Federal Voting Assistance Program (FVAP), 173
Federal Web Locator, 10
Federal Writers' Project, 224
Federal Y2K Commercial Off-the-Shelf (COTS)
   Product Database, 75
Federation of American Scientists, 84, 175
FedLaw, 11
FEDNET, 164
FedStats, 11
FedWorld, 11-12
FEMA (Federal Emergency Management Agency), 71,
   116
FERRET, 93
Fertilizer, 36
Fibromyalgia, 207, 211
Fibrous dysplasia, 216
Filename extensions, 288
Files, 289
File transfer protocol (FTP), 289
FinanceNet, 19, 21, 56, 57, 174
Financial aid, 58, 105, 109, 111, 112
Financial and Contractual Status (FACS) On-Line
   Query System, 59
Financing strategies, 47
FindLaw, 238-239
Finger, 289
Fingerprints, 251
Fire
   Fire Administration, 116-117
   fire ecology, 139
   fire safety, 116-117, 176, 235
   fires and firefighting, 116-117
   fire weather, 116, 133
   forest fires, 34
Firearms, 248, 250
First ladies, 180, 224
First 150 Years, The: The Traveling Exhibition, 40
Fish and fishing, 132, 135, 140, 142, 256
Fish and Wildlife Service, 132, 136, 142, 254
   Fish and Wildlife Service Manual, 136
   fws-news mailing list, 132
   Region 7-Alaska, 142
Fisheries, 132, 133
Fish kills, 128
FJOB (Federal Job Opportunity Board), 12
Floods, 116, 262, 268
Flu, 207
FOIA (Freedom of Information Act), 10, 20, 23, 146,
   150, 151
Folk arts, 96
Folklife, 106
Food and Drug Administration. *See* FDA

Food and nutrition, 33, 34, 36, 106, 201-203, 212
   Center for Food Safety and Applied Nutrition, 201
   chemical contaminants in food, 201
   consumer information, 14
   dietary guidelines, 23, 33, 201, 215
   dietary supplements, 190, 202-203
   diet programs, 19, 188, 201
   drug interactions, 202
   eating disorders, 201, 207, 216, 221
   fast food, 201
   food additives, 201, 202
   food allergies, 201, 207, 211
   Food and Nutrition Information Center, 34, 201
   Food and Nutrition Research Briefs, 32
   *Food and Nutrition Resource Guide for Homeless
      Shelters, Soup Kitchens, and Food Banks,* 201
   food pyramid, 201
   food safety, 33, 34, 201, 202
   labels, 201
   National Food Safety Database, 202
   NutriBase, 202
   nutrients in food, 201, 202
   Office of Dietary Supplements, 202-203
   pesticides in diets of children, 23
   publications, 17, 22
   research, 33
   spending on, 36
   sports nutrition, 201
   vegetarian nutrition, 201
Foodborne illness, 33, 201, 202
*Foodborne Pathogenic Microorganisms and Natural
   Toxins,* 201
Foreign affairs, 15, 144-159, 168
   Agency for International Development, 150
   Bosnia Report, 144
   Bureau of Consular Affairs Home Page, 144
   Bureau of Diplomatic Security, 144-145
   Caucasus Report, 145
   Center for the Study of Intelligence, 145
   Central Intelligence Agency, 145-146
   CIA Electronic Document Release Center, 146
   embassies and consulates, 16, 144, 150, 151-157,
      159
   Foreign Affairs Manual, 151
   Foreign Affairs Network Listservs, 147
   foreign aid, 15, 150
   foreign assets, 50
   Foreign Commercial Service, 151
   foreign governments, 146
   foreign service officers, 144
   Information Agency, 96, 147, 151, 158
   Institute of Peace, 158-159
   International Broadcasting Bureau Servers, 147
   Overseas Security Advisory Council, 148
   Peace Corps, 148
   policy, 150, 158, 159

Radio Free Asia, 148-149
Radio Free Europe/Radio Liberty, 144, 145, 149
RFE/RL Newsline, 149
Secretary of State, 149-150
State Department, 144, 147, 148, 149, 150, 159
State Department Electronic Reading Room, 150-151
trade, 22, 50
Travel-Advisories Mailing List, 150
Foreign agents, 171
Foreign countries, 12, 106, 144, 145, 147, 148, 150, 159, 167. *See also names of specific countries*
Foreign exchange rates, 54
Foreign labor, 92
Foreign languages, 98, 102-103, 106, 112
Foreign trade, 22, 50
Forests
    forest fires, 34
    forests and forestry, 33, 34, 129
    Forest Service, 71, 142
    national forests, 141, 142
Forms, 23
Franklin D. Roosevelt Library and Museum, 225
Fraud, 54, 83, 144, 168, 208, 209, 251, 252
    computers, 252
    health care, 201, 208
    online, 14
    postal, 52
    reporting complaints, 20
Free Application for Federal Student Aid (FAFSA), 105, 112
Freedom of Information Act (FOIA), 10, 20, 23, 146, 150, 151
Freedom of the press, 158
FREE (Federal Resources for Educational Excellence), 106
Freeware, 53, 289
French language, 106
Frequently Used Sites Related to U.S. Federal Government Information, 12-13
Frogs, 133
Fruits and vegetables, 32
FTC (Federal Trade Commission), 14, 19-20
FTP (file transfer protocol), 289
Fuels
    alternative, 120, 121, 124
    biofuels, 120
    diesel, 123
    gasoline, 122, 123
    natural gas, 122-123
    processing facilities, 124
Fulbright grant program, 158
Funerals, 19
Furman v. Georgia, 240
Furniture, 176

Fusion, 257
FVAP (Federal Voting Assistance Program), 173
Fws-news mailing list, 132

Galaxies, 278
Galileo mission, 273
Gambling, 64
Gangs, 113, 249, 250, 251
GAO (General Accounting Office), 11, 16, 22, 84, 168
    GAO Daybook, 164, 168
    GAO Reports, 25
Garbage, 289
Gardening, 32, 34
Gasoline stocks and prices, 122, 123
Gateways, 10-16, 289
    Center for Information Law and Policy, 10
    Federal Information Center, The, 10-11
    FedLaw, 11
    FedWorld, 11-12
    Frequently Used Sites Related to U.S. Federal Government Information, 12-13
    Government Information Exchange, 13
    INFOMINE, 13
    Meta-Index for U.S. Legal Research, 14
    NonProfit Gateway, 14
    University of Michigan Documents Center, 16
    U.S. Consumer Gateway, 14
    U.S. Federal Government Agencies Directory, 15
    U.S. Government Information, 15
    U.S. State and Local Gateway, 15
    Yahoo!—U.S.Government, 16
Gays in the military, 82
GC-NRR mailing list, 121-122
Genealogical research, 227
General Accounting Office. *See* GAO
General Services Administration (GSA), 17, 49, 60-61, 75
    Federal Acquisition Regulation, 57
    Federal Electronic Commerce Program Office, 46
    Federal Information Center, 10-11
    Government Information Exchange, 13
    Office of Governmentwide Policy, 174-175
Genetics, 188, 189, 190, 211, 214, 235
Genocide, 158
Genome research, 211, 257
Geography, 111, 272
Geological Survey, 71, 128, 254, 255, 256
Geology, 140, 256
George Bush Presidential Library and Museum, 226
Georgetown University Legal Explorer, 239
George Washington University, 102
Georgia State University College of Law, 14
Geospatial and Statistical Data Center, 93-94
German language, 106
Getting Online: A Friendly Guide for Teachers, Students, and Parents, 99

Gettysburg Address, 27
GIF (graphics interchange format), 289
Gifted education, 69, 98, 100-101, 103
GILS (Government Information Locator Service), 25
Gingrich, Newt, 2, 167
Ginnie Mae: Government National Mortgage Association, 57
Glaciers, 133, 254
Glass Ceiling Commission, 236
Glaucoma, 210
Global change, 106, 255
    Global Change Data and Information System, 255
    Global Change Research Act of 1990, 255
Global marketplace, 23
Global warming, 42, 120
Gold Rush, 225
Gore, Al, 97, 174, 178
Gore, Tipper, 178
Government, 167
    financial management of, 174
    GOVBOT database, 13
    Government Documents Round Table, 12
    Government Information Exchange, 13
    Government Information Locator Service (GILS), 25
    Government Information Sharing Project, 20-21
    Government Performance and Results Act, 174
    Government-wide Performance Plan for FY 1999, 179
    GOVINFO mailing list, 21
    GOVNEWS, 21-22
    reinventing, 130, 174, 175
    secrecy in, 175-176
    See also Congress; Elections; Policies, regulations, and operations; White House
Government contractors. See Contracts
Government National Mortgage Association (Ginnie Mae), 57
Government Printing Office (GPO), 17, 18, 24-26, 56, 121, 165
Government publications. See Publications
Govsales mailing list, 57-58
Gov.topic.forsale.misc newsgroup, 57-58
Gov.us.fed.doc.cbd.forsale newsgroup, 56-57
GPO Access, 24-26
GPO (Government Printing Office), 17, 18, 24-26, 56, 121, 165
GPS satellite timing operations, 260
Grand Canyon National Park, 140
Grants, 10, 16, 17, 22, 56-61, 80
    electronic, 46
    EPA, 130
    Fulbright grants, 158
    List of Defaulted Borrowers, 58
    NASA Acquisition Internet Service (NAIS) Home Page, 59-60
    National Endowment for the Arts, 40-41
    National Endowment for the Humanities, 60

National Research Initiative Competitive Grants Program, 33
National Science Foundation, 60
nonprofit organizations, 14
Graphics interchange format (GIF), 289
Grateful Med, 190
Greenhouse effect, 133
Griswold v. Connecticut, 240
Gross national product, 54
GSA. See General Services Administration
Guatemala, 151
Gulf War, 217-218
Gulf War illness, 83, 217-218
    GulfLINK, 217
    Missing GulfLINK Files, 217
    Persian Gulf War Illnesses Task Force, 146
    Presidential Advisory Committee on Gulf War Veterans' Illnesses, 218
Gun Dealer Licensing and Illegal Gun Trafficking, 248
Guns, 248, 250

Habitat protection, 133
Hale-Bopp comet, 271
Hamilton, Calvin, 279
Handbook of International Economic Statistics, 146
Harmonized Tariff Schedule of the United States, 51
Harvard University, 94
Hatch Act, 177
Hate crimes, 23, 248
Hate Crime Statistics, 23
Hazardous materials and waste, 29, 128, 129, 131, 134, 135, 235, 286
HazDat database, 128
Headaches, 213
Head Start, 68
Health and health care, 12, 15, 166, 168, 191, 204-216
    access to health care, 93
    administration of, 190
    Agency for Health Care Policy and Research, 204
    allocation of resources, 189
    alternative medicine, 214
    behavioral risk factors, 206
    bibliographic information, 188-191
    CDC Diabetes and Public Health Resource, 205
    CDC's Tobacco Information and Prevention Source (TIPS), 206
    CDC Travel Information, 205-206
    CDC WONDER, 205, 206
    Center for Food Safety and Applied Nutrition, 201
    Centers for Disease Control and Prevention, 205
    Combined Health Information Database, 188
    Committee on Commerce Tobacco Documents, 207
    complementary medicine, 214
    Consumer Health Information, 207
    consumer information, 14, 17, 207
    Diabetes in America, 207-208

directories, 194-195
Dr. Felix's Free MEDLINE Page, 188
education, 104
fraud, 201, 208
Health and Human Services Department, 194
Health Care Financing Administration, 208, 209
Healthfinder, 194
Health Information for International Travel, 205
health insurance, 93, 94, 162, 197, 204
Health Resources and Services Administration, 58
HealthSTAR database, 189-190
Healthy People 2010 initiative, 215
herbal medicine, 32, 201
hospital discharges, 206
information resources, 189
Initiative to Eliminate Racial and Ethnic Disparities
  in Health, 208
Internet FDA, 209
Internet Grateful Med, 189-190
literacy and, 108
long-term care, 204, 209
managed care, 35, 209
maternal and child health, 188, 190
medical screening, 257
Medicare, 10, 66, 197, 208, 209-210
minorities and, 215
National Bioethics Advisory Commission, 210
National Center for Health Statistics, 205
National Eye Institute, 210
National Health Information Center, 194
National Health Interview Survey, 93
National Heart, Lung, and Blood Institute, 210-211
National Human Genome Research Institute, 211
National Institute of Allergy and Infectious Diseases,
  184, 211
National Institute of Arthritis and Musculoskeletal
  and Skin Diseases, 211-212, 216
National Institute of Dental Research, 212
National Institute of Diabetes and Digestive and
  Kidney Diseases, 207, 212
National Institute of Neurological Disorders and
  Stroke, 212-213
National Library of Medicine, 29, 184, 189, 190-191,
  226
national observances, 194
National Sudden Infant Death Syndrome Resource
  Center, 213
National Women's Health Information Center
  (NWHIC), 213
and nuclear, biological, and chemical weapons, 78,
  79
nursing homes, 17, 208, 209, 235
Office of Alternative Medicine, 214
Office of Animal Care and Use, 214
Office of Disease Prevention, 214-215

Office of Disease Prevention and Health Promotion,
  215
Office of Minority Health Resource Center, 215
Office of Rare Diseases, 215-216
organ and tissue donation, 189, 216
Osteoporosis and Related Bone Diseases National
  Resource Center, 216
planning, 190
policy, 167, 189
pollution and, 29
privacy of electronic health data, 23, 190, 257
promotion, 188, 215
publications, 17, 22-23
PubMed, 191
in rural America, 35
search engines, 194-195
statistics, 204
technology and, 166
teenage attitudes about, 93
transplantation, 189, 210, 211, 216
travel and, 205, 206
See also Aging; AIDS and HIV; Alcohol and alcohol
  abuse; Cancer; Disabilities; Diseases; Drugs and
  drug abuse; Environmental health; Food and
  nutrition; Gulf War illness; Human radiation
  experiments; Medications; Medicine; Mental health
  and illness; National Institutes of Health (NIH)
Health and Human Services Department, 69, 194,
  219
  Agency for Toxic Substances and Disease Registry,
    128
  Disabilities and Managed Care, 196-197
  Health Care Financing Administration, 208,
    209
  Initiative to Eliminate Racial and Ethnic Disparities
    in Health, 208
  LTCARE-L mailing list, 209
  Office of the Assistant Secretary for Planning and
    Evaluation, 70
  Organ Donation, 216
  Web Pages for Kids around the Federal Government,
    71
  YouthInfo, 71
Hearing impairments, 61, 100, 188, 204, 207, 214
Heart disease, 201, 207, 208, 210, 214
Heart transplants, 210
Hematologic disorders, 212
Hemingway, Ernest, 227
Hepatitis, 206
Herbal medicine, 32, 201
Herbicides, 32
Herbs and herb gardening, 32
Heroin, 186, 190
High blood pressure, 210
Higher education. *See* Colleges and universities
Highways, 162, 285-286, 287

Hiking, 140
HillSource, 164
Hindenburg disaster, 248
Hip replacement, 211-212
Hispanics, 104
HISTLINE database, 190
Historical Census Data Browser, 94
Historic preservation, 224
Historic sites, 141
History, 60, 98, 99, 111, 158, 224-228
    Advisory Council on Historic Preservation, 224
    American Memory, 224-225
    Architect of the Capitol Home Page, 225
    Franklin D. Roosevelt Library and Museum, 225
    George Bush Presidential Library and Museum, 226
    historic documents and exhibits, 15, 16, 18
    Images from the History of Medicine, 226
    Jimmy Carter Library, 226
    John F. Kennedy Library Home Page, 227
    Lyndon B. Johnson Library and Museum, 227
    of medicine, 190, 226
    National Archives and Records Administration, 227-
    228
    U.S. Colored Troops, 228
Hitler, Adolf, 248
HIV. *See* AIDS and HIV
HIV/AIDS Surveillance Report, 185, 205
HIV/AIDS Treatment Information Service, 185
Hobbies, 17
Homeless programs, 18, 113
Home Mortgage Disclosure Act, 63
Home page, 289
Homes
    financing and refinancing, 19, 63, 134
    home-based small businesses, 48
    home improvement loans, 134
    home ownership, 18, 63
    HomePath, 63
    mortgages, 18, 19, 54, 57, 62, 63
Home schooling, 98, 101, 103
Homesteads, 34
Homosexuals, 82
Hormone replacement therapy, 210
Horticulture, 34
Hospital discharges, 206
Hotel and Motel Fire Safety Act of 1990, 117
Household products, 176
House of Representatives, 164, 165, 168, 170
    calendar and schedule, 24, 162, 165
    committees, 163, 165, 167
    ethics manual, 168
    hearings, 167, 168
    HillSource, 164
    House Republican Conference, 164
    Independent Counsel's Report to the U.S. House of
    Representatives, 165

Internet Law Library, 26
    members, 165
    Office of the Clerk On-line Information Center, 165
    Office of the Majority Whip, 165-166
    rules, 25, 165, 167, 169
    Subcommittee on Rules and Organization of the
    House, 167
    travel expenses, 171
    votes, 163, 165, 168
    Whip Notice, The, 165, 170
    Whipping Post, The, 165, 170
    women in, 165
Housing, 15, 17, 18, 20, 35, 94, 134
Housing and Urban Development Department, 18, 57,
71
How Our Laws Are Made, 168
How to Effectively Locate Federal Government
    Information on the Web, 22
HREX (Human Radiation Experiments Information
    Management System), 219
HSRPROJ database, 190
Human Genome Project, 106, 211
Humanities, 35, 60, 98, 240
Human radiation experiments, 89, 125, 219
Human Radiation Experiments Information
    Management System (HREX), 219
Human research, 190, 210
Human rights, 151, 158, 159
Hungary, 124
Hurricane Bonnie, 116
Hurricanes, 116, 133, 261, 262, 272
Hustler Magazine v. Falwell, 240
Hybrid Electric Vehicle Program, 257
Hyperparathyroidism, 216
Hypophosphatasia, 216

IBM Patent Server, 46-47
Illegal aliens, 177
Illinois Institute of Technology, Chicago-Kent College
    of Law, 10, 245
Images from the History of Medicine, 226
Immigration, 167, 177, 227
    education and, 113
    Immigration and Naturalization Service, 177
    Immigration to the United States, 23-24
Immunizations, 206, 208
Immunotoxicity studies, 200
Impact hazards, 270
Impeachment, 16, 178
Imports, 51, 251
Impotence, 214
Income, 25, 93, 94
Income tax preparation services, 19
Incontinence, 207
Independent agencies, 15
Independent Counsel and Impeachment, The, 178

Independent Counsel's Report to the United States
  House of Representatives, 165
Indexes, 12
Indiana University, 99, 103
Indian education, 104
Indian tribes, 17, 61
Indoor air quality, 176, 235, 257
Industrial production, 94
I-net-bulletin mailing list, 92
Infant mortality, 208
Infectious diseases, 79, 184, 205, 211. *See also* AIDS and
  HIV
Infomercials, 19
INFOMINE, 13
Information
  ERIC Clearinghouse on Information and
    Technology, 28, 96, 102
  information science, 121
  information technology, 75, 166
  information technology policy, 75
  infrastructure, 51
  law and policy, 10
Information access, 10-29, 35, 146, 175
  gateways, 10-16
  government publications, 17-26
  libraries, 27-29, 111
Information Agency, U.S., 96, 147, 151, 158
Information Security Oversight Office, 175
Infrastructure, 81, 85
Inhalant abuse, 186, 207
Initiative to Eliminate Racial and Ethnic Disparities in
  Health, 208
Insects, 32, 33, 34, 140
Insignia Publishing Company, 217
INS (Immigration and Naturalization Service), 177
Insomnia, 210
Inspectors general, 83
Institute of Peace, 158-159
Instructional Computing Group (Harvard University),
  94
Insurance, 48, 93, 94, 162, 197, 204
Intellectual property, 10, 51, 257
Intelligence, 16, 84, 145, 146
  Intelligence in the War for Independence, 146
  Intelligence Reform Program, 84
  See also CIA (Central Intelligence Agency)
Intelligent Mechanisms Group, 257-258
Interactive Weather Information Network (IWIN), 261
Interior Department, 71, 254, 255
Interior design, 224
Internal Revenue Information Services (IRIS), 65-66
Internal Revenue Service (IRS), 50, 65, 66
International Broadcasting Bureau Servers, 147
International Child Labor Study Office, 236
International conflict, 158
International Development Agency, 150

International Govnews Project, 21
International laws, 26, 27
International Nuclear Safety Center, 124
International Nuclear Safety Program, 124
International relations, 158
International Space Station, 272-273
International Trade Administration, 49, 50-51
International Trade Commission, 50-51
Internet, 257, 289
  addresses, 5
  bandwidth issues, 62
  federal sites, 2-3
  Getting Online, 99
  safety, 248, 251
  searches, 4
  universal service, 62
Internet FDA, 209
Internet Grateful Med, 189-190
Internet Newsbrief, 130
Internships, 23
Inter-University Consortium for Political and Social
  Research, 94, 250
Inventions, 51
Invertebrate zoology, 42
Investments, 52, 54
Iraq, 158
IRIS (Internal Revenue Information Services), 65-66
Irrigation, 32
IRS (Internal Revenue Service), 50, 65, 66
Issnews mailing list, 273
IT Policy On-Ramp, 75
IWIN (Interactive Weather Information Network), 261

JAN (Job Accommodation Network), 233
Jet propulsion, 260
Jet Propulsion Laboratory, 258, 259, 270, 273, 279,
  282
Jimmy Carter Library, 226
Job openings, 174, 230, 232
  agriculture, 32
  AHCPR, 204
  CBO, 162
  Defense Department, 83
  DIA, 81
  FBI, 248
  FCC, 62
  Federal Bureau of Prisons, 249
  Interior Department, 254
  NASA, 275
  NSF, 60
  OMB, 179
  ORNL, 259
  TVA, 125
  VA, 83
  Year 2000, 76
  See also Employment; Federal employment

Jobs, 230-232
America's Career InfoNet, 230
America's Job Bank, 230
Corporation for National Service, 231
Job Accommodation Network (JAN), 233
job ads, 19
job market, 230, 231
job training programs, 18
Office of Personnel Management Home Page, 231
Planning Your Future: A Federal Employee's Survival
Guide, 231
USA Jobs, 232
See also Careers; Employment; Federal employment
John F. Kennedy Center for the Performing Arts, 40, 96
John F. Kennedy Library Home Page, 227
Johnson, Lyndon B., 227
Johnson Space Center, 272, 276
Jones v. Clinton, 246
Journal of Transportation and Statistics, The, 284
JPL Robotics, 258
Judges, 238
Jupiter, 273, 282
Jury duty, 238, 246
Justice, 12, 23, 248-252
Bureau of Alcohol, Tobacco, and Firearms, 248
Bureau of Justice Statistics, 238, 250
Commission on Civil Rights Home Page, 252
criminal justice, 12, 167, 249, 250
Customs Service Web Site, 251
Federal Bureau of Investigation, 71, 93, 248
Federal Bureau of Prisons, 249
Federal Judicial Center Home Page, 238
Federal Judiciary Center Home Page, 238
judicial branch, 15, 16, 176
Judicial Conference of the United States, 238
Justice Department, 18, 20, 71, 251
Justice Information Center, 249
Justice Information Distribution List 250
juvenile justice, 249, 250
Juvenile Justice Electronic Mailing List (JUVJUST),
250
National Archive of Criminal Justice Data, 250
National Criminal Justice Reference Service, 249, 250
Office of Justice Programs, 250-251
Sentencing Commission, 252
Sourcebook of Criminal Justice Statistics, 24
See also Courts; Crime; Prisons and prisoners

Kennedy, Edward, 227
Kennedy, Jacqueline Bouvier, 227
Kennedy, John F., 84, 227, 228
Kennedy, Robert, 227
Kennedy Center for the Performing Arts, 40, 96
Kennedy Space Center, 274
Kepler, Johannes, 280
Kepler Mission: A Search for Habitable Planets, 280

KGB, 84
Kidnapping, 159, 248, 251
Kidney diseases, 188, 207, 212, 214
Kids Corner, 13
King, Martin Luther, Jr., 158
Knee problems, 207, 211
Korean language, 106
Korean War, 228
Kosovo, 158
Ksc-press-release mailing list, 274

Labor
Bureau of Labor Statistics, 92, 93, 235
Commission on the Future of Worker-Management
Relations, 236
Equal Employment Opportunity Commission, 21,
236
Federal Labor Relations Authority, 18
foreign labor, 92
Job Accommodation Network (JAN), 233
Labor Department, 71, 92, 230, 231, 235-236
labor force, 92, 93, 94
labor-management cooperation, 236
laws and regulations, 233-236
Monthly Labor Review, 23
National Labor Relations Act, 233
National Labor Relations Board, 233
Occupational Safety and Health Administration, 49,
233-234, 235
Pension Benefit Guaranty Corporation, 234
President's Committee on Employment of People
with Disabilities, 234-235
productivity, 92
statistics, 92, 93
Technical Links, 235
WorkNet@IRL, 236
Laboratory animals, 214
Laboratory methods, 29
Land Management Bureau, 139-140, 141, 142, 254
Landscape painting, 110
Landscaping, 34, 123
Language arts, 103, 106, 110
Languages and linguistics, 98, 102-103, 106, 108, 112
La Nina weather system, 116
Laos, 148
Latin America, 27
Launch vehicles, 260
Law and legal issues, 10, 11
administrative law, 23, 240
civil litigation, 238
election law, 172
Law Journal Extra!, 239
Legal Information Institute, 239-240
legal research, 11, 14
See also Laws and legislation
Law enforcement, 249

Law Enforcement Bulletin, 248
Laws and legislation, 11, 12, 13, 15, 16, 18, 22, 26, 167, 176
  banks, 62
  Code of Federal Regulations, 14, 18, 24, 235
  costs and benefits of federal regulations, 179
  on disabilities, 197
  education, 98
  environment, 130
  fair housing, 18
  information law, 19
  international law, 26, 27
  labor, 233-236
  legislative branch, 15, 16, 169
  legislative process, 167, 169
  Legislative Resource Center, 165
  legislative resources, 23
  on population, 190
  in Portuguese-speaking countries, 28
  in Spanish-speaking countries, 28
  state laws, 11, 26
  tax law, 10, 65
  territorial laws, 11, 26
  U.S. Code, 14, 18, 26, 169, 240
  See also Congress; Courts; Crime; Justice; Law and legal issues; Policies, regulations, and operations
Lead, 199, 205
Learn and Serve America, 231
Learning disabilities, 100, 108, 112, 207, 213, 221
Legal Information Institute, 239-240
Legal issues. *See* Law and legal issues
Legal research, 11, 14
Legislation. *See* Laws and legislation
Legislative Branch, U.S., 169
Lennon, John, 248
Letter bombs, 248
Lewinsky, Monica, 2
Libraries, 111
  American Library Association, 12
  Colorado Alliance of Research Libraries (CARL) Databases, 17
  federal depository libraries, 18, 24, 26
  Franklin D. Roosevelt Library and Museum, 225
  John F. Kennedy Library Home Page, 227
  Library of Congress, 2, 27, 28, 167, 169, 224
  Library of Congress Home Page, 27
  Library of Congress Information System (LOCIS), 28
  LM_NET, 28
  Lyndon B. Johnson Library and Museum, 227
  National Institutes of Health Library Catalog, 29
  National Library of Medicine, 29, 184, 189, 190-191, 226
  National Library Service for the Blind and Physically Handicapped, 27

National Transit Library, 285
National Transportation Library, 284
NLM Locator, 29
Online Library System (OLS), 29
presidential, 225, 226, 227
school library media, 28
technology and, 105
Vatican library, 27
Library and information science, 102, 111
Library of Congress, 2, 167, 169, 224
  Home Page, 27
  Information System (LOCIS), 28
Life sciences, 259
Lightning, 262
Liibulletin mailing list, 240
Limited Test Ban Treaty, 86
LingNet, 106
Linguistics, 98, 102-103, 106, 108, 112
List of Defaulted Borrowers, 58
Listserv, 289
Literacy, 108, 109, 111
Literature, 60, 98, 158
  literary arts, 96
  literary festivals, 27
Livestock, 33
L.L. Bean, 141
LM_NET mailing list, 28
Loans, 10, 17. *See also* Mortgages
Lobbying, 171, 172
Local governments, 35, 176
LOCIS (Library of Congress Information System), 28
Login, 5, 289
Long-term care, 204, 209
Loren Data Corp., 58
Los Alamos National Laboratory, 111
Lotteries, 64
Louisiana State University Libraries, 15
Low Income Home Energy Assistance, 68
Low-input farming, 32
LTCARE-L mailing list, 209
Lunar Prospector, 274-275
Lung transplants, 210
Lupus, 207, 211
Lyme disease, 205, 207, 211
Lyndon B. Johnson Library and Museum, 227

Macedonian constitution, 106
Macular degeneration, 210
Magna Carta, 96
Mail, 52, 175
  addressing and packaging, 49
  classification reform, 52
  tracking express mail, 52
Mail bombs, 52, 248
Mailing lists, 5, 289
  agriculture, 36-37

ALZHEIMER, 220
Census Bureau, 92
CIAC-Bulletin, 74
courts, 240
education, 97-98, 105, 107, 110
energy, 121-122
environment, 130, 131, 132
EPA, 130
FCC, 105
Federal Register, 19
Fish and Wildlife Service, 132
government sales, 56-58
justice, 250
Nuclear Regulatory Commission, 121-122
PARENTING-L, 70-71
space, 271, 273, 274, 278, 281
State Department, 147
travel and tourism, 48-49, 150
Mail order merchandise rule, 19
Mail server, 289
Mainstreaming, 100
Malamud, Carl, 2
Malaria, 190, 205, 206, 211
Mammals, 132, 133, 140
Managed care, 35, 209
Mantle, Mickey, 248
Manufacturing, 23, 94, 134, 259
Maps and mapping, 94, 106, 146, 256
Map Stats, 94
Marijuana, 179, 207
Marine accidents, 286
Marine biology, 256
Marine Corps, 83, 84
Marine fisheries, 132
Marine forecasts, 262
Marine geology, 256
MarineLINK, 84
Marine mammals, 132, 133
Marine safety and accidents, 87
Marine Sanctuary, 255
Marriage abroad, 144
Marriage certificates, 205
Mars, 259, 275, 280-281
Marshall, Thurgood, 248
Marshall Plan, 27, 158
Marshall Space Flight Center Procurement Site, 59
Marshals Service, 17, 251
Mass transit, 285
Materials science, 121, 259
Maternal and child health, 188, 190
Mathematics, 106, 107, 111
Maxwell Technologies Inc., 66
MCI Communications Corp., 98
McKinley, William, 224
Media and film, 96
Medicaid, 10, 197, 208

Medical devices, 209
Medicare, 10, 66, 197, 208, 209-210
Medications, 204
    effects of, 190
    for mental illness, 221
    reactions with food, 202
    See also FDA (Food and Drug Administration)
Medicinal herbs, 32, 201
Medicine, 191
    aerospace medicine, 260
    animal research, 189, 199
    biomedicine, 29, 189, 214
    effects of drugs, 190
    ethics, 189
    history of medicine and related professions, 190, 226
    human experimentation, 189, 210
    medical databases, 189
    medical sciences, 22
    National Library of Medicine, 29, 184, 189, 190-191, 226
    patient outcomes, 190
    patient rights, 189
    preclinical sciences, 189, 191
    research, 190, 191, 257
    resources, 23
    telemedicine, 191
    veterinary medicine, 189, 191
    See also Health and health care
MEDLARS system, 189
MEDLINE, 189, 190, 191
Melanoma, 214
Memory loss, 204
Menopause, 207
Mental health and illness, 189, 220-222
    alternative approaches, 221
    Alzheimer's disease, 188, 207, 220, 221
    managed care and, 221, 222
    medications, 221
    National Center for Mental Health Services, 221
    National Institute of Mental Health, 221
    National Mental Health Services Knowledge
        Exchange Network, 221
    organizations and agencies, 221
    statistics, 221
    substance abuse and, 222
    Substance Abuse and Mental Health Services
        Administration, 222
Mentoring programs, 113
Mercury in fish, 201
Message, for mailing lists, 5
Meta directory, 289
Meta-Index for U.S. Legal Research, 14
Meteorology, 261. *See also* Weather
Meteors, 270, 278, 279. *See also* Asteroids and comets
Methamphetamine, 186
Methanol, 120

Mexican Americans, 104
MGS-Status mailing list, 281
MIAs, 27, 146
Microsoft antitrust case, 251
Midair collisions, 286
MIDDLE-L mailing list, 107
Middle schools, 23, 107
Migrants, 70
    education and, 104
    farmworkers, 104
Military, 13, 16
    acronyms, 82
    Air Force, 80, 81
    Army, 2, 27, 78, 79, 86-87
    base closure and realignment, 47, 82, 162
    books, 85
    in Bosnia, 81
    Coast Guard, 87
    domestic preparedness, 82
    draft lotteries, 86
    gays in, 82
    housing, 80
    Marine Corps, 83, 84
    NATO and, 82
    Navy, 87
    records, 17, 83, 86, 227-228
    Selective Service System, 10, 86
    strategy, 24
    World Military Expenditures and Arms Transfers, 24,
        86
Milk and dairy products, 33
Minerals, 42, 139, 254
Minerals Management Service, 254
Minimum wage law, 235
Mining, 129, 131
    Mine Safety and Health Administration, 235
Minorities
    in colleges and universities, 107, 113
    disabilities and, 197
    health care and, 215
    Minority Health Resource Pocket Guide, 215
    minority-owned businesses, 48, 53
    teachers, 113
    See also African Americans
Mint, U.S., 50, 61
Mirror site, 290
Mir space station, 277
Missiles, 86
Missing children, 250, 251
Missing GulfLINK Files, The, 217
Missing in action, 27, 146
Mississippi, 248
Modem, 290
Money, 14, 17, 50, 55, 61
Money laundering, 251, 252
Monroe, Marilyn, 248

Monthly Catalog of United States Government
    Publications, 25
Monthly Labor Review, 23
Moon, 273, 274, 275, 278, 279
Morbidity and Mortality Weekly Report, 184, 185, 205
Mortality, 184, 185, 205, 206
Mortgages, 18, 19, 54, 57, 62, 63
Motion pictures, 224-225
Motor vehicles. See Vehicles
Moving, 52
Multiple sclerosis, 213
Murder in families, 250
Muscular dystrophy, 213
Musculoskeletal diseases, 188, 211-212, 216
Museums. See Arts and museums
Music, 96

NAFTA (North American Free Trade Agreement), 47
NAIS Email Notification Service, 59
NARA Archival Information Locator (NAIL), 227
NASA (National Aeronautics and Space
    Administration), 2, 71, 255
    Acquisition Forecast, 59
    Acquisition Internet Service (NAIS), 59-60
    Ames Research Center, 258, 281
    Asteroid and Comet Impact Hazards, 270
    Center for Mars Exploration (CMEX), 280
    Headquarters, 275
    Homepage, 275
    Image eXchange (NIX), 276
    Jet Propulsion Laboratory, 258, 259, 270, 273, 279,
        282
    Johnson Space Center, 272
    Johnson Space Center Digital Image Collection, 276
    Kennedy Space Center, 274
    launch passes, 275, 277
    mailing lists, 272, 273, 274, 278, 281
    NasaNews, 276
    NASA Pocket Statistics, 275
    NASA Search, 277
    National Space Science Data Center, 278
    Near-Live Comet Watching System, 271
    photo databases, 276
    Planetary Data System Imaging Node, 281
    Planetary Photojournal, 282
    Planetary Rings Node, 282
    press releases, 276, 278
    procurement, 59-60
    Quest, 109
    Shuttle-Mir Web, 277
    Shuttle Web, 277
    Spacelink, 272, 277-278
    Space Telerobotics Program, 258
    Stardust, 271
    Trading Post 3, 279
National Academy of Sciences, 22, 201

National Academy Press, 22-23, 166
National Action Plan on Breast Cancer, 192-193
National Adult Literacy and Learning Disabilities
  Center, 108
National Aeronautics and Space Administration. *See*
  NASA
National Agricultural Library, 32, 34, 35, 37, 201
National Agricultural Statistics Service, 36
National Air and Space Museum, 40
National Archive of Criminal Justice Data, 250
National Archives, 85, 151
National Archives and Records Administration, 227-
  228
National Arthritis and Musculoskeletal and Skin
  Diseases Information Clearinghouse, 212
National Association for the Education of Young
  Children, 97, 110
National Bioethics Advisory Commission, 210
National Biological Service, 254
National Cancer Institute, 192, 193
National Cemetery System, 83
National Center for Biotechnology Information, 191
National Center for Education Statistics, 20, 107
National Center for Health Statistics, 205
National Center for Infectious Diseases, 205
National Center for Mental Health Services, 221
National Child Care Information Center (NCCIC), 69
National Church Arson Task Force, 248
National Clearinghouse for Alcohol and Drug
  Information, 187
National Clearinghouse for ESL Literacy Education
  (NCLE), 108
National Clearinghouse on Child Abuse and Neglect
  Information, 69
National Commission on Retirement Policy, 236
National Council on Disability, 197
National Credit Union Administration, 63-64
National Criminal Justice Reference Service, 249, 250
National Cryptologic Museum, 84
National Defense Panel, 82
National Digestive Diseases Information
  Clearinghouse, 212
National Earthquake Information Center, 256
National Education Goals, 108
National Endowment for the Arts, 40-41, 96
National Endowment for the Humanities, 60, 98, 240
National Eye Institute, 210
National Food Safety Database, 202
National forests, 141, 142
National Gallery of Art, 41
National Gambling Impact Study Commission, 64
National Health Information Center, 194
National Health Interview Survey, 93
National Heart, Lung, and Blood Institute, 210-211
National Highway Traffic Safety Administration, 285-
  286, 287

National Historic Preservation Act of 1966, 224
National Human Genome Research Institute, 211
National Hurricane Center, 261
National Income and Products Accounts, 93
National Information Infrastructure, 51
National Institute for Literacy, 108, 109
National Institute for the Environment, 129
National Institute of Allergy and Infectious Diseases
  (NIAID), 184, 211
National Institute of Arthritis and Musculoskeletal and
  Skin Diseases, 211-212, 216
National Institute of Dental Research, 212
National Institute of Diabetes and Digestive and
  Kidney Diseases, 207, 212
National Institute of Environmental Health Sciences,
  71, 199
National Institute of Mental Health, 221
National Institute of Neurological Disorders and
  Stroke, 212-213
National Institute of Standards and Technology, 49, 74,
  75, 258-259
National Institute on Alcohol Abuse and Alcoholism,
  186
National Institute on Disability and Rehabilitation
  Research (NIDRR), 196, 197, 198
National Institute on Drug Abuse, 186
National Institutes of Health (NIH), 2, 23, 32, 188, 194,
  195, 202, 207, 214
  Library Catalog, 29
  National Eye Institute, 210
  National Human Genome Research Institute, 211
  National Institute of Arthritis and Musculoskeletal
    and Skin Diseases, 211-212
  National Institute of Dental Health, 212
  National Institute of Diabetes and Digestive Kidney
    Diseases, 212
  NIH Web Search, 195
  Office of Alternative Medicine, 214
  Office of Animal Care and Use, 214
  Office of Rare Diseases, 215-216
National Interagency Fire Center, 116
National Labor Relations Act, 233
National Labor Relations Board (NLRB), 233
National Library of Education, 104
National Library of Medicine, 29, 184, 189, 190-191,
  226
National Library Service for the Blind and Physically
  Handicapped, 27
National Literacy Advocacy, 108, 109
National Marine Fisheries Service, 132
National Marine Sanctuary, 255
National Mental Health Services Knowledge Exchange
  Network, 221
National Military Strategy of the United States, 24
National Museum of American Art, 41
National Museum of Natural History, 42

National Oceanic and Atmospheric Administration (NOAA), 49, 133, 135, 255, 256, 262

National Ocean Service, 255

National Organ and Tissue Donation Initiative, 216

National Parent Information Network (NPIN), 69-70

National parks, 17, 139, 140-141

National Park Service, 140, 141, 142, 228, 254

National Partnership for Reinventing Government, 174, 175

National Performance Review, 15, 49, 174

National Pesticide Telecommunications Network, 199

National Portrait Gallery, 42

National Public School Locator Search, 107

National Rehabilitation Information Center, 197-198

National Renewable Energy Laboratory, 120, 124-125, 257

National Research Council, 214

National Research Initiative Competitive Grants Program, 33

National Science Foundation Bulletin, 60

National Science Foundation (NSF), 21, 60, 71, 240

National security, 16, 82

    National Security Agency, 84-85

    National Security Council, 85

National Senior Service Corps, 231

National Severe Storms Laboratory, 261-262

National Space Science Data Center, 278

National Sudden Infant Death Syndrome Resource Center, 213

National symbols and songs, 16

National Tech Corps, 97

National Technical Information Service, 49

National Telecommunications and Information Administration, 49

National Toxicology Program, 200

National Transit Library, 285

National Transportation Library, 284

National Transportation Safety Board (NTSB), 286

National Trust for the Humanities, 98

National Weather Service, 116, 261, 262

    Alaska Region, 262

    forecasts, 34

    offices, 262-267

    River Forecast Centers, 268

National Wetlands Inventory, 132-133

National Wildlife Refuge System, 140

National Women's Health Information Center (NWHIC), 213

National Zoo, 42

Native Americans, 17, 42, 61, 104

NATO, 82, 158

Natural gas production and prices, 122, 123

Natural history, 42

Naturalization, 177, 227

Natural resources, 12, 22, 33, 36, 129

NatureNet, 140-141

Naval Observatory, 260

Navy, 87

NCCIC (National Child Care Information Center), 69

NCLE (National Clearinghouse for ESL Literacy Education), 108

Near-Earth Asteroid Tracking Home Page, 270

Near-Live Comet Watching System, 271

Nelson, Baby Face, 248

Neptune, 282

Nervous system disorders, 212

Neurological disorders, 212-213

Nevada Test Site, 88

News events, 16

Newsgroups, 290

New York City, 224

New York Law Publishing Company, 239

New York Times v. Sullivan, 240

NIAID (National Institute of Allergy and Infectious Diseases), 184, 211

Nicotine dependence, 186, 206

NIDRR (National Institute on Disability and Rehabilitation Research), 196, 197, 198

Nigeria, 158

NIH. *See* National Institutes of Health

NIH Web Search, 195

Nitrates, 33

NIX (NASA Image eXchange), 276

Nixon, Richard M., 178, 228

NLM Locator, 29

NLRB (National Labor Relations Board), 233

NOAA (National Oceanic and Atmospheric Administration), 49, 133, 135, 255, 256, 262

NOAA Web Sites, 133

NonProfit Gateway, 14

Nonprofit organizations, 14

Non-Proliferation Treaty, 86

North American Free Trade Agreement (NAFTA), 47

North American Reporting Center for Amphibian Malformations, 133

North Carolina Cooperative Extension Service, 34-35

Northern Prairie Wildlife Research Center, 133

North Korea, 148

Northwestern University, 240

Notes, 54

NPIN (National Parent Information Network), 69-70

NRC (Nuclear Regulatory Commission), 121, 125, 126

NSF (National Science Foundation), 21, 60, 71, 240

NSF Guide to Programs, 60

NTSB (National Transportation Safety Board), 286

Nuclear, Biological, and Chemical Medical Defense Information Server, 78

Nuclear physics, 260

Nuclear power, 123, 124, 126

Nuclear reactors and plants, 121, 124, 126, 137

Nuclear Regulatory Commission (NRC), 121, 125, 126

Nuclear safety, 124, 126

Nuclear science, 257

Nuclear testing, 86, 88, 125

Nuclear waste, 137-138

   Nuclear Waste Technical Review Board, 137

   Office of Civilian Radioactive Waste Management, 137

   Yucca Mountain Site Characterization Project, 137-138

Nuclear Waste Policy Act of 1982, 137

Nuclear Waste Technical Review Board, 137

Nuclear weapons, 86, 88-89

   Defense Nuclear Facilities Safety Board Server, 88

   Department of Energy Nevada Operations Office, 88

   Environment, Safety, and Health Technical Information Services, 88-89

   Explorer, 89

   plants, 88, 89

   testing, 86, 88, 125

Nuclear weapons-free zones, 86

Nursing, 189, 191

Nursing homes, 17, 208, 209, 235

NutriBase, 202

Nutrition. *See* Food and nutrition

Nutrition and Your Health: Dietary Guidelines for Americans, 215

Oak Ridge National Laboratory (ORNL), 259

Obesity, 104, 210, 212

Obsessive-compulsive disorder, 221

Occupational injuries, 89

Occupational Outlook Handbook, 23, 92

Occupational Safety and Health Act of 1970, 234

Occupational Safety and Health Administration, 49, 233-234, 235

Ocean drilling, 133

Oceanography, 55, 110, 256, 260

Office of Alternative Medicine, 214

Office of Animal Care and Use, 214

Office of Civilian Radioactive Waste Management, 137

Office of Defects Investigation, 285

Office of Dietary Supplements, 202-203

Office of Disease Prevention, 214-215

Office of Disease Prevention and Health Promotion, 215

Office of Economic Conversion Information, 47

Office of Federal Procurement Policy, 56

Office of Foreign Assets Control, 50

Office of General Counsel, 234

Office of Government Ethics Home Page, 177

Office of Governmentwide Policy, 174-175

Office of Human Radiation Experiments, 219

Office of Information Technology, 75

Office of Justice Programs, 250-251

Office of Juvenile Justice and Delinquency Prevention, 250

Office of Management and Budget (OMB), 16, 175, 179, 180

   circulars and bulletins, 11

   OMB Watch, 134

   regulatory review process, 130

Office of Minority Health Resource Center, 215

Office of National Drug Control Policy, 179

Office of Personnel Management, 231, 232

Office of Rare Diseases, 215-216

Office of Scientific and Technical Information, 125

Office of Special Counsel, 177

Office of Surface Mining, 254

Office of System Safety Home Page, 286

Office of Technology Assessment, 166

Office of the Assistant Secretary for Planning and Evaluation, 70

Office of the Clerk On-line Information Center, 165

Office of the Majority Whip, 165-166

Office of the Secretary of Defense, 173

Office of the U.S. Trade Representative's Homepage, 47

Office supply scams, 20

Offshore oil and gas wells, 123

Ohio State University, 100

Oil market, 122

Oil spills, 87, 135

Oklahoma City bombing, 116

Older Americans Act, 204. *See also* Aging

OLDMEDLINE database, 190

Olestra, 201

OLS (Online Library System), 29

OMB. *See* Office of Management and Budget

Online fraud, 14

Online Library System (OLS), 29

Online Women's Business Center, 47-48

Open Skies Treaty, 86

Operating Experience Weekly Summary, 88

Opiate addiction, 214

Oppt-newsbreak mailing list, 130

Oral contraceptives, 207

Oral health, 188, 204, 212

Oregon State University, 20, 199

Organ and tissue donation, 189, 216

Organic farming, 32

Organized crime, 250

OSHA (Occupational Safety and Health Administration), 49, 233-234, 235

Osteogenesis imperfecta, 216

Osteoporosis, 201, 216

Osteoporosis and Related Bone Diseases National Resource Center, 216

Ostriches, 32

OTA Legacy, 166

Outdoor education, 104

Overseas Security Advisory Council, 148

Oyez Project, 240-241

Ozone layer, 23

Pace University School of Law, 245
Package bombs, 248
Paget's disease, 216
Paintings, 41, 43, 106
Paleobiology, 42
Panic disorder, 214, 221
Paperwork Reduction Act, 179
Parenting, 69, 70
    involvement with education, 113
    parental rights, 70, 98
    PARENTING-L mailing list, 70-71
    Parent News, 70
    Parents and Children Together, 103
    See also Children and families
Parkinson's disease, 213
Parks and public lands, 129, 139-142, 167
    Alaska Public Lands Information Centers, 139
    America's National Parks Electronic Bookstore, 139
    Bureau of Land Management, 139-140, 141, 142, 254
    Fish and Wildlife Service, 132, 136, 142, 254
    Fish and Wildlife Service Region 7—Alaska, 142
    Forest Service Home Page, 142
    Grand Canyon National Park, 140
    National Wildlife Refuge System, 140
    NatureNet, 140-141
    ParkNet, 141
    Park Search, 141
    Public Lands Statistics, 139
    Recreation.GOV, 142
    state parks, 139, 141
Partnership for a New Generation of Vehicles (PNGV), 259
Passports, 49, 144
Passwords, 5, 290
Patents, 12, 15, 16, 46, 51, 52, 257
    Patent and Trademark Office, 46, 49, 51, 52
    Patent Bibliographic Database, 52
Pathfinder, 163
Patient rights, 189
Patterns of Global Terrorism, 159
PDF files, 290
PDS Geosciences Node, 259
PDS Mars Explorer for the Armchair Astronaut, 281
Peace Corps, 148
Penkovsky, Oleg, 146
Penny Hill Press, 166-167
Pension Benefit Guaranty Corporation, 234
Pentagon, 82
Pentagon Book Store Online, 85
Periodicals, 23
Persian Gulf illness. *See* Gulf War illness
Persian Gulf War, 217-218
Personal property, 94, 175
Personnel management, 231, 232
Pest control, 32, 33, 202
Pesticides, 23, 129, 131, 135, 199, 201, 202

Petroleum market, 122
Philippine Insurrection, 225
Philosophy, 60
Phonics instruction, 110
Photographs, 224-225
Photovoltaics, 124
Physical education, 106
Physically handicapped. *See* Disabilities
Physical science, 259
Physics, 121, 257
Picasso, Pablo, 248
Pipeline accidents, 286
Plain Language Action Network, 175
Planes. *See* Aviation
Planets, 278, 279, 280-282
    Center for Mars Exploration (CMEX), 280
    detection, 280
    Jupiter, 273, 282
    Kepler Mission: A Search for Habitable Planets, 280
    Mars, 259, 275, 280-281
    MGS-Status mailing list, 281
    Neptune, 282
    PDS Mars Explorer for the Armchair Astronaut, 281
    Planetary Data System (PDS) Geosciences Node, 259
    Planetary Photojournal, 282
    Planetary Rings Node, 282
    Saturn, 282
    Uranus, 282
    Venus, 273
    Welcome to the Planets, 282
    See also Asteroids and comets; Space
Planned Parenthood v. Casey, 240
Planning Your Future: A Federal Employee's Survival Guide, 231
Plants, 32, 132, 140
    Botanical Garden, 225
    botany, 42
    invasive and nonnative, 141
    pathology, 34
    pests and diseases, 34
    plant science, 34
    rare plants, 142
    weeds, 139
Playground safety, 104
PNGV (Partnership for a New Generation of Vehicles), 259
Poison control centers, 199
Poisoning prevention, 176
Policies, regulations, and operations, 21, 174-177
    Access Board, 196
    children and youth, 70
    Consumer Product Safety Commission, 71, 176
    FinanceNet, 174
    Immigration and Naturalization Service, 177
    National Partnership for Reinventing Government, 174

National Performance Review, 15, 49, 174
  Office of Government Ethics Home Page, 177
  Office of Governmentwide Policy, 174-175
  Office of Special Counsel, 177
  Plain Language Action Network, 175
  Project on Government Secrecy, 175-176
  REGINFO.GOV, 176
Political action committees, 171, 172
Political books, 85
Political correctness, 103
Politics, 16, 163, 170
Pollution, 29, 129, 130, 131, 134, 135
Polygraph testing, 251
POPLINE database, 190
Population, 20, 54, 93, 94, 135, 177
  law and policy, 190
  migration in rural areas, 35
Population Estimates by Age, Sex and Race, 20
Pornography, 251
Portraits, 42, 224
Postal Service, 52
Postal Inspection Service, 52
postal rates, 52
Post-polio syndrome, 213
Poverty, 35, 70, 94
Powers, Francis Gary, 146
POWs, 27, 146
Prayer in schools, 240
Pregnancy, 70, 186, 188, 201
Prescription medicines. See Medications
Presidential Advisory Committee on Gulf War
  Veterans' Illnesses, 218
Presidents, 16, 18
  biographies, 180
  budget proposals, 12
  elections, 110, 172
  environmental issues and, 131
  executive branch, 12, 15, 16, 177
  executive orders, 11, 16, 85, 146, 175, 177,
    180
  first ladies, 180, 224
  impeachment, 16, 178
  libraries, 225, 226, 227
  portraits, 42, 180, 224
  radio addresses, 180
  speeches, 12, 180
  vetoes, 167
  vice presidents, 12
President's Commission on Critical Infrastructure
  Protection, 85
President's Committee on Employment of People with
  Disabilities, 233, 234-235
President's Committee on the Arts and the Humanities,
  68
President's Council on Year 2000 Conversion, 76
Presley, Elvis, 228, 248

Press releases, 16
  Census Bureau, 92
  DOT, 287
  EIA, 122
  EPA, 130
  FAA, 285
  Fish and Wildlife Service, 132
  Kennedy Space Center, 274
  NASA, 276, 278
  Nuclear Regulatory Commission, 121
  press-release mailing list, 92, 278
  White House, 12, 180
PREVline (Prevention Online), 187
Price indexes, 54, 55, 92
Prime rate, 54
Princeton University, 166
Prisoners of war, 27, 146
Prisons and prisoners
  drug enforcement and treatment, 249
  executions, 249
  Federal Bureau of Prisons, 249
  federal prisons, 249
  HIV, 249
  literacy programs, 100, 249
  mandatory minimum prison terms, 238, 252
  recidivism, 250
  women, 250
  See also Crime; Justice
Privacy, 14
  of health data, 23, 190, 257
  online, 20
  Privacy Act, 10, 20, 146, 151
Private schools, 104
Privatization, 22
Procurement, 175, 179
  Acquisition Reform Network (ARNet), 56
  ACQWeb, 80
  CBDNet, 56
  Commerce Business Daily, 18, 23, 49, 56, 58, 59
  Customs Service, 251
  Federal Acquisition Regulation, 57
  Loren Data Corp., 58
  Marshall Space Flight Center Procurement Site, 59
  NAIS Email Notification Service, 59
  NASA Acquisition Internet Service (NAIS) Home
    Page, 59-60
  for nonprofit organizations, 235
  Office of Federal Procurement Policy, 56
  Procurement Reference Library, 59
  SBA PRO-Net, 48
  Treasury Department, 50
Producer price index, 92
Product-announce mailing list, 92
Production, 25
Product safety, 14
Project EASI 109

Project Gemini, 275
Project Mercury, 276
Project on Government Secrecy, 175-176
Project Vote Smart, 170
Prompt, 290
PR-OPA mailing list, 121-122
Propane, 122
Prostate problems, 204
Protease inhibitors, 185
Psoriasis, 211
Publications, 10, 17-26
    Colorado Alliance of Research Libraries (CARL)
        Databases, 17
    consumer information, 14
    Consumer Information Center, 17
    Consumer Product Safety Commission, 176
    Core Documents of U.S. Democracy, 18
    on education, 22, 98, 107, 111-112
    on employment, 17
    on energy, 121, 123
    on environment, 17, 22, 135
    Federal Bulletin Board, 18-19
    Federal Register Mailing Lists, 19
    Federal Trade Commission Home Page, 19-20
    on food and nutrition, 17, 22
    Freedom of Information Act, 20
    General Services Administration, 60-61
    Government Information Sharing Project, 20-21
    Government Printing Office, 17, 18, 24-26, 56, 121,
        165
    GOVINFO, 21
    GOVNEWS, 21-22
    on health and health care, 17, 22-23
    House of Representatives Internet Law Library, 26
    Housing and Urban Development Department, 18
    How to Effectively Locate Federal Government
        Information on the Web, 22
    Insignia Publishing Company, 217
    National Academy Press, 22-23
    Penny Hill Press, 166-167
    Pentagon Bookstore Online, 85
    political books, 85
    on science, 22-23
    taxes, 12, 65, 66
    Uncle Sam, 23
    U.S. Government Documents Ready Reference
        Collection, 23-24
    White House, 180-181
Public debt, 50, 54
Public health, 128, 190, 205
Public Health Service, 185, 213
Public lands. See Parks and public lands
Public Lands Statistics, 139
Public safety, 13, 15
Public service, 235
PubMed, 191

Quasi-official agencies, 15
Quest, 109

Radar images, 261, 262, 268
Radiation, 89, 125, 131, 137
    electromagnetic, 260
    human experiments, 89, 125, 219
Radioactive waste, 126, 137
Radioactivity, 88
Radio and TV Marti, 147
Radio Free Asia, 148-149
Radio Free Europe/Radio Liberty, 144, 145, 149
Railroads, 106, 225, 284, 286, 287
Rainfall prediction, 133
Range resources, 33
Rare diseases, 188, 215-216
Raymond, Tony, 172
Reading, 17, 23, 98, 100, 103, 110, 111, 112
READPRO mailing list, 110
ReadyWeb, 110
RealAudio software, 164, 240
Real estate, 18, 60, 94, 175
Real Estate Settlement Procedures Act, 18
Recalls, 10, 209
Recidivism, 250
Recreation, 142, 176
Recreation.GOV, 142
Reengineering, 16
Refugees, 113
Regenerative agriculture, 32
Regents of the University of California v. Bakke, 240
REGINFO.GOV, 176
Regional Economic Information System, 21
Regulations. See Laws and legislation; Policies,
    regulations, and operations
Regulatory research, 11
Rehabilitation, 112, 196, 197-198, 214
Rehabilitation Act of 1973, 236
Reinventing government, 130, 174, 175
Relevant Knowledge, 2
Renewable energy, 120, 121, 122-125, 257
Report of the Commission on Protecting and Reducing
    Government Secrecy, 175
Reproductive technology, 189
Reproductive toxicity studies, 200
Reptiles, 140
Republican Party, 164
Research, 257
    animals in, 32-33
    human research, 210
    laboratories, 16
    National Research Council, 214
    regulatory, 11
    research guides, 23
Restless legs syndrome, 213
Resumes, 230, 231

Retirement, 66, 204, 231, 236
Retirement communities, 35
RFE/RL Newsline, 149
Rheumatoid arthritis, 211
Riparian areas, 139
River Forecast Centers, 268
River trips, 140
Robinson, Jackie, 225, 248
Robotics, 257, 258, 273
Rockets, 274, 275
Rocky 7, 259
Rocky Mountain Arsenal, 78
Roe v. Wade, 240
Roosevelt, Franklin D. and Eleanor, 225
Rosenberg, Ethel and Julius, 146
Roswell Incident, 80
RTK NET, 134
Rural areas, 33, 34, 35, 36, 167, 224
    crime, 35, 249
    education, 35, 104
    health care, 35
    rural development, 33, 35
    Rural Information Center, 34, 35
    See also Agriculture
Russia, 27, 106, 124, 277
    Russian archives, 27
    Russian church, 27
    Russian language, 106

Safety
    aviation, 286, 287
    child safety seats, 285
    consumer products, 21, 176
    food, 33, 34, 201, 202
    mining, 235
    nuclear, 124, 126
    occupational, 49, 233-234, 235
    playgrounds, 104
    public safety, 13, 15
    recreational, 176
    Safe Places to Play, 71
    in schools, 106
    systems, 286
    toys, 176
    traffic, 285-286, 287
    transportation, 286
    workplace, 233-234
Saint Valentine's Day Massacre, 248
Sales, 17, 22, 56-61, 62, 174, 251
    CBDNet, 56
    daily-sales mailing list, 56-57
    General Services Administration, 60
    govsales mailing list, 57-58
    List of Defaulted Borrowers, 58
    NASA Acquisition Internet Service (NAIS) Home
      Page, 59-60

    seized property, 17
    U.S. Mint, 61
SALP (systemic assessment of licensee performance)
    reports, 126
SAMHSA (Substance Abuse and Mental Health
    Services Administration), 194, 222
Sanctions, 46, 50
San Francisco, California, 224
Satellite images, 261, 262, 268
Saturn, 282
Savings
    savings bonds, 10, 50, 54
    savings deposits, 54, 162
    savings institutions, 62, 63
SBA. *See* Small Business Administration
SBA PRO-Net, 48
SCAN, 260
Schools
    crime in, 250
    local area networks for, 102
    middle schools, 23, 107
    private schools, 104
    school buses, 285
    School District Data Book Profiles, 21
    school health, 188
    school prayer, 240
    size and enrollment, 93, 101
    small schools, 104
    violence in, 101, 103, 107, 111, 112, 113
    See also Education
Science
    bibliographies, 27
    ethics, 22, 257
    Federation of American Scientists, 84, 175
    future of, 257
    museums and centers, 126
    National Academy of Sciences, 22, 201
    National Science Foundation, 21, 60, 71, 240
    policy, 167
    publications, 22-23
    See also Earth sciences; Technology; Weather
Scientific reports, 12
Sculptures, 41, 43
SDILINE database, 190
Search and rescue, 116
Search engines, 4, 22
Searches, 4
Sea turtles, 133
SEC (Securities and Exchange Commission), 2, 52-53
SEC News Digest, 52
Second language development, 98, 102-103
Secrecy in government, 175-176
Secrecy Policy Board, 175
Secretary of Defense, 173
Secretary of State, 149-150
Sector Facility Indexing Project, 134-135

Securities, 52, 54, 57
Securities and Exchange Commission (SEC), 2, 52-53
Seismology, 255. *See also* Earthquakes
Seized property, 17, 50
Selected Current Aerospace Notices, 260
Selective Service System, 10, 86
Semi-Annual Regulatory Agenda, 26
Senate, 169-170
    calendar and schedule, 24, 162, 169
    committees, 163, 167, 169
    members, 169
    rules, 169
    Senate Committee on Governmental Affairs, 18
    Senate Manual, 26
    votes, 163, 169
Senior citizens. *See* Aging
Sentencing Commission, 252
Sentencing guidelines, 238, 250, 252
Serials, 23
Servers, 290
Sex crimes and offenders, 249, 252
Sexual abuse, 249
Sexual harassment, 99, 102, 236
Sexually transmitted diseases, 185, 211
Shakespeare, William, 103
Shareware, 53, 290
Ships and ship wrecks, 87, 133
Shoemaker-Levy 9 comet, 273
Shuttle Reference Manual, 274
Shuttle-status mailing list, 274
Sickle-cell disease, 210
Single-sex education, 113
SIRIS (Smithsonian Institution Research Information System), 43
Skin diseases, 188, 211-212, 216
Ski reports, 133
Slave ownership, census data on, 94
Sleep apnea, 210, 213
Small business, 17, 23, 47-48, 59, 60
    SBA PRO-Net, 48
    Small Business Administration (SBA), 47, 48, 53
    Small Business Handbook, 235
Small Business Administration (SBA), 47, 48, 53
Small-scale farming, 32
Smart cards, 46
Smithsonian Education, 110-111
Smithsonian Institution, 40, 41, 42-43
Smithsonian Institution Research Information System (SIRIS), 43
Smoking, 23, 206, 210
    nicotine dependence, 186, 206
    prenatal, 188
    See also Tobacco
Smuggling, 177, 251
Social sciences, 22, 99

Social Security, 10, 66, 162
    paying taxes, 49
    Social Security Administration, 66, 71, 75
    Social Security Handbook, 23, 66
    Social Security Online, 66
Social services, 168
Social studies, 99, 106
Socks the Cat, 180
Soft money contributions, 171, 172
Software, 53, 102, 288
Software patents, 51
Soil conservation and management, 33, 34
Solar space power, 260
Solar system, 273, 278, 279, 282
Solid waste, 131, 135
Sonic boom, 260
Sourcebook of Criminal Justice Statistics, 24
Southern Regional Education Board, 110
Soviet KGB, 84
Soviet Union, 27, 145, 149
Space, 106, 166, 260, 272-279
    astronauts, 275, 277
    commercialization of, 260
    Earth from Space, 272
    EXPRESS, 272
    history, 275, 278
    International Space Station, 272-273
    issnews mailing list, 273
    Jet Propulsion Laboratory, 273
    Kennedy Space Center, 274
    ksc-press-release mailing list, 274
    life sciences, 190
    Lunar Prospector, 274-275
    NASA Headquarters, 275
    NASA Homepage, 275
    NASA Image eXchange (NIX), 276
    NASA Johnson Space Center Digital Image Collection, 276
    NasaNews, 276
    NASA Search, 277
    NASA Shuttle-Mir Web, 277
    NASA Shuttle Web, 277
    NASA Spacelink, 277-278
    National Air and Space Museum, 40
    National Space Science Data Center, 278
    press-release mailing list, 278
    shuttle-status mailing list, 274
    Space Calendar, 279
    spacecraft, 271, 273, 278, 282
    SPACELINE database, 190
    space probes, 260, 278
    space shuttle, 40, 274, 276, 277, 278
    space stations, 260, 272, 273, 275, 277
    Trading Post 3, 279
    Views of the Solar System, 279
    See also Asteroids and comets; Planets

Spanish-American War, 225
Spanish language, 106
Speaker of the House, 165, 167
Special education, 112, 197
Special interest groups, 170
Specialty crops, 36, 37
Speeches, 11, 180, 224
Spellman, Francis Cardinal, 248
Spies, 146
Spinal cord injuries, 196, 213
Squid, giant, 42
SR71 Blackbird spy plane, 40
Stamps, 52, 106
Standard Industrial Classification Manual, 93
Standards, 49, 74, 75, 258-259
Stardust Mailing List, 271
Stardust mission, 271
Starr, Kenneth, 2, 165, 178
Stars, 278
State and Metropolitan Area Data Book, 11, 23
State Court Locator, 10
State courts, 10, 239
State Department, 144, 147, 148, 149, 150, 159
State Department Electronic Reading Room, 150-151
State government, 176
State laws, 11, 26
State of the Coast, 135
State parks, 139, 141
State Web Locator, 10
Statistical Abstract of the United States, 11, 18, 23, 26, 94
Statistics
    Federal Interagency Council on Statistical Policy, 11
    FedStats, 11
    See also Demographic data
Statutes. *See* Laws and legislation
Storms, 116, 261-262
Strategic Arms Reduction Treaty, 86
Stress management, 231
Strokes, 204, 207, 212-213
Structural mechanics, 260
Student loans and aid, 58, 105, 109, 111, 112
Subcommittee on Rules and Organization of the House, 167
Subject directories, 13
Subject line, 5
Substance abuse, 70
    Substance Abuse and Mental Health Services Administration (SAMHSA), 194, 222
    See also Alcohol and alcohol abuse; Drugs and drug abuse
Sudden infant death syndrome, 207, 213
Suicide, 221
Sun, 278, 279
Superfund sites, 128, 129, 134, 135
Supplemental Security Income, 66

Supreme Court, 12, 25, 238-239
    building tour, 240
    calendar, 240
    decisions, 11, 12, 18, 25, 26, 239-240
    members, 163, 240
    opinions, 10, 14, 18, 238, 247
    oral arguments, 240
    orders, 18
    rules, 238, 240
    syllabi of decisions, 240
Surface mining, 254
Surgery, 17, 204
Surplus listings, 56
Survey of Income and Program Participation, 93
Survivors benefits, 66
Sustainable farming, 32
Sustainable Fisheries Act of 1996, 132
Sweatshops, 235
Syracuse University, 102
Systemic assessment of licensee performance (SALP) reports, 126
System safety, 286

Tariffs, 51
Task Force on Excellence in State and Local Government through Labor-Management Cooperation, 236
Task Force Russia, 27
Taxes, 10, 16, 17, 50, 65-66
    for businesses, 49, 65
    Digital Daily, The, 65
    Digital Dispatch, 65
    forms, 10, 12, 65, 66
    income tax preparation services, 19
    Internal Revenue Service, 50, 65, 66
    IRIS (Internal Revenue Information Services), 65-66
    nonprofit organizations, 14
    publications, 12, 65, 66
    reform, 162
    regulations, 65
    statistics, 65
    Taxing Times, 66
    tax law, 10, 65
    Tax Law Locator, 10
    Taxpayer Relief Act of 1997, 33
    Tele-Tax telephone numbers, 66
T-bills, 54
TDD/TTY numbers, 61, 198
Teachers and teaching, 101, 104, 105, 109, 113
    American Federation of Teachers, 96
    minority teachers, 113
    qualifications, 98
    teacher education, 104
    teacher-parent differences, 101
    working conditions, 107
Technical assistance programs, 17

Technical Links, 235
Technical reports, 12
Technology, 257-260
  bibliographies, 27
  consumer information, 14
  education and, 102, 105, 106, 112
  ERIC Clearinghouse on Information and
    Technology, 28, 96, 102
  Ernest Orlando Lawrence Berkeley National
    Laboratory, 257
  Hybrid Electric Vehicle Program, 257
  Intelligent Mechanisms Group, 257-258
  JPL Robotics, 258
  NASA Space Telerobotics Program, 258
  National Institute of Standards and Technology, 49,
    74, 75, 258-259
  Oak Ridge National Laboratory (ORNL), 259
  Office of Technology Assessment, 166
  Partnership for a New Generation of Vehicles
    (PNGV), 259
  publications, 22-23
  Rocky 7, 259
  SCAN, 260
  technophobia, 48
  Time Service Department, 260
Technology transfer, 34, 211, 278
Technology Transfer Information Center, 34
Teen pregnancy, 70
Telecommunications, 49
Telemarketing, 19, 20, 62
Telemedicine, 191
Telephone bills, 62
Telephone directories, 13
Telephone order merchandise rule, 20
Tele-Tax, 66
Telnet, 290
Tennessee Valley Authority (TVA), 125
Teratology studies, 200
Territorial laws, 11, 26
Terrorism, 24, 81, 117, 144, 148, 159, 248
Terrorism in the United States, 24, 248
Textiles, 36, 131, 235
Thai language, 106
Thalidomide, 190
Theater, 96
This is MEGA Mathematics!, 111
THOMAS, 167
Threatened species. *See* Endangered species
Thrift institutions, 62
Thunderstorms, 262
Tibet, 148
Time Service Department, 260
Time Warner, 163
Time zones, 260
Tobacco
  Bureau of Alcohol, Tobacco, and Firearms, 248

CDC's Tobacco Information and Prevention Source
  (TIPS), 206
Committee on Commerce Tobacco Documents, 207
nicotine dependence, 186, 206
regulation, 209
smoking, 23, 188, 206, 210
tobacco settlement, 162
Tornadoes, 262
Tourism. *See* Travel and tourism
Tourism mailing list, 48-49
Touro Law Center, 245
Toxic substances, 29, 128, 130, 131
  Agency for Toxic Substances and Disease Registry,
    128
  National Toxicology Program, 200
  toxic chemicals, 128, 129, 134, 135
  toxicity studies, 200
  toxicology, 199
  Toxic Release Inventory, 129, 130, 134
  TOXLINE database, 190
Toy ads, 19
Toy safety, 176
Trace Research and Development Center, 198
Trade, 13, 15
  agriculture, 34, 36, 37
  electronic commerce, 46, 49, 50, 59, 175
  exports, 46, 49, 86, 151, 251
  Federal Trade Commission, 14, 19-20
  foreign trade, 22, 50
  imports, 51, 251
  International Trade Commission, 49, 50-51
  Office of the United States Trade Representative's
    Homepage, 47
  sanctions, 46
  statistics on, 51, 94
Trademarks, 12, 15, 51, 240
Trading Post 3, 279
Traffic safety, 285-286, 287
Trains, 106, 225, 284, 286, 287
Transplantation, 189, 210, 211, 216
Transportation, 123, 166, 175, 284-287
  accidents, 286
  Amtrak, 284
  Bureau of Transportation Statistics, 284, 287
  consumer information, 14
  FAA Y2K Program Office, 284
  fatigue management, 287
  Federal Aviation Administration, 12, 285, 286, 287
  Federal Transit Administration, 285
  intelligent systems, 284, 285
  Journal of Transportation and Statistics, The, 284
  National Highway Traffic Safety Administration,
    285-286, 287
  National Transit Library, 285
  National Transportation Library, 284
  National Transportation Safety Board, 286

Office of Defects Investigation, 285
Office of System Safety Home Page, 286
policy, 80
Transportation Department, 284, 287
Transportation Statistics Annual Report, 284
Transportation Statistics Bureau, 284
White House Commission on Aviation Safety and
   Security, 287
Travel and tourism, 12, 13, 17, 35, 175
   abroad, 10, 144, 148, 150, 151, 159, 205
   CDC Travel Information, 205-206
   Customs Service, 251
   health and, 205, 206
   hotel and motel fire safety, 117
   for older Americans, 144
   safety, 144, 148
   Tourism mailing list, 48-49
   by train, 284
   Travel-Advisories Mailing List, 150
   to Washington, D.C., 168
   See also Aviation; Parks and public lands
Treasury Building, 50
Treasury Department, 50
Treaties and agreements, 25, 26, 86
Tropical Prediction Center, 261
Trotsky, Leon, 248
Tuberculosis, 185, 211
Tutoring, 102
TVA (Tennessee Valley Authority), 125

Uncle Sam, 23
Unemployment, 25, 92, 93, 162. *See also* Employment
Unidentified flying objects (UFOs), 84, 146, 248
Unified Agenda, 26
Uniform Commercial Code, 240
Uniform Crime Report, 24, 93
Uniform resource locator (URL), 290
Unison Institute, 134
United Nations Charter, 96
U.S. Bankruptcy and District Courts, 241
U.S. Business Advisor, 49
U.S. Circuit Court of Appeals Decisions, 241
U.S. Circuit Courts of Appeals, 241
U.S. Code, 14, 18, 26, 169, 240
U.S. Colored Troops, 228
U.S. Consumer Gateway, 14
U.S. Courts for the Ninth Circuit, 246
U.S. Courts of Appeals
   decisions, 14, 239, 241
   District of Columbia Circuit, 239
   Eighth Circuit, 246
   Eleventh Circuit, 247
   Federal Circuit, 239, 241, 247
   Fifth Circuit, 245
   First Circuit, 247
   Fourth Circuit, 247

   Ninth Circuit, 10
   Second Circuit, 245
   Seventh Circuit, 245
   Sixth Circuit, 247
   Tenth Circuit, 246
   Third Circuit, 10
U.S. Department of Agriculture (USDA). *See*
   Agriculture Department
U.S. Federal Courts Finder, 247
U.S. Federal Government Agencies Directory, 15
U.S. Government Documents Ready Reference
   Collection, 23-24
U.S. Government Electronic Commerce Policy, 50
U.S. Government Information, 15
United States Government Manual, 18, 25, 176
U.S. Imports/Exports History, 21
U.S. State and Local Gateway, 15
University of California, 13, 22, 257
University of California, Los Angeles, 99
University of Chicago at Urbana-Champaign, 101
University of Colorado, Government Publications
   Library, 15
University of Illinois at Chicago, 147
University of Massachusetts, 13
University of Memphis Library, 23
University of Michigan Documents Center, 16
University of North Texas, 178
University of Oregon, 101
University of Virginia, 93
University of Wisconsin-Madison, 198
Uploading, 290
Uranus, 282
Urban development, 22
Urban education, 69, 112-113
Urban Education Web, 112-113
Urban technology, 260
Urinary problems, 207
URL (uniform resource locator), 290
Urologic diseases, 188, 212
USA Counties, 20
USA Jobs, 232
USDA Agricultural Baseline Projections to 2007, 33
USDA Cooperative State Research, Education, and
   Extension Service, 35
USDA Economics and Statistics System, 36
USDA Forest Service Home Page, 142
USDA Home Page, 36
USDA Reports Electronic Mailing List, 36-37
USDA (U.S. Department of Agriculture). *See*
   Agriculture Department
Usenet newsgroups, 21, 290
Users, 290
USGS Branch of Earthquake and Geomagnetic
   Information On-line System, 256
USPTO Patent Databases, 52
Utilities, 35, 123

Vaccinations, 205
Vasectomy, 207
Vatican library, 27
Vaudeville, 224
V-chip, 62
Vechten, Carl Van, 224
Vegetables, 32, 36, 37
Vegetarian nutrition, 201
Vehicles, 17
  alternative fuel, 120, 121
  carjacking, 250
  crash tests, 285
  defects investigations, 285
  Hybrid Electric Vehicle Program, 257
  leasing, 19, 54
  Partnership for a New Generation of Vehicles, 259
  space vehicles, 260
  theft, 251
VENONA project, 84, 145
Venus, 273
Vertebrate zoology, 42
Veterans, 17, 53, 168, 231, 232
Veterans Affairs Department, 83, 219
Veterinary medicine, 189, 191
Vice presidents, 12
Vietnam, 145, 148
Vietnam War, 27, 86, 146, 228
Views of the Solar System, 279
Villanova University School of Law, 10
Violence, 249, 250, 251
  domestic violence, 70, 251
  drug abuse and, 179
  families and, 23
  political violence against Americans, 144
  in schools, 101, 103, 107, 111, 112, 113
  Violence Against Women Office, 251
  workplace, 233, 250
Virginia Declaration of Rights, 96
Viruses (computers), 74, 75
Visible Human Project, 190-191
Visual arts, 96
Visual impairments, 27, 28, 196, 210
Vital records, 17
Vocational education, 19, 100, 106
Vocational rehabilitation, 197
Voice communication, between humans and machines, 23
Voice of America, 147
Volcanoes, 133, 254, 256, 258
Vote Smart Web, 170
Voting, 12
  Federal Voting Assistance Program, 173
  Project Vote Smart, 170
  registration, 172, 173

Voting Assistance Guide, 173
  See also Elections
Voyager mission, 282

Wallenberg, Raoul, 151
Washburn University School of Law, 246
Washington, D.C., 42-43, 168, 225
Washington, George, 225
Washington University Alzheimer's Disease Research Center, 220
Washington University School of Law, 246
Waste conversion, 120
Wastewater treatment facilities, 130
Water
  conservation and management, 33, 37, 129
  discharge permits, 130
  heating, 123
  pollution, 29, 33, 132
  quality, 33, 37, 129, 131, 135, 140
  use conflicts in the West, 162
  Water Quality Information Center, 37
  water resources, 34, 139, 256, 272
Water Quality Information Center, 37
Wayne, John, 248
Weapons, 82, 86. *See also* Chemical and biological weapons; Nuclear weapons
Weather, 15, 256, 261-268, 272
  agriculture and, 36
  climate, 15, 33, 129, 133, 162, 256, 262
  current conditions, 261
  El Niñno system, 133
  fire weather, 116, 133
  forecasts, 116, 260, 261, 262, 268
  Interactive Weather Information Network (IWIN), 261
  La Nina system, 116
  maps, 261
  marine forecasts, 262
  models, 133
  National Hurricane Center, 261
  National Severe Storms Laboratory, 261-262
  National Weather Service, 116, 261, 262
  National Weather Service Alaska Region, 262
  National Weather Service Offices, 262-267
  precipitation predictions, 268
  River Forecast Centers, 268
  satellite and radar images, 261, 262, 268
  severe weather, 133, 261, 262
  thunderstorms, 262
  tornadoes, 262
  Tropical Prediction Center, 261
  warnings, 116, 261, 262
  winter weather and storms, 116
Web directories, 16
Web Pages for Kids around the Federal Government, 71
Weeds, 139

Weekly Compilation of Presidential Documents, 18
Weight control, 19, 188, 201. *See also* Obesity
Welcome to the Planets, 282
Welcome to the White House, 179-180
Welfare, 12, 15
   literacy and, 108
   reform, 15, 23, 68, 70
   welfare-to-work programs, 70
Westinghouse Works, 224
Wetlands, 129, 132-133, 135, 136, 140, 256
Whales, 132
Wheelchairs, 196
Where to Write for Vital Records, 24
Whip Notice, The, 165, 170
Whipping Post, The, 165, 170
Whistleblowers, 83, 177
White House, 16, 71, 178-181
   documents, 12, 18, 180
   E-Mail to the White House, 178
   Independent Counsel and Impeachment, The, 178
   kids and pets, 180
   news conferences, 12
   Office of Management and Budget, 179
   Office of National Drug Control Policy, 179
   offices and agencies, 180
   photographs, 180
   press releases and briefings, 12, 180
   publications, 180-181
   speeches, 12, 180
   tours, 180
   Welcome to the White House, 179-180
   White House for Kids, 180
   White House Publications, 180-181
White House Commission on Aviation Safety and
   Security, 287
White House Conference on Aging, 204
Whitman, Walt, 225
WhoWhere? Edgar, 53
Wild and scenic rivers, 140
Wildcards, 290
Wildfires, 116, 262
Wild horses and burros, 139
Wildlife, 133, 136, 139, 140, 141, 142
   refuges, 136, 139, 140, 141
   stewardship, 34
Wild 2 comet, 271
WINDandSEA, 256
Wind technology, 124
Winter weather and storms, 116
Wiretaps, 238
Women, 167
   credit histories, 19

   drug abuse and, 186
   health, 199, 213
   journalists during World War II, 27
   media guidebook for, 158
   Online Women's Business Center, 47-48
   prisoners, 250
   suffrage, 225
   victims of violent crime, 250
   women-owned businesses, 47-48
   Women's Business Assistance Centers, 48
   in the workplace, 235, 236
Woodrow Wilson School of Public and International
   Affairs, 166
Work-at-home schemes, 19
Workforce development, 15
WorkNet@IRL, 236
Workplace issues, 10, 13
   health and safety, 61, 89, 92, 235
   injury and illness statistics, 234
   learning, 100
   literacy, 100, 108
   substance abuse, 235
   violence and theft, 61, 235, 250
   women, 235, 236
World Agricultural Outlook Board, 36
World Factbook, 145
World Military Expenditures and Arms Transfers, 24, 86
WORLDNET Television and Film Service, 147
World's Fair (Buffalo), 224
World War I, 224
World War II, 151, 228
World Wide Web (WWW), 290. *See also* Internet
Wright, Frank Lloyd, 27
Writing, 103, 111, 175, 224
Writing User-Friendly Documents, 175

X-ray research, 257

Yahoo!—U.S.Government, 16
Year 2000, 13, 15, 63, 75, 76, 158, 168, 284
Year 2000 Information and Readiness Disclosure Act,
   76
Year-round education, 113
Yellow Pages, 13
YouthInfo, 71
Yucca Mountain Site Characterization Project, 137-138

Zaire, 158
Zip Codes, 52
Zipped files, 288
Zoo, 42
Zoology, 42